KU-716-467

EVERY ONE
A WITNESS
The Tudor Age

COMMENTARIES OF AN ERA

A. F. SCOTT

WHITE LION PUBLISHERS
London   New York   Sydney   Toronto

Copyright © Scott & Finlay Ltd., 1975

First published in the United Kingdom
by White Lion Publishers, 1975

ISBN 0 7274 0045 2

Made and printed in
Great Britain
for White Lion Publishers Limited
138 Park Lane, London W1Y 3DD
by
Hendington Limited
Deadbrook Lane, Aldershot, Hampshire

Photoset in 10 on 11 pt Baskerville
by Blackfriars Press Limited
Smith Dorrien Road, Leicester
LE5 4BS

CONTENTS

v

LIST OF ILLUSTRATIONS

The author and publisher acknowledge with thanks permission to reproduce the illustrations listed below.

ACKNOWLEDGEMENTS

The author and publishers are grateful to the authorities named for permission to use copyright material. Furthermore, the publishers have tried to trace the owners of all copyright material, and apologise for any omissions. Should these be made known to us proper acknowledgements will be made in future editions.

To My Irish Cousins

All the parts of the whole year, as winter, summer, months, nights and days, continue in their order. All kinds of fishes in the sea, rivers and waters, with all fountains and springs, yea, the seas themselves, keep their comely course and order. And man himself also hath all his parts both within and without, as soul, heart, mind, memory, understanding, reason, speech, with all and singular corporal members of his body, in a profitable, necessary, and pleasant order. Every degree of people, in their vocation, calling, and office, hath appointed to them their duty and order. Some are in high degree, some in low; some kings, and princes, some inferiors and subjects; priests and laymen, masters and servants, fathers and children, husbands and wives, rich and poor; and every one have need of other.

The Book of Homilies, 1562

PREFACE

by Lord Wolfenden

Arthur Scott is indefatigable. Here he adds yet another to the collection of anthologies which he has prepared for our edification and delight. Those who know the earlier ones need only to be told that this one is well up to their standard of excellence: those who come to him for the first time are on the threshold of a new and exhilarating experience.

The distinctive features of these anthologies are three. First, they are derived entirely from contemporary sources. There is nothing here that is second-hand, or derivative, or distorted by subsequent commentary. Everything is reported as it was seen at its own time. Secondly, they cover an astonishing variety of habits, practices, customs, persons, and events. *Humani nil a se alienum putat* Arthur Scott. Thirdly, they are concerned with the whole spectrum, or kaleidoscope, of the Age, not merely with Kings and Princes and the other Great Figures whom alone we normally meet in history books. We meet ordinary people going about their ordinary daily business and pleasures.

The illustrations, contemporary also, are a genuine embellishment in the literal sense of that word.

The choice of passages and pictures is, as always, masterly, a rare combination of historical scholarship with human concern. Arthur Scott has put us yet further in his debt by his astonishing skill in bringing our distant forefathers to life before our eyes.

Royalty

HENRY VII

His politic wisdom in governance it was singular, his wit always quick and ready, his reason pithy and substantial, his memory fresh and holding, his experience notable, his counsels fortunate and taken by wise deliberation, his speech gracious in diverse languages, his person goodly and amiable, his natural complexion of the purest mixture, his eyes fair and in good number, leagues and confederacies he had with all Christian princes, his mighty power was dreaded everywhere, not only within his realm but without also, his people were to him in as humble subjection as ever they were to king, his land many a day in peace and tranquillity, his prosperity in battle against his enemies was marvellous, his dealing in time of perils and dangers was cold and sober with great hardiness. If any treason were conspired against him it came out wonderfully, his treasure and riches incomparable, his buildings most goodly and after the newest cast all of pleasure. But what is all this now unto him, all be but *fumus & umbra*. A smoke that soon vanisheth, and a shadow soon passing away.

The funeral sermon preached by Bishop Fisher at St Paul's, 10 May 1509. *The English Works of John Fisher*

HENRY VIII

His Majesty is twenty-nine years old and extremely handsome. Nature could not have done more for him. He is much handsomer than any other sovereign in Christendom; a great deal handsomer than the King of France; very fair and his whole frame admirably proportioned. On hearing that Francis I wore a beard, he allowed his own to grow, and as it is reddish, he has now a beard that looks like gold. He is very accomplished, a good musician, composes well, is a most capital horseman, a fine jouster, speaks good French, Latin, and Spanish, is very religious, hears three masses daily when he hunts, and

1

1. Henry VII in 1505 holding the red rose of Lancaster. He was perhaps 'rather cold in manner, rather hard at heart, certainly fond of money.' But he was a patron of Caxton the printer; through his encouragement Newfoundland was discovered; and he was a great builder.

2. Henry VIII after Holbein. 'I seem to see in him,' says a historian, 'a grand gross figure, very far removed from ordinary human sympathies, self-engrossed, self-confident, self-willed, unscrupulous in act.' Yet judged by the standards of his own day, he must be seen 'as a great and to a large extent a successful king'.

3. The King's Lock, taken from house to house during Royal Progresses, and always used for the King's Bedchamber to maintain absolute security: now, appropriately enough, at Hever Castle, the ancestral home of the Boleyn family.

sometimes five on other days. He hears the office every day in the Queen's chamber, that is to say, vesper and compline. He is very fond of hunting, and never takes his diversion without tiring eight or ten horses, which he causes to be stationed beforehand along the line of country he means to take, and when one is tired he mounts another, and before he gets home they are all exhausted. He is extremely fond of tennis, at which game it is the prettiest thing in the world to see him play, his fair skin glowing through a shirt of the finest texture.

Despatch of Giustiani, the Venetian Ambassador

ANNE BOLEYN AT DINNER TELLS OF HER HATRED OF CARDINAL WOLSEY

And I heard it reported by them that waited upon the King at dinner, that Mistress Anne Boleyn was much offended with the King, as far as she durst, that he so gently entertained my lord,

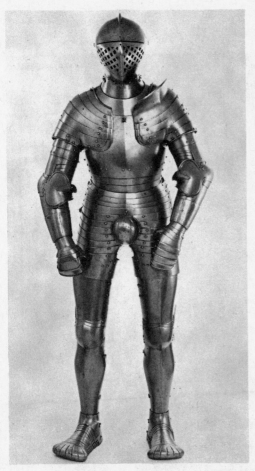

4. Armour of King Henry VIII made about 1535 in his own workshops at Greenwich.

Reproduced by gracious permission of Her Majesty the Queen.

saying, as she sat with the King at dinner, in communication of him, 'Sir,' quoth she, 'is it not a marvellous thing to consider what debt and danger the cardinal hath brought you in with all your subjects?' 'How so, sweetheart?' quoth the King. 'Forsooth,' quoth she, 'there is not a man within all your realm, worth five pounds, but he hath indebted you unto him; by his means' (meaning by a loan that the King had but late of his subjects). 'Well, well,' quoth the King, 'as for that there is in him no blame; for I know that matter better than you, or any other.' 'Nay, Sir,' quoth she, 'besides all that, what things hath he wrought within

5.   Catherine of Aragon wearing an English hood, with her hair covered by
striped 'rolls', *c.* 1520. Thomas Cromwell said of her that 'Nature wronged the
Queen in not making her a man. But for her sex she would have surpassed all
the heroes of history'. The people of England loved her and always showed their
affection.

this realm to your great slander and dishonour. There is never a nobleman within this realm that if he had done but half so much as he hath done, but he were well worthy to lose his head. If my Lord of Norfolk, my Lord of Suffolk, my lord my father, or any other noble person within your realm had done much less than he, but they should have lost their heads on this.' 'Why, then I perceive,' quoth the King, 'ye are not the cardinal's friend?' 'Forsooth, Sir,' then quoth she, 'I have no cause, nor any other that loveth your grace, no more have your grace, if he consider well his doings.' At this time the waiters had taken up the table, and so they ended their communication.

George Cavendish, The Life and Death of Thomas Wolsey, 1557

EDWARD VI

All the graces were in him. He had many tongues when he was yet but a child; together with the English, his natural tongue, he had both Latin and French; nor was he ignorant, as I hear, of the Greek, Italian and Spanish, and perhaps some more. But for the English, French, and Latin, he was exact in them and apt to learn everything. Nor was he ignorant of logic, of the principles of natural philosophy, nor of music. The sweetness of his temper was such as became a mortal, his gravity becoming the majesty of a King, and his disposition suitable to his high degree. In sum, that child was so bred, had such parts, was of such expectation that he looked like a miracle of a man. These things are not spoken rhetorically and beyond the truth, but are indeed short of it. He was a marvellous boy. When I was with him he was in the fifteenth year of his age, in which he spake Latin as politely and as promptly as I did . . . And indeed the ingenuity and sweetness of his disposition had raised in all good and learned men the greatest expectation of him possible. He began to love the liberal arts before he knew.them; and to know them before he could use them: and in him there was such an attempt of nature, that not only England, but the world has reason to lament his being so early snatched away. How truly was it said of such extraordinary persons, that their lives are short and seldom do they come to be old. He gave us an essay of virtue, though he did not live to give a pattern of it. When the gravity of the King was needful, he carried himself like an old man; and yet he was always affable and gentle, as became his age. He played on the lute, he meddled in affairs of state; and for bounty he did in

6. Edward VI by Guillium Scrots or Stretes, *c.* 1550. He could speak four languages, had the Tudor love of music, and interest in astronomy. A strong Protestant, he was widely read in theology, and had marked powers of argument.

7. Edward VI's coronation procession moving down Cheapside towards Westminster. We see here the Tower of London and Old St Paul's.

that emulate his father; though he, even when he endeavoured to be too good, might appear to have been bad: but there was no ground of suspecting any such thing in the son, whose mind was cultivated by the study of philosophy.

Giralamo Cardano, an Italian physician visiting the King in 1552

MARY I

The Most Serene Madame Mary is entitled Queen of England and of France, and Defendress of the Faith. She was born on 18th Feb. 1515 [1516 N.S.] so she yesterday completed her 38th year and six months. She is of low stature, with a red and white complexion, and very thin; her eyes are white and large, and her hair reddish; her face is round, with a nose rather low and wide; and were not her age on decline, she might be called handsome rather than the contrary. She is not of a strong constitution, and of late she suffers from headache and serious affection of the heart, so that she is often obliged to take medicine, and also to be blooded. She is of very spare diet, and never eats until 1 or 2 p.m., although she rises at day-break, when, after saying her prayers and hearing mass in private, she transacts business incessantly, after midnight, when she retires to rest; for she chooses to give audience not only to all the members of her Privy Council, and to hear from them every detail of public business, but also to all other persons who ask it of her. Her Majesty's countenance indicates great benignity and clemency, which are not belied by her conduct, for although she has had many enemies, and though so many of them were by

8. Mary I by Hans Eworth. Few people could have been unhappy. She loved her husband, Philip II of Spain, but was not loved by him. She went to war for his sake and lost Calais. She persecuted the Protestants. By so doing she made their final triumph a certainty.

law condemned to death, yet had the executions depended solely on her Majesty's will, not one of them perhaps would have been enforced; but deferring to her Council in everything, she in this matter likewise complied with the wishes of others rather than with her own. She is endowed with excellent ability, and more than moderately read in Latin literature, especially with regard to Holy Writ, and besides her native tongue she speaks Latin, French, and Spanish, and understands Italian perfectly, but does not speak it. She is also very generous, but not to the extent of letting it appear that she rests her chief claim to commendation on this quality.

She is so confirmed in the Catholic religion that although the King her brother and his Council prohibited her from having mass celebrated according to the Roman Catholic ritual, she nevertheless had it performed in secret, nor did she ever choose by any act to assent to any other form of religion, her belief in that in which she was born being so strong that had the opportunity offered she would have displayed it at the stake. Her Majesty takes great pleasure in playing on the lute and spinet, and is a very good performer on both instruments; and

9. *Queen Elizabeth confounding the Goddesses,* an allegorical painting by Hans Eworth, 1569. Elizabeth was thirty-six at the time, and this is the first painting of her as the Queen.

indeed before her accession she taught many of her maids of honour. But she seems to delight above all in arraying herself elegantly and magnificently . . . She also makes great use of jewels in which she delights greatly, and although she has a great plenty of them left her by her predecessors, yet were she better supplied with money than she is, she would doubtless buy many more.

Giacomo Soranzo, the Venetian Ambassador, 18 August 1554

ELIZABETH I

First went Gentlemen, Barons, Earls, Knights of the Garter, all richly dressed and bare-headed; next came the Chancellor, bearing the Seals in a red-silk purse, between two: one of which carried the Royal Sceptre, the other the Sword of State, in a red scabbard, studded with golden *Fleurs de Lis,* the point upwards: Next came the Queen, in the sixty-fifth year of her age, as we were told, very majestic; her face oblong, fair, but wrinkled; her

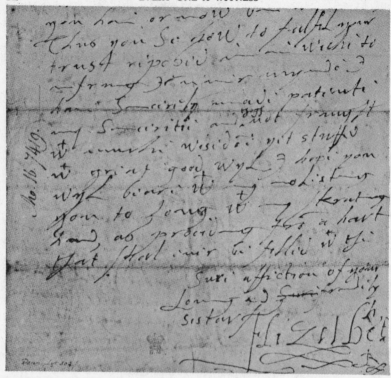

10. A letter from Queen Elizabeth to King James VI of Scotland (later James I), explaining in friendly terms her policy regarding the King of Spain.

eyes small, yet black and pleasant; her nose a little hooked; her lips narrow, and her teeth black (a defect the English seem subject to, for their too great use of sugar); she had in her ears two pearls, with very rich drops; she wore false hair, and that red; upon her head she had a small crown, reported to be made of some of the gold of the celebrated Lunebourg Table. Her bosom was uncovered, as all the English Ladies have it, till they marry; and she had on a necklace of exceeding fine jewels; her hands were small, her fingers long, and her stature neither tall nor low; her air was stately, her manner of speaking mild and obliging. That day she was dressed in white silk, bordered with pearls of the size of beans, and over it a mantle of black silk, shot with silver threads; her train was very long, the end of it borne by a marchioness; instead of a chain, she had an oblong collar of gold and jewels. As she went along in all this state and

11. One of the grandest surviving portraits of Queen Elizabeth at the height of her powers.

'She could be furious, abusive and formidable, yet (as Sir John Harington said) her smile "was pure sunshine". She could be disloyal to her ministers, but she never lost their loyalty: she could speak the most bitter words, yet she could write the most enchanting and heart-warming letters . . . She had a wonderful flair for politics and a most discerning eye in foreign affairs . . .

'The secret of her astounding success she herself revealed in her last speech: "though God hath raised me high, yet this I count the glory of my reign, that I have reigned with your loves".' C. R. N. Routh.

12. Mary, Queen of Scots. Miniature attributed to Nicholas Hilliard. One week old, she became Queen of Scots. She married the Dauphin, Francis, in 1558, and the same year became heir apparent to the English throne, and the following year Queen of France. When her husband died she returned to Scotland. She was now Elizabeth's 'ever-present yet ever-distant rival', a constant focus of Catholic discontent. Her marriage to her cousin, Lord Darnley, ended in his murder at Kirk O'Field. On her abdication, their son was crowned James VI of Scotland. Mary, who had fled to England, was imprisoned for 19 years and beheaded in 1587.

magnificence, she spoke very graciously, first to one, then to another, whether foreign ministers, or those who attended for different reasons, in English, French and Italian; for, besides being well skilled in Greek, Latin, and the languages I have mentioned, she is mistress of Spanish, Scotch and Dutch: whoever speaks to her, it is kneeling; now and then she raises some with her hand. While we were there, W. Slawata, a Bohemian Baron, had letters to present to her; and she, after pulling off her glove, gave him her right hand to kiss, sparkling with rings and jewels, a mark of particular favour: wherever she turned her face, as she was going along, everybody fell down on their knees. The Ladies of the Court followed next to her, very handsome and well-shaped, and for the most part dressed in white; she was guarded on each side by the Gentlemen Pensioners, fifty in number, with gilt battleaxes. In the Antichapel next the Hall where we were, petitions were presented to her, and she received them most graciously, which occasioned the acclamation of, *Long Live Queen Elizabeth!* She answered it with, *I thank you, my good people!* In the Chapel was excellent music; as soon as it and the service was over, which scarce exceeded half an hour, the Queen returned in the same state and order, and prepared to go to dinner.

Paul Hentzner, *A Journey into England in the Year 1608*

ELIZABETH I

Now, if ever any person had either the gift or the skill to win the hearts of people, it was this Queen; and if ever she did express the same, it was at that present, in coupling mildness with majesty as she did, and in stately stooping to the meanest sort. All her faculties were in motion, and every motion seemed a well guided action: Her eye was set upon one, her ear listened to another, her judgment ran upon a third, to the fourth she addressed her speech. Her spirit seemed to be everywhere, and yet so entire in herself, as it seemed to be nowhere else. Some she commended, some she pitied, some she thanked, at others she pleasantly and wittily jested, contemning no person, neglecting no office; and generally casting forth such courteous countenances, gestures and speeches, that thereupon the people again redoubled the testimonies of their joy, and afterwards, raising everything to the highest strain, filled the ears of all men with immoderate extolling their Prince.

Sir John Hayward, *With the beginning of the Raigne of Queene Elizabeth*, 1636

London

LONDON THROUGH ITALIAN EYES

This is from a private report drawn up by the Venetian envoy for the information of his government, about 1500. It gives a glowing account of London.

It abounds with every article of luxury, as well as with the necessaries of life. But the most remarkable thing in London is the wonderful quantity of wrought silver. I do not allude to that in private houses, but to the shops of London. In one single street, named the Strand, leading to St Paul's, there are fifty-two goldsmith's shops, so rich and full of silver vessels, great and small, that in all the shops in Milan, Rome, Venice, and Florence put together, I do not think there would be found so many of the magnificence that are to be seen in London. And these vessels are all either salt cellars, or drinking cups, or basins to hold water for the hands, for they eat off that fine tin [pewter], v ııch is little inferior to silver. These great riches of London are not occasioned by its inhabitants being noblemen or gentlemen; being all, on the contrary, persons of low degree, and artificers who have congregated there from all parts of the island, and from Flanders, and from every other place.

Italian Relation of England, 1500

THE GOVERNMENT OF LONDON

'Within London the Lord Mayor is next unto the King in all manner of things.' *The Mayor held a position of great responsibility and renown, and took a leading part not only in civic functions but on all royal occasions.*

No one can be mayor or alderman of London, who has not been an apprentice in his youth; that is, who has not passed the seven or nine years in that hard service described before. Still, the citizens of London are thought quite as highly of there, as the Venetian gentlemen are at Venice.

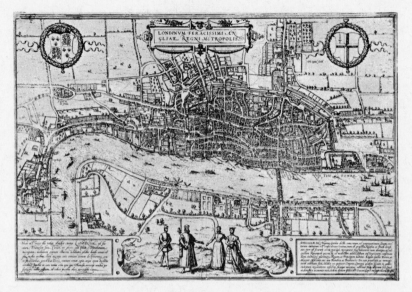

13. *Civitates Orbis Terrarum,* by G. Braun and F. Hohenberg (Cologne, 1577-88 edition). This map of London will reward examination with a magnifying glass, though it is not accurate in all small details. It shows the extent of London with outlying fields, gardens and orchards, and open spaces in the city itself. It shows the Tower, London Bridge, Bridewell, Lambeth Palace and in the centre old St Paul's with its spire, which had, in fact, fallen down in 1561.

The city is divided into several wards, each of which has six officers. But superior to these, are twenty-four gentlemen who are called aldermen, which in their language signifies old or experienced men. And, of these aldermen, one is elected every year by themselves, to be a magistrate named the mayor, who is in no less estimation with the Londoners, than the person of our most serene lord, the Doge, is with us, or than the Gonfaloniero at Florence. And the day on which he enters upon his office, he is obliged to give a sumptuous entertainment to all the principal people in London, as well as to foreigners of distinction. And I, being one of the guests, together with your Magnificence, carefully observed every room and hall, and the court, where the company were all seated, and was of opinion that there must have been 1000 or more persons at table.

A no less magnificent banquet is given when two other officers named *sheriffs* are appointed; to which I went, being anxious to see every thing well. At this feast, I observed the infinite profusion of victuals, and of plate, which was for the most part gilt. And amongst other things, I noticed how punctiliously they sat in their order, and the extraordinary silence of every one.

Italian Relation of England, 1500

LONDON AND THE RIVER THAMES

At present, all the beauty of this island is confined to London; which, although sixty miles distant from the sea, possesses all the advantages to be desired in a maritime town; being situated on the river Thames, which is very much affected by the tide, for many miles above it. And London is so much benefited by this ebb and flow of the river, that vessels of 100 tons burden can come up to the city, and ships of any size to within five miles of it. Yet the water in this river is fresh for twenty miles below London. Although this city has no buildings in the Italian style, but of timber or brick like the French, the Londoners live comfortably, and, it appears to me, that there are not fewer inhabitants than at Florence or Rome.

Italian Relation of England, 1500

IN HONOUR OF THE CITY OF LONDON

London, thou art of townes *A per se*.
  Soveraign of cities, seemliest in sight,
Of high renoun, riches and royaltie;
  Of lordis, barons, and many a goodly knyght;
  Of most delectable lusty ladies bright;
Of famous prelatis, in habitis clericall;
  Of merchauntis full of substaunce and of myght:
London, thou art the flour of Cities all.

William Dunbar, 1501

LONDON SUBURBS

The manner of the most gentlemen and noblemen is to house themselves (if possibly they may) in the suburbs of the city, because the air there being somewhat at large, the place is healthy; and through the distance from the body of the town, the noise not much and so consequently quiet. Also for comfort, we find many lodgings, both spacious and roomy, with gardens and orchards very delectable.

Civil and Uncivil Life, 1579,
W. C. Hazlett: *Inedited Tracts*

WATER FOR LONDON
This year Bevis Bulmar, a most ingenious gentleman, set up an engine at Brokenwharf, thereby, from thence to convey Thames water up into the city, sufficient to serve the whole west part thereof, being conveyed into men's houses by pipes of lead.

John Stow, *The Annales of England,* 1580

LORD POMP
Lord Pomp, let nothing that's magnifical,
Or that may tend to Londons graceful state,
Be unperform'd, as shows and solemn feasts,
Watches in armour, triumphs, cresset-lights;
Bonfires, bells, and peals of ordinance
And pleasure, see that plays be published,
May-games and masques, with mirth and minstrelsy
Pageants and school-feasts, bears and puppet plays.

*The Pleasant and Stately Morall of
the Three Lordes and Three Ladies
of London,* 1590

LONDON TO A FOREIGNER
London is a large, excellent and mighty city of business, and the most important in the whole kingdom; most of the inhabitants are employed in buying and selling merchandize, and trading in almost every corner of the world, since the river is most useful and convenient for this purpose, considering that ships from France, the Netherlands, Sweden, Denmark, Hamburg and other Kingdoms, come almost up to the city, to which they convey goods and receive and take away others in exchange.

It is a very populous city, so that one can scarcely pass along the streets, on account of the throng.

The inhabitants are magnificently apparelled, and are extremely proud and overbearing; and because the greater part, especially the tradespeople, seldom go into other countries, but always remain in their houses in the city attending to their business, they care little for foreigners, but scoff and laugh at them; and moreover one dare not oppose them, else the street-boys and apprentices collect together in immense crowds and strike to the right and left unmercifully without regard to person; and because they are the strongest, one is obliged to put up with insult as well as the injury.

The women have much more liberty than perhaps in any

other place; they also know well how to make use of it, for they
go dressed out in exceedingly fine clothes, and give all their
attention to their ruffs and stuffs, to such a degree indeed, that,
as I am informed, many a one does not hesitate to wear velvet in
the streets, which is common with them, whilst at home perhaps
they have not a piece of dry bread. All the English women are
accustomed to wear hats upon their heads, and gowns cut after
the old German fashion — for indeed their descent is from the
Saxons.

The Journal of Frederick, Duke of Würtemberg, 1592

LONDON'S DRINKING-WATER SUPPLY

The sweet [pure] water is preserved in various parts of the city,
in large well-built stone cisterns, to be drawn off by cocks, and
the poor water-bearers carry it on their shoulders to the
different houses and sell it in a peculiar kind of wooden vessels,
broad at the bottom, but very narrow at the top, and bound with
iron hoops.

Jacob Rathgeb, 1592, quoted in Rye:
England as Seen by Foreigners

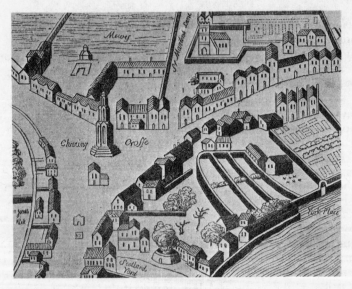

14.   The village of Charing in the sixteenth century. It stood at the western end
of the Strand, London, and was the site of one of the eight crosses set up by
Edward I in memory of his queen, Eleanor. The cross was removed later in the
seventeenth century.

ENGLISH SNOBBERY

In London, the rich disdain the poor. The courtier the citizen. The citizen the country man. One occupation disdaineth another. The merchant the retailer. The retailer the craftsman. The better sort of craftsman the baser. The shoemaker the cobbler. The cobbler the carman. One nice dame disdains her next neighbour should have that furniture to her house, or dainty dish or device, which she wants. She will not go to church, because she disdains to mix herself with base company, and cannot have her close pew by herself. She disdains to wear that everyone wears, or hear that preacher which everyone hears. So did Jerusalem disdain God's prophets, because they came in the likeness of poor men. She disdained Amos, because he was a keeper of oxen, as also the rest, for they were of the dregs of the people. But their disdain prospered not with them. Their house, for their disdain, was left desolate unto them.

Thomas Nashe, *Christs Teares over Ierusalem*, 1593

THE TOWER OF LONDON

For Stow, the chronicler, London was 'the fairest, largest, richest and best inhabited city in the world', and he gave it the care and study he thought it deserved. His Survey of London *is invaluable for the detailed information it gives about this ancient city.*

This tower is a citadel, to defend or command the city: a royal place for assemblies, and treaties. A prison of estate, for the most dangerous offenders: the only place of coinage for all England at this time: the armoury for warlike provision: the treasury of the ornaments and jewels of the crown, and general conserver of the most records of the King's courts of justice at Westminster.

John Stow. *A Survey of London*, 1598

LONDON TRAFFIC

The number of cars, drays, carts, and coaches more than hath been accustomed, the streets and lanes being straitened, must needs be dangerous, as daily experience proveth. The coachman rides behind the horse tails, lasheth them and looketh not behind him; the drayman sitteth and sleepeth on his dray and letteth his horse lead him home. I know that by the good laws and customs of this city, shod carts are forbidden to enter the same except upon reasonable causes, as the service of the prince or suchlike, they be tolerated; also that the forehorse of every

15.   A miniature of the White Tower of London from the manuscript poems of
Charles D'Orléans, who was captured at Agincourt in 1415, and held prisoner in
England till 1440.

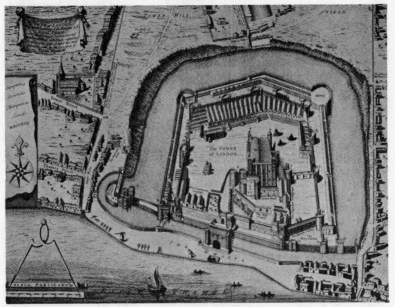

16. The Tower of London in 1597. It was the Royal mint from the thirteenth century to 1834, and a prison from the eleventh century. Traitors' Gate, standing behind The Wharfe, recalls the time when Anne Boleyn, Lady Jane Grey and the Earl of Essex were executed in the Tower.

carriage should be led by hand — but these good orders are not observed. Now of late years the use of coaches brought out of Germany is taken up and made so common as there is neither distinction of time nor difference of persons observed; for the world runs on wheels with many whose parents were glad to go on foot.

John Stow, *A Survey of London*, 1598

SUBJECTS OF THIS REALM

The multitude (or whole body) of this populous city is two ways to be considered, generally and specially: generally they be natural subjects, a part of the commons of this realm, and are by birth for the most part a mixture of all countries of the same, by blood gentlemen, yeoman, and of the basest sort, without distinction: and by profession busy bees, and travailers for their living in the hive of this commonwealth; but specially considered, they consist of these three parts, merchants handicraftsmen, and labourers.

Merchandise is also divided into these three sorts, navigation — by the which merchandises are brought and carried in and out over the seas — invection — by the which commodities are gathered into the city and dispersed from thence into the country by land — and negotiation, which I may call the keeping of a retailing or standing shop. In common speech they of the first sort may be called merchants, and both the other retailers. Handicraftsmen be those which do exercise such arts as require both labour and cunning as goldsmiths, tailors, and haberdashers, skinners, etc. Labourers and hirelings I call those *quorem opere non artes emunter*, as Tullie sayeth, of which sort be porters, carmen, watermen, etc. Again these three sorts may be considered in respect of their wealth, or number: in wealth, merchants and some of the chief retailers have the first place; the most part of retailers and all artificers, the second or mean place; and hirelings the lowest room: but in number they of the middle place be first, and do far exceed both the rest: hirelings be next, and merchants be the last.

John Stow, *A Survey of London,* 1598

17. London, *c.* 1616 by the Dutch artist, Claes Visscher, with buildings on both sides of the river and on London Bridge, a street in itself, with many shops and houses. Southwark Cathedral stands on the south bank.

18. A model of Elizabethan London with the Globe Theatre; and to the left the Bear Garden on the south bank of the Thames, with old St Paul's away on the left. (Still from the film *Henry V*).

LONDON'S DRINKING-WATER

The supply of water for the public at this time was not very satisfactory. An Elizabethan working man would pay as much as eight pence for water during one week.

Spring or drinking-water is enclosed in great well-sealed stone cisterns in different parts of the town, is let off through cocks into special wooden iron-bound vessels with broad bottoms and narrow tops, which poor labourers carry to and fro to the houses on their shoulders and sell.

Thomas Platter, Travels in England, 1599

HOG LANE, 1603

John Stow, writing of Hog Lane in 1603, said,

within these forty years, had on both sides fair hedgerows of elm trees, with bridges and easy stiles to pass over into the pleasant fields, very commodious for citizens therein to walk, shoot, and otherwise to recreate and refresh their dull spirits in the sweet and wholesome air, which is now within a few years made a continual building throughout, of garden houses, and small cottages: and the fields on either side be turned into garden plots, teynter yards [for stretching cloth], bowling alleys, and such like, from Houndes ditch in the west, so far as White Chappell, and further towards the East.

Towns – Buildings – Gardens

AN ENGLISH HOME

'Come on, you shall go see my house the while. It is not like your large country houses; victuals be here at such high prices that much money is soon consumed; nevertheless, assure yourself that no man is welcomer than you to such cheer as you find.' And bringing me through divers well-trimmed chambers, the worst of them decorated with rich tapestries, some with rich cloth of arras, all with beds, chairs and cushions of silk and gold. So down we came again into the parlour and what should I say more, but to dinner we went.

Gilbert Walker, *A Manifestation of Dice-play*, 1532

HOUSES OF THE HUSBANDMEN

. . . walls of earth, low thatched roofs, few partitions, no planchings or glass windows, and scarcely any chimneys, other than a hole in the wall to let out the smoke: their bed, straw and a blanket: as for sheets, so much linen cloth had not yet stepped over the narrow channel, between them and Brittaine [Brittany]. To conclude, a mazer [drinking-cup] and a pan or two, comprised all their substance: but now most of these fashions are universally banished, and the Cornish husbandman conformeth himself with a better supplied civility to the Eastern pattern.

Richard Carew, *Survey of Cornwall*, *c.*1580

MAYOR OF RYE IN 1581 TELLS THE MAYORS OF WINCHELSEA, HASTINGS, ROMNEY, HYTHE, DOVER AND SANDWICH ABOUT THE IRON INDUSTRY

By sundry iron works and glass houses [for glass blowing] already erected, the woods growing near unto the three towns of Hastings, Winchelsea and Rye are marvellously wasted and decayed; and if speedy remedy be not had the said woods will in

26

short time be utterly consumed, in sort as there will not any
timber be had for shipping, waterworks, house building, nor
wood for fuel.

Rye MS., 1581

HOUSES AND FURNITURE

The greatest part of our building in the cities and good towns of
England consisteth only of timber, for as yet few of the houses
of the commonalty (except here and there in the west-country
towns) are made of stone, although they may, in my opinion, in
divers other places be builded so good cheap of the one as of the
other. In old time the houses of the Britons were slightly set up
with a few posts and many raddles [laths], with stable and all
offices under one roof, the like whereof almost is to be seen in
the fenny countries and northern parts unto this day, where for
lack of wood they are enforced to continue this ancient manner
of building . . .

19. A fifteenth-century yeoman's cottage at Bignor, N.W. Sussex. In Domesday
'Bigeneure', the village, is on the old Roman Stane Street.

20. The north front of Eastington Hall, a fifteenth-century timber-built manor house near the village of Longdon in S. Worcestershire.

Certes this rude kind of building made the Spaniards in Queen Mary's days to wonder, but chiefly when they saw what large diet was used in many of these so homely cottages; insomuch that one of no small reputation amongst them said after this manner — 'These English,' quoth he, 'have their houses made of sticks and dirt, but they fare commonly so well as the king.' Whereby it appeareth that he liked better of our good fare in such coarse cabins than of their own thin diet in their prince-like habitations and palaces. In like sort as every country house is thus apparelled on the outside, so is it inwardly divided into sundry rooms above and beneath; and, where plenty of wood is, they cover them with tiles, otherwise with straw, sedge or reed, except some quarry of slate be near hand, from whence they have for their money much as may suffice them. The clay wherewith our houses are impanelled is either white, red or blue; and of these the first doth participate very much of the nature of our chalk, the second is called loam, but the third eftsoons changeth colour as soon as it is wrought, notwithstanding that it looks blue when it is thrown out of the pit . . .

The walls of our houses on the inner sides in like sort be either hanged with tapestry, arras work, or painted cloths, wherein either divers histories, or herbs, beasts, knots and such like are stained, or else they are ceiled with oak of our own, or wainscot brought hither out of the east countries, whereby the rooms are not a little commended, made warm and much more close than otherwise they would be. As for stoves, we have not hitherto used them greatly, yet do they now begin to be made in divers houses of the gentry and wealthy citizens, who build them not to work and feed in, as in Germany and elsewhere, but now and then to sweat in, as occasion and need shall require it.

This also hath been common in England, contrary to the customs of all other nations, and yet to be seen (for example, in most streets of London), that many of our greatest houses have outwardly been very simple and plain to sight, which inwardly have been able to receive a duke with his whole train, and lodge them at their ease. Hereby, moreover, it is come to pass that the fronts of our streets have not been so uniform and orderly builded as those of foreign cities, where (to say truth) the outer side of their mansions and dwellings have oft more cost bestowed upon them than all the rest of the house, which are often very simple and uneasy within, as experience doth

21. A long gallery, Lanhydrock House, Cornwall. This Tudor house stands in a well-wooded park on the river Fowey, and was the seat of the Robartes family.

22.   Many of the old timbered houses in Lavenham, Suffolk, are fine examples of sixteenth-century architecture.

confirm. Of old time, our country houses, instead of glass, did use much lattice, and that made either of wicker or fine rifts of oak in chequerwise. I read also that some of the better sort, in and before the times of the Saxons (who notwithstanding used some glass also since the time of Benedict Biscop, the monk that brought the feat of glazing first into the land), did make panels of horn instead of glass, and fix them in wooden calms [frames]. But as horn in windows is now quite laid down in every place, so our lattices are also grown into less use, because glass is come to be so plentiful and within a very little so good cheap, if not better than the other . . .

The furniture of our houses also exceedeth, and is grown in manner even to passing delicacy: and herein I do not speak of the nobility and gentry only, but likewise of the lowest sort in most places of our south country that have anything at all to take to. Certes in noblemen's houses it is not rare to see abundance of arras, rich hangings of tapestry, silver vessel, and so much other plate as may furnish sundry cupboards to the sum oftentimes of a thousand or two thousand pounds at the least, whereby the value of this and the rest of their stuff doth grow to be almost

23. The great screen on the west side of King's College Chapel, Cambridge, c. 1531-1535, with Italianate Renaissance design.

inestimable. Likewise in the houses of knights, gentlemen, merchantmen, and some other wealthy citizens, it is not geason [rare] to behold generally their great provision of tapestry, Turkey work, pewter, brass, fine linen, and thereto costly cupboards of plate, worth five or six hundred or a thousand pounds to be deemed by estimation. But, as herein all these sorts do far exceed their elders and predecessors, and in neatness and curiosity the merchant all other, so in time past the costly furniture stayed there, whereas now it is descended yet lower even unto the inferior artificers and many farmers, who, by virtue of their old and not of their new leases, have for the most part learned also to garnish their cupboards with plate, their joined beds with tapestry and silk hangings, and their tables with carpets and fine napery, whereby the wealth of our country (God be praised therefore, and give us grace to employ it well) doth infinitely appear. Neither do I speak this in reproach of any man. God is my judge, but to shew that I do rejoice rather to see how God hath blessed us with his good gifts: and whilst I

24. Bishop Hooper's Lodging, Westgate Street, Gloucester. In this double-gabled house he spent the night before he was burned at the stake as a heretic, in 1553.

25. Little Sodbury Manor, Gloucestershire, from the west.

behold how that, in a time wherein all things are grown to most excessive prices, and what commodity so ever is to be had is daily plucked from the commonalty by such as look into every trade, we do yet find the means to obtain and achieve such furniture as heretofore hath been unpossible.

There are old men yet dwelling in the village where I remain which have noted three things to be marvellously altered in England within their sound remembrance, and other three things too too much increased.

One is the multitude of chimneys lately erected, whereas in their young days there were not above two or three, if so many, in most uplandish towns of the realm (the religious houses and manor places of their lords always excepted, and peradventure some great personages), but each one made his fire against a reredos [brick or stone back of a fireplace] in the hall, where he dined and dressed his meat.

The second is the great (although not general) amendment of lodging; for, said they, our fathers, yea and we ourselves also, have lain full oft upon straw pallets, on rough mats covered only with a sheet, under coverlets made of dogswain [rough cloth] or hopharlots [coarse coverlet] (I use their own terms), and a good round log under their heads instead of a bolster or pillow. If it were so that our fathers or the goodman of the house had within seven years after his marriage purchased a mattress or flock bed, and thereto a sack of chaff to rest his head upon, he thought himself to be as well lodged as the lord of the town, that peradventure lay seldom in a bed of down or whole feathers, so well were they contented, and with such base kind of furniture: which also is not very much amended as yet in some parts of Bedfordshire, and elsewhere, further off from our southern parts. Pillows (said they) were thought meet only for women in childbed. As for servants, if they had any sheet above them, it was well, for seldom had they any under their bodies to keep them from the pricking straws that ran oft through the canvas of the pallet and rased [scratched] their hardened hides.

The third thing they tell of is the exchange of vessel, as of treen [wooden] platters into pewter, and wooden spoons into

26. Little Moreton Hall, Cheshire, from the south. This moated, black-and-white timbered manor house, completed by William Moreton and his son, John, in the late sixteenth century, is one of the most picturesque of its kind in Cheshire.

27. Thomas Wolsey, subsequently Cardinal and Lord Chancellor of England, started to build Hampton Court in 1514. He offered it to Henry VIII in 1526 to regain favour, but soon fell from power. Between 1531 and 1536 the King added the Great Hall to this royal palace, improved the Chapel, made other additions. This became Henry's favourite country home, with its park bordered by the Thames.

silver or tin. For so common were all sorts of treen stuff in old time that a man should hardly find four pieces of pewter (of which one was peradventure a salt) in a good farmer's house, and yet for all this frugality (if it may so be justly called) they were scarce able to live and pay their rents at their days without selling of a cow or a horse or more, although they paid but four pounds at the uttermost by the year. Such also was their poverty that, if some one odd farmer or husbandman had been at the ale-house, a thing greatly used in those days, amongst six or seven of his neighbours, and there in a bravery, to shew what store he had, did cast down his purse, and therein a noble or six shillings in silver, unto them (for few such men then cared for gold, because it was not so ready payment, and they were oft enforced to give a penny for the exchange of an angel [gold coin]), it was very likely that all the rest could not lay down so much against it; whereas in my time, although peradventure four pounds of old rent be improved to forty, fifty or a hundred pounds, yet will the farmer, as another palm or date tree, think his gains very small towards the end of his term if he have not six or seven years' rent lying by him, therewith to purchase a new lease, beside a fair garnish of pewter on his cupboard, with so much more in odd vessel going about the house, three or four feather beds, so many coverlets and carpets of tapestry, a silver salt, a bowl for wine (if not a whole nest), and a dozen of spoons to furnish up the suit.

William Harrison, *Description of England,* 1587

GARDENS AND ORCHARDS

If you look into our gardens annexed to our houses, how wonderfully is their beauty increased, not only with flowers . . . and variety of curious and costly workmanship, but also with rare and medicinable herbs sought up in the land within these forty years: so that, in comparison of this present, the ancient

28. Longleat, Wiltshire, built in the classical style for Sir John Thynne between 1558 and 1580. Though a deal of interest lies in its splendid contents, the beauty of its four palatial facades places it among the chief architectural glories of England.

29. Wollaton Hall, Nottinghamshire, showing the west front from the south west. This splendid example of Elizabethan Renaissance architecture was designed by Robert Smythson 1580-1588. He had worked with Sir John Thynne rebuilding Longleat House in Wiltshire. Wollaton Hall was original as it had no courtyards, the hall stood central in the form of a great tower, and ornamented towers rose at the four corners of this massive building.

gardens were but dunghills and laystows [refuse places] to such as did possess them. How art also helpeth nature in the daily colouring, doubling and enlarging the proportion of our flowers, it is incredible to report: for so curious and cunning are our gardeners now in these days that they presume to do in manner what they list with nature, and moderate her course in things as if they were her superiors. It is a world also to see how many strange herbs, plants and annual fruits are daily brought unto us from the Indies, Americans, Taprobane [Ceylon], Canary Isles, and all parts of the world: the which, albeit that in respect of the constitutions of our bodies they do not grow for us, because that God hath bestowed sufficient commodities upon every country for her own necessity, yet, for delectation sake unto the eye and their odoriferous savours unto the nose, they are to be cherished, and God to be glorified also in them, because they are his good gifts, and created to do man help and service. There is not almost one nobleman, gentleman or merchant that hath not great store of these flowers, which now also do begin to wax so well acquainted with our soils that we may almost account of them as parcel of our own commodities. They have no less regard in like sort to cherish medicinable herbs fetched out of other regions nearer hand, insomuch that I have seen in some one garden to the number of three hundred or four hundred of them, if not more, of the half of whose names within forty years past we had no manner knowledge. But herein I find some cause of just complaint, for that we extol their uses so far that we fall into contempt of our own, which are in truth more beneficial and apt for us than such as grow elsewhere, sith (as I said before) every region hath abundantly within her own limits whatsoever is needful and most convenient for them that dwell therein . . .

30. Montacute House, Somerset, one of the most beautiful country houses built in the reign of Elizabeth. The possible designer was Thomas Arnold, who built it in 1588-1601 for Sir Edward Phelips, It has fine windows and garden balustrades. The house contains splendid heraldic glass, plasterwork and panelling. Hospitality is shown by the inscription over the door:

  Through this wide-opening gate
  None come too early, none return too late.

And even as it fareth with our gardens, so doth it with our orchards, which were never furnished with so good fruit nor with such variety as at this present. For, beside that we have most delicate apples, plums, pears, walnuts, filberts, etc., and those of sundry sorts, planted within forty years past, in comparison of which most of the old trees are nothing worth, so have we no less store of strange fruit, as apricots, almonds, peaches, figs, corn-trees [cornelian cherry] in noblemen's orchards. I have seen capers, oranges and lemons, and heard of wild olives growing here, beside other strange trees brought from far, whose names I know not. So that England for these commodities was never better furnished, neither any nation under their clime more plentifully endued with these and other blessings from the most high God, who grant us grace withal to use the same to his honour and glory, and not as instruments and provocations unto further excess and vanity, wherewith his displeasure may be kindled, lest these his benefits do turn unto thorns and briers unto us for our annoyance and punishment, which he hath bestowed upon us for our consolation and comfort.

William Harrison, *Description of England*, 1587

THEOBALDS

[in Herts] . . . went to see the magnificent palace Theobalds, belonging to the Lord High Treasurer of England, which is reckoned one of the most beautiful houses in England, as in truth it is.

First of all his Highness inspected the handsome and delightful hall, which is so ornamental and artistic that its equal is not easily to be met with; for, besides other imbellishments in it, there is a very high rock, of all colours, made of real stones, out of which gushes a splendid fountain that falls into a large circular bowl or basin, supported by two savages. This hall has no pillars: it is about sixty feet in length and upwards of thirty wide.

The ceiling or upper floor is very artistically constructed: it contains the twelve signs of the zodiac, so that at night you can see distinctly the stars proper to each; on the same stage the sun performs its course, which is without doubt contrived by some concealed ingenious mechanism. On each side of the hall are six trees, having the natural bark so artfully joined, with birds' nests and leaves as well as fruit upon them, all managed in such a manner that you could not distinguish between the natural and these artificial trees; and, as far as I could see, there was no difference at all, for when the steward of the house opened the windows, which looked upon the beautiful pleasure-garden, birds flew into the hall, perched themselves upon the trees, and began to sing. In a word, this hall is so elegantly adorned with paintings and otherwise that it is right royal, and well worth the seeing.

There are also many other spacious halls and fine galleries in this splendid palace, with very artistic paintings and correct landscapes of all the most important and remarkable towns in Christendom, as well as tables of inlaid-work and marble of various colours, all of the richest and most magnificent description.

In another hall is depicted the Kingdom of England, with all its cities, towns and villages, mountains and rivers; as also the armorial bearings and domains of every esquire, lord, knight, and noble who possess lands and retainers to whatever extent. In short, all the apartments and rooms are adorned with beautiful tapestries and the like to such a degree that no king need be ashamed to dwell there.

Some rooms in particular have very beautiful and costly ceilings, which are skilfully wrought in joiner's work and elegantly coloured.

The Journal of Frederick, Duke of Würtemberg, 1592

31. Speke Hall, within the boundaries of Liverpool, is one of the finest of half-timbered Elizabethan manor-houses. The house has 'all sorts of annexes approached by secret doors in the wainscoting — an eavesdropping chamber from which every word spoken in the hall can be overheard; also hideaways with escape routes through the walls . . .' Probably for use in troubled times for the Norreys family, who built and extended the house, was Catholic.

32. The Bodleian Library, Oxford, one of the most important libraries in the world. The original library was founded in 1480 by Humphrey, Duke of Gloucester, son of Henry IV. A diplomat, Sir Thomas Bodley, re-arranged it in 1598, and, by adding his own private collection, established it firmly.

THE GARDEN OF THEOBALDS

. . . the garden, encompassed with a ditch full of water, large
enough for one to have the pleasure of going in a boat, and
rowing between the shrubs; here are great variety of trees and
plants; labyrinths made with a great deal of labour; a jet d'eau,
with its basin of white marble; and columns and pyramids of
wood and other materials up and down the garden. After seeing
these, we were led by the gardener into the summer-house, in
the lower part of which, built semicircularly, are the twelve
Roman emperors in white marble, and a table of touchstone; the
upper part of it is set round with cisterns of lead, into which the
water is conveyed through pipes, so that fish may be kept in
them, and in summertime they are very convenient for bathing;
in another room for entertainment very near this, and joined to
it by a little bridge, was an oval table of red marble.

Paul Hentzner, *Travels in England*, 1598

THE GARDENS AT HAMPTON COURT

. . . the gardener conducted us into the royal pleasaunce.

By the entrance I noticed numerous patches where square
cavities had been scooped, as for paving stones; some of these
were filled with red brick-dust, some with white sand, and some
with green lawn, very much resembling a chess-board. The
hedges and surrounds were of hawthorn, bush firs, ivy, roses,
juniper, holly, English or common elm, box and other shrubs,
very gay and attractive.

There were all manner of shapes, men and women, half men
and half horse, sirens, serving-maids with baskets, French lilies
and delicate crenellations all round made from the dry twigs
bound together and the aforesaid evergreen quick-set shrubs, or
entirely of rosemary, all true to the life, and so cleverly and
amusingly interwoven, mingled and grown together, trimmed
and arranged picturewise that their equal would be difficult to
find.

And just as there is a park on the one hand, so opposite this in
the middle of the other side there is a maze, similarly decorated
with plants and flowering trees, and two marble fountains, so
that time shall not drag in such a place; for should one miss
one's way, not only are taste, vision and smell delighted, but the
glad-some birdsongs and plashing fountains please the ear,
indeed it is like an earthly paradise.

Thomas Platter, *Travels in England*, 1599

THREE COUNTIES IN 1599

Lancashire: a district plentiful of oats and great bodied beeves.
Northumberland: chiefly noted for swift horses and sea coals, a
rough country and hardly tilled, inhabited by a fierce people.
Sussex: divided into downs full of sheep and woodland full of
iron mines, and some good pasturage.

British Museum, Harleian MSS. 3813

BARNET

This Barnet is a place of great resort,
And commonly upon the market days
Here all the country gentlemen appoint
A friendly meeting; some about affairs
Of consequence and profit — bargain, sale,
And to confer with chapmen, some for pleasure,
To match their horses, wager on their dogs,
Or try their hawks; some to no other end
But only meet good company, discourse,
Dine, drink and spend their money.

Thomas Heywood, *English Traveller*

Family

SOCIAL LIFE

THE ENGLISH IN THE SIXTEENTH CENTURY
They eat very frequently, at times more than is suitable, and are particularly fond of young swans, rabbits, deer and sea birds. They often eat mutton and beef, which is generally considered to be better here than anywhere else in the world. This is due to the excellence of their pastures. They have all kinds of fish in plenty and great quantities of oysters which come from the sea-shore. The majority, not to say everyone, drink that beverage [beer] I have spoken of before, and prepare it in various ways. For wine is very expensive, as the vine does not grow in the island; nor does the olive, and the products of both are imported from France and Spain . . .

They have several harsh laws and customs, one of which, still in force to-day, we would consider the most severe of all. This lays down that, at death, a man must leave all his property to his wife, completely excluding the children, for whom they show no affection, lavishing all their love on their wives. And consequently, since the wives have the same dislike for their children, they choose in the end a husband from among the servants and ignore the children. This custom, apart from being contrary to nature, may also be objected to as impious and profane.

Andreas Franciscus, *Itinerarium Britanniae, c.* 1497.
This Latin MS. was translated by C. V. Malpatti

A FOREIGN VIEW OF ENGLAND
The English are, for the most part, both men and women of all ages, handsome and well-proportioned; though not quite so much so, in my opinion, as it had been asserted to me, before your Magnificence went to that kingdom; and I have understood from persons acquainted with these countries that the Scotch are much handsomer; and that the English are great lovers of themselves, and of everything belonging to them; they think that

there are no other men than themselves, and no other world but England: and whenever they see a handsome foreigner, they say that 'he looks like an Englishman', and that 'it is a great pity that he should not be an Englishman'; and when they partake of any delicacy with a foreigner, they ask him, 'whether such a thing is made in their country?' They take great pleasure in having a quantity of excellent victuals, and also in remaining a long time at table, being very sparing of wine when they drink it at their own expense . . . and they think that no greater honour can be conferred or received than to invite others to eat with them, or to be invited themselves; and they would sooner give five or six ducats to provide an entertainment for a person, than a groat to assist him in any distress.

They all from time immemorial wear very fine clothes, and are extremely polite in their language; which, although it is as well as the Flemish derived from the German, has lost its natural harshness, and is pleasing enough as they pronounce it. In addition to their civil speeches, they have the incredible courtesy of remaining · with their heads uncovered with an admirable grace, whilst they talk to each other. They are gifted with good understandings, and are very quick at everything they apply their minds to; few, however, excepting the clergy, are addicted to the study of letters; and this is the reason why anyone who has learning, though he may be a layman, is called by them a clerk. And yet they have great advantages for study, there being two general universities in the kingdom, Oxford and Cambridge; in which are many colleges founded for the maintenance of poor scholars. And your Magnificence lodged at one named Magdalen, in the University of Oxford, of which the founders have been prelates, so the scholars are also ecclesiastics.

The common people apply themselves to trade, or to fishing, or else they practise navigation; and they are so diligent in mercantile pursuits, that they do not fear to make contracts on usury.

Although they all attend mass every day, and say many Paternosters in public (the women carry long rosaries in their hands, and any who can read taking the office of Our Lady with them, and with some companion reciting it in the church verse by verse, in a low voice, after the manner of churchmen), they always hear mass on Sunday in their parish church, and give liberal alms, because they may not offer less than a piece of money of which fourteen are equivalent to a golden ducat; nor do they omit any form incumbent upon good Christians; there are, however, many who have various opinions concerning religion.

They have a very high reputation in arms; and from the great fear the French entertain of them, one must believe it to be justly acquired. But I have it on the best information, that when the war is raging most furiously, they will seek for good eating, and all their other comforts, without thinking of what harm might befall them . . .

The want of affection in the English is strongly manifested towards their children; for after having kept them at home till they arrive at the age of seven or nine years at the utmost, they put them out, both males and females, to hard service in the houses of other people, binding them generally for another seven or nine years. And these are called apprentices, and during that time they perform all the most menial offices; and few are born who are exempted from this fate, for every one, however rich he may be, sends away his children into the houses

33. A four-poster Tudor bed with the decorated tester or rectangular framed canopy (from which hung the bed-curtains) supported by two posts. The headboard is enriched with elaborate heraldic carving.

of others whilst he, in return, receives those of strangers into his own. And on inquiring their reason for this severity, they answered that they did it in order that their children might learn better manners. But I, for my part, believe that they do it because they like to enjoy all their comforts themselves, and that they are better served by strangers than they would be by their own children. Besides which the English being great epicures, and very avaricious by nature, indulge in the most delicate fare themselves and give their household the coarsest bread, and beer, and cold meat baked on Sunday for the week, which, however, they allow them in great abundance.

Venetian Relation, c. 1498

WIFE AND HUSBAND

It is convenient for a husband to have sheep of his own, for many causes, and then may his wife have part of the wool, to make her husband and herself some clothes. And at the least way, she may have the locks of the sheep, either to make clothes or blankets and coverlets, or both. And if she have no wool of her own, she may take wool to spin of cloth-makers, and by that means she may have a convenient living, and many times do other works. It is a wife's occupation, to winnow all manner of corns, to make malt, to wash and wring, to make hay, shear corn, and in time of need to help her husband to fill the muck-wain or dung-cart, drive the plough, to load hay, corn and such other. And to go or ride to the market, to sell butter, cheese, milk, eggs, chickens, capons, hens, pigs, geese, and all manner of corns. And also to buy all manner of necessary things belonging to household, and to make a true reckoning and account to her husband, what she hath paid. And if the husband go to the market, to buy or sell, as they oft do, he then to show his wife in like manner. For if one of them should use to deceive the other, he deceiveth himself, and he is not likely to thrive. And therefore they must be true either to other.

John Fitzherbert, *Boke of Husbondrye,* 1523

A PUBLIC FUNERAL IN 1560

The 23rd day of July was buried my good lady, the wife of Sir William Chester, knight and draper and alderman and merchant of the staple, and the house and the church and the street hung with black and ensigns of arms. And she gave to twenty poor women good russet gowns, and he gave unto four aldermen black gowns and other men gowns and coats to the number of a hundred . . . And there were two heralds of arms; and then came the corpse and four mourners bearing of four pennons of arms about, and came mourners before and after, and the clerks singing. And master Beycon did preach over night; and the morrow after to the house to dinner; six dozen of skochyons [ensigns] and a half dozen ensigns of buckram.

The Diary of Henry Machyn, citizen and
merchant-taylor of London, 1550-1563

SERVANTS

Verses painted on the kitchen wall of Winchester College portray a servant in the 1560s.

A trusty servant's portrait would you see,
This emblematic figure we'll survey.
The porker's snout — not nice in diet shows;
The padlock's shut — no secret he'll disclose;
Patient the ass — his master's wrath will bear;
Swiftness in errand — the stag's feet declare;
Loaded his left hand — apt to labour saith;
The vest — his neatness; open hand — his faith;
Girt with his sword, his shield upon his arm,
Himself and master, he'll protect from harm.

'THE PARADISE OF MARRIED WOMEN'

Although the women there are entirely in the power of their husbands except for their lives, yet they are not kept so strictly as they are in Spain or elsewhere. Nor are they shut up, but they have the free management of the house or housekeeping, after the fashion of those of the Netherlands and others their neighbours. They go to market to buy what they like best to eat. They are well dressed, fond of taking it easy, and commonly leave the care of household matters and drudgery to their servants. They sit before their doors, decked out in fine clothes, in order to see and be seen by the passers-by. In all banquets and feasts they are shown the greatest honour; they are placed at the upper end of the table, where they are the first served; at the lower end they help the men. All the rest of their time they employ in walking and riding, in playing at cards or otherwise, in visiting their friends and keeping company, conversing with their equals (whom they term 'gossips') and their neighbours, and making merry with them at childbirths, christenings, churchings, and funerals; and all this with the permission and knowledge of their husbands, as such is the custom. Although

34. The Great Bed of Ware, nearly twelve feet square, was made by a carpenter, James Fosbrooke, in 1463. Its first home may have been Ware Park in Hertfordshire. It was moved to the Saracen's Head Inn at Ware. It is referred to by Shakespeare, Jonson and Farquhar.

the husbands often recommend to them the pains, industry, and care of the German or Dutch women, who do what men ought to do both in the house and in the shops, for which services in England men are employed, nevertheless the women usually persist in retaining their customs. This is why England is called 'The Paradise of Married Women'. The girls who are not yet married are kept much more rigorously and strictly than in the Low Countries.

The women are beautiful, fair, well-dressed and modest, which is seen there more than elsewhere, as they go about the streets without any covering either of huke [cape] or mantle, hood, veil, or the like. Married women only wear a hat both in the street and in the house; those unmarried go without a hat, although ladies of distinction have lately learnt to cover their faces with silken masks or vizards, and feathers, — for indeed they change very easily, and that every year, to the astonishment of many.

Emanuel Van Meteren, *Nederlandtsche Historie*, 1575

A DAY IN THE LIFE OF ROBERT LANEHAM, 1575

A-mornings I rise ordinarily at seven o'clock. Then ready, I go into the Chapel: soon after eight, I get me commonly into my Lord's Chamber, or into my Lord President's. There, at the cupboard, after I have eaten the manchet [a loaf of bread served out as allowance], served over-night for livery, (for I dare be as bold, I promise you, as any of my friends the servants there: and indeed, could I have fresh if I would tarry: but I am of wont jolly and dry a-mornings) I drink me up a good bowl of Ale: when in a sweet pot it is defecated [freed from dregs] by all night's standing, the drink is the better; take that of me: and a morsel in a morning, with a sound draught, is very wholesome and good for the eyesight. Then I am as fresh all the forenoon after as had I eaten a whole piece of beef. Now, sir, if the Council sit, I am at hand, wait at an inch, I warrant you. If any make babbling, 'Peace!' (say I) 'Wot ye where ye are?' If I catch a listener, or a prier in at the chinks or at the lock hole, I am by and bye in the bones of him [giving him a dig in the ribs]; but now they keep good order; they know me well enough: if he be a friend or such one as I like, I make him sit down by me on a form or a chest: let the rest walk, a God's name! And here doth my languages now and then stand me in good stead, my French, my Spanish, my Dutch, and my Latin, sometime among Ambassadors' men, if their Master be within the Council, sometimes with the Ambassador himself, if he bid me call his lackey, or ask me what's o'clock: and I warrant ye I answer him roundly, that they marvel to see such a fellow there: then laugh I, and say nothing. Dinner and supper I have twenty places to go to and heartily prayed to. And sometimes get I to Master Pinner, by my faith a worshipful Gentleman, and as careful for his charge as any her Highness hath: there find I always good store of very good viands: we eat and be merry, thank God and the Queen! Himself in feeding very temperate and moderate as ye shall see any: and yet by your leave, of a dish — as a cold pigeon or so, that hath come to him at meat, more than he looked for, — I have seen him even so by and bye surfeited, as he hath plucked off his napkin, wiped his knife, and eat not a morsel more: like enough to stick in his stomach a two days after . . . In afternoons and a nights, sometimes am I with the right worshipful Sir George Howard, as good a gentleman as any likes: and sometimes at my good Lady Sidney's chamber, a Noblewoman that I am as much bound unto, as any poor man may be unto so gracious a Lady. And sometime in some other

place; but always among the Gentlewomen by my good will (O,
ye know that comes always of a gentle spirit); and when I see
company according, then can I be as lively too. Sometimes I foot
it with dancing; now with my Gittern, [guitar], and else with my
Cittern, [like a guitar, but with wire strings], then at the
Virginals — ye know nothing comes amiss to me — then carol I
up a song withal, that by and bye they come flocking about me
like bees to honey: and ever they cry, 'Another, good Laneham,
another!' . . . By my truth, countryman, it is sometime by
midnight ere I can get from them. And thus have I told ye most
of my trade, all the live-long day: what will ye more? God save
the Queen and my Lord! I am well, I thank you.

Robert Laneham's Letter, as edited by Dr. Furnivall

INSTRUCTIONS TO CHILDREN AND SERVANTS

When that thou comest to the Church, thy prayers for to say,
See thou sleepe not, nor yet talke not, devoutly looke thou pray,
Ne cast thyne eyes to ne fro, as thinges thou wouldst still see;
So shall wyse men judge thee a foole, and wanton for to bee.
When thou are in the Temple, see thou do thy Churchly warkes;
Heare thou Gods word with diligence, crave pardon for thy
     fautes.

. . . . . .

Looke that your knyfe be sharp & kene to cut your meate
     withall;
So the more cleanlyer, be sure, cut your meate you shall.
Or thou put much bread in thy pottage, looke thou doe it assay:
Fill not thy spoone to full, least thou loose somewhat by the way.

. . . . . .

And sup not lowde of thy Pottage, no tyme in all thy lyfe:
Dip not thy meate in the Saltseller, but take it with thy knyfe.
When thou haste eaten thy Pottage, doe as I shall thee wish:
Wype clean thy spone, I do thee read, leave it not in the dish;
Lay it downe before thy trenchoure, therefore be not afrayde;
And take heede who takes it up, for feare it be convayde.
Cut not the best peece for thy selfe, leave thou some parte
     behynde:
Bee not greedye of meate and drinke; be liberall and kynde.
Burnish no bones with thy teeth, for that is unseemely;
Rend not thy meate asunder, for that swarves from curtesy;
And if a straunger syt neare thee, ever among now and than
Reward thou him with some daynties: shew thyselfe a
     Gentleman.

If your fellow sit from his meate and cannot come thereto,
Then cutte for him such as thou haste; he may lyke for thee
     doe.

. . . . . .

Scratche not thy head with thy fyngers when thou arte at thy
     meate;
Nor spytte you over the table boorde; see thou doest not this
     forget.
Pick not thy teeth with thy Knyfe nor with thy fingers ende,
But take a stick, or some cleane thyng, then doe you not
     offende.

. . . . . .

Fyll not thy mouth to full, leaste thou perhaps of force must
     speake;
Nor blow not out thy crums when thou doest eate.
Fowle not the place with spitting whereas thou doest syt,
Least it abhore some that syt by: let reason·rule thy wyt.
If thou must spit, or blow thy nose, keepe thou it out of sight,
Let it not lye upon the ground, but treade thou out right.
  Hugh Rhodes, *The Boke of Nurture, or Schoole of good maners*, 1577

35.   A sixteenth-century marriage feast at Bermondsey, by Joris Hofnagel.

LAP-DOGS

That plausible proverb, therefore, verified sometime upon a tyrant, namely that he loved his sow better than his son, may well be applied to some of this kind of people, who delight more in their dogs [spaniels], that are deprived of all possibility of reason, than they do in children that are capable of wisdom and

36. Long Cover (detail). Early seventeenth century. It is made of linen, 'embroidered with silver-gilt, silver thread and coloured silks in stem. chain, buttonhole, herringbone, and plaited braid stitches with couched work'. Barbara J. Morris.

judgment. Yea, they oft feed them of the best, where the poor man's child at their doors can hardly come by the worst. But the former abuse peradventure reigneth where there hath been long want of issue, else where barrenness is the best blossom of beauty, or, finally, where poor men's children for want of their own issue are not ready to be had. It is thought of some that it is very wholesome for a weak stomach to bear such a dog in the bosom, as it is for him that hath the palsy to feel the daily smell and savour of a fox. But how truly this is affirmed, let the learned judge: only it shall suffice for Dr Cains to have said thus much of spaniels and dogs of the gentle kind.

William Harrison, *Description of England*, 1587

PRIDE OF MERCHANTS' WIVES
Mistress Minx, a merchant's wife, that will eat no cherries, forsooth, but when they are at twenty shillings a pound, that looks as simperingly as if she were besmeared [befouled], and jets [walks pompously] it as gingerly as if she were dancing the Canaries [Spanish dance]: she is so finical in her speech, as though she spake nothing but what she had first sewed over before in her samplers, and the puling accent of her voice is like a feigned treble, or one's voice that interprets to the puppets. What should I tell how squeamish she is in her diet, what toil she puts her poor servants unto, to make her looking-glasses in the pavement? how she will not go into the fields, to cower on the green grass, but she must have a coach for her convoy; and spends half a day in pranking herself if she be invited to any strange place? Is not this the excess of pride, signior Satan? Go to, you are unwise, if you make her not a chief saint in your calendar.

Thomas Nashe, *Pierce Penilesse*, 1592

HOUSEHOLD RULES
Rules similar to those drawn up by John Harrington for the master of a household:
A servant must not be absent from morning or evening meals or prayers without excuse lest he be fined twopence each time.

Any servant late to dinner would be fined twopence.

Any man waiting at table without a trencher in his hand, except for good excuse, would be fined one penny.

For each oath, a servant would be fined one penny.

37. Wash day.

Any man provoking another to strike or striking another would be liable to dismissal.

For a dirty shirt on Sunday or a missing button, the fine would be six pence.

After 8:00 A.M. no bed must be found unmade and no fireplace or candle box left unclean, or the fine would be one penny.

The hall must be cleaned in an hour.

Any man leaving a door open he had found shut would be fined one penny unless he could show good cause.

The whole house must be swept and dusted each Friday.

THE INVENTORY OF THOMAS HEARNE, 1597

An inventory taken the twelfth day of November 1597 of all and singular the goods and chattels and implements as were Thomas Hearne of Harwell in the county of Berks deceased as followeth:

	£	s	d
In the hall			
Imprimis a table, a form, a plank, two chairs, two shelves and painted cloths		4	0
Brass			
Item one brass pot, three kettles, two brass pans, a basin and two candlesticks		16	0
Pewter			
Item four platters, three pottengers, a salt cellar and a saucer		5	4
Item a meal bowl, a pair of bellows and dishes		1	0
In the chamber			
Item an old bedstead, a cupboard, an old press, an old chest and painted cloths		5	0
Item in apples		10	0
Item an axe, a hatchet, a wedge, a bill, a broche, a pair of andirons and pothangers		5	4
The chamber in the entry			
Item a plain bedstead, a flocked bolster and a coverlet		12	0
Item an old bedstead, a coffer and a kever		3	0
In the kitchen			
Item a *yoting vat* three close barrels and two other barrells, a yeldvat and two spinning wheels		11	0
Item a *quern* and pothangers		3	4

	£	s	d
In the barn			
Item in wheat and barley	4	15	0
Item in hay and pulse	1	0	0
Item ladders, sieves and other *lumbells*		2	6
Item one cow and two young bullocks	2	10	0
Item the tilth on the ground this year	1	10	0
Item two pairs of sheets, two tablecloths and two pillowberes		13	3
Items his wearing apparel		6	8
Summa	14	13	6

Appraised by us EDWARD POPE and WILLIAM WISE, their marks.

FOOD AND DRINK

DAILY DIET OF THE DUCHESS OF SOMERSET IN THE TOWER, 1552

		Mutton stewed with potage	8d.	
		Beef boiled	8d.	
	Dinner	Boiled mutton, one leg	5d.	5s. 9d.
		Veal, roast	10d.	
		Capon, roast, one	2s. 4d.	
		Coneys, two	10d.	
		Mutton and potage	6d.	
By		Sliced beef	7d.	
the	Supper	Mutton, roast	8d.	3s. 1d.
Day		Coneys, two	10d.	
		Larks or other, one dozen	10d.	
	Dinner	Bread	10d.	
	and	Beer	8d.	2s. 2d.
	Supper	Wine	8d.	

Sum of these diets as appear } Per sum by the week 77s.

{ Wood, coals, and candle by the week } 20s.

That the lieutenant doth find the said duchess all napery, plate, pewter vessels, spices, the roasting of her meat, butter to baste

the same, with different other charges which be needed, as
vinegar, mustard, various, onions, salads, and other.

Also the lady Page being for the most part with the said
duchess with two gentlewomen, and one man attending on her,
for whom is none allowance to the lieutenant.

Lansdown Manuscripts No. 113 (32)

A DOCTOR'S ADVICE

There is nothing that doth comfort the heart so much beside
God as honest mirth and good company. And wine moderately
taken doth comfort the heart, and good bread doth confirm and
steady a man's heart. And all good and temperate drinks the
which doth engender good blood doth comfort the heart. All
manner of cordials and restoratives and all sweet and soothing
things doth comfort the heart, and so doth nutmeg and ginger,
and poached eggs not hard, their yolks be a cordial.

Andrew Boorde, *Breviary of Helthe*, 1547

INSTRUCTIONS TO WAIT AT TABLE

When your master will go to his meat, cover your table and set
on salt, bread, and trenchers, the salt before the bread, the
trenchers before the salt, and set your napkins and spoons on

38. Dining at home, early seventeenth century. From 'A pleasant Countrey new
Ditty: Merrily showing how to drive the cold Winter away. To the tune of When
Phoebus did rest; &c. Printed at London for H.G.' Roxburghe Collection. These
ballads with woodcuts were hawked about by pedlars in towns and villages.

the cupboard ready and lay every man a trencher and a napkin and a spoon. And some do use to set before every man a loaf of bread and his cup. Also see you have voiders in readiness for to avoid [clear away] the morsels that they do leave on their trenchers. Then with your trencher knife take off such fragments and put them in your voider and set clean again. And when men have well eaten and do begin to wax weary of eating, you shall take up the meat and void the table, and then set down cheese or fruits. Notice if your master is used to wash at the table or standing and cast a clean towel upon your table-cloth and set down your basin and ewer before him.

Hugh Rhodes, The Booke of Nurture, 1568

HOW DIFFERENT PEOPLE DINE AND SUP

With us the nobility, gentry and students do ordinarily go to dinner at eleven before noon and to supper at five, or between five and six in the afternoon. The merchants dine and sup seldom before twelve at noon and six at night, especially in London. The husbandmen dine also at high noon as they call it and sup at seven or eight. As for the poorest sort they generally dine and sup when they may, so that to talk of their order of repast is useless.

William Harrison, A Description of England, 1577

FOOD IN ENGLAND

The situation of our region, lying near unto the north, doth cause the heat of our stomachs to be of somewhat greater force: therefore our bodies do crave a little more ample nourishment than the inhabitants of the hotter regions are accustomed withal, whose digestive force is not altogether so vehement, because their internal heat is not so strong as ours, which is kept in by the coldness of the air that from time to time (especially in winter) doth environ our bodies.

It is no marvel therefore that our tables are oftentimes more plentifully garnished than those of other nations, and this trade hath continued with us even since the very beginning . . .

In number of dishes and change of meat the nobility of England (whose cooks are for the most part musical-headed Frenchmen and strangers) do most exceed, sith there is no day in manner that passeth over their heads wherein they have not only beef, mutton, veal, lamb, kid, pork, cony [rabbit], capon, pig or so many of these as the season yieldeth, but also some portion of the red or fallow deer, beside great variety of fish and

39. A meal at the inn. From 'A Bill of Fare, For, A Saturday Night's Supper, A Sunday morning Breakfast, and A Munday Dinner, Described in a pleasant new Merry Dittie. To the tune of Cooke Laurell or Michelmas Terme. London. Printed by H.P. for Fr. Grove, near the Sarazens Head without Newgate.' Roxburghe Collection.

wild-fowl, and thereto sundry other delicates wherein the sweet hand of the seafaring Portingal [Portuguese] is not wanting: so that for a man to dine with one of them, and to taste of every dish that standeth before him (which few use to do, but each one feedeth upon that meat him best liketh for the time, the beginning of every dish notwithstanding being reserved unto the greatest personage that sitteth at the table, to whom it is drawn up still by the waiters as order requireth, and from whom it descendeth again even to the lower end, whereby each one may taste thereof), is rather to yield unto a conspiracy with a great deal of meat for the speedy suppression of natural health, than the use of a necessary mean to satisfy himself with a competent repast to sustain his body withal. But as this large feeding is not seen in their guests no more is it in their own persons, for sith they have daily much resort unto their tables (and many times unlooked for) and thereto retain great numbers of servants, it is very requisite and expedient for them to be somewhat plentiful in this behalf.

The chief part likewise of their daily provision is brought in before them (commonly in silver vessel, if they be of the degree of barons, bishops and upwards) and placed on their tables, whereof, when they have taken what is pleaseth them, the rest is reserved and afterward sent down to their serving men and waiters, who feed thereon in like sort with convenient moderation, their reversion also being bestowed upon the poor which lie ready at their gates in great numbers to receive the same. This is spoken of the principal tables whereat the nobleman, his lady and guests are accustomed to sit; besides which they have a certain ordinary allowance daily appointed for their halls, where the chief officers and household servants (for all are not permitted by custom to wait upon their master), and with them such inferior guests do feed as are not of calling to associate the nobleman himself; so that, besides those aforementioned, which are called to the principal table, there are commonly forty or three score persons fed in those halls, to the great relief of such poor suitors and strangers also, as oft be partakers thereof and otherwise like to dine hardly. As for drink it is usually filled in pots, goblets, jugs, bowls of silver, in noblemen's houses; also in fine Venice glasses of all forms; and, for want of these elsewhere, in pots of earth of sundry colours and moulds, whereof many are garnished with silver, or at the leastwise in pewter, all which notwithstanding are seldom set on the table, but each one, as necessity urgeth, calleth for a cup of such drink as him listeth to have, so that, when he hath tasted of it, he delivereth the cup again to some one of the standers by, who, making it clean by pouring out the drink that remaineth, restoreth it to the cupboard from whence he fetched the same . . .

It is a world to see in these our days, wherein gold and silver most aboundeth, how that our gentility, as loathing those metals (because of the plenty) do now generally choose rather the Venice glasses, both for our wine and beer, than any of those metals or stone wherein before time we have been accustomed to drink; but such is the nature of man generally that it most coveteth things difficult to be attained; and such is the estimation of this stuff that many become rich only with their new trade unto Murano (a town near to Venice, situate on the Adriatic Sea), from whence the very best are daily to be had, and such as for beauty do well near match the crystal or the ancient *Murrhina vasa* [vessel made of precious stone] whereof now no man hath knowledge. And as this is seen in the gentility, so in the wealthy commonalty the like desire of glass is not neglected, whereby the gain gotten by their purchase is yet much more increased to the benefit of the merchant. The poorest also will have glass if they may; but, sith the Venetian is somewhat too dear for them, they content themselves with such as are made at home of fern and burnt stone; but in fine all go one way — that is, to shards at the last, so that our great expenses in glasses (besides that they breed much strife toward such as have the charge of them) are worst of all bestowed in mine opinion, because their pieces do turn unto no profit . . .

At such time as the merchants do make their ordinary or voluntary feasts, it is a world to see what great provision is made of all manner of delicate meats, from every quarter of the country, wherein, beside that they are often comparable herein to the nobility of the land, they will seldom regard anything that the butcher usually killeth, but reject the same as not worthy to come in place. In such cases also gellifs [jellies] of all colours, mixed with a variety in the representation of sundry flowers, herbs, trees, forms of beasts, fish, fowls and fruits, and thereunto marchpane [marzipan] wrought with no small curiosity, tarts of divers hues and sundry denominations, conserves of old fruits, foreign and home-bred, suckets [sweetmeats], codiniacs [quince-marmalade], marmalades, marchpane, sugar-bread, ginger-bread, florentines [meat-pies], wild-fowl, venison of all sorts, and sundry outlandish confections, altogether seasoned with sugar (which Pliny called *mel ex arundinibus,* a device not common nor greatly used in old time at the table, but only in medicine, although it grew in Arabia, India, and Sicilia), do generally bear the sway, besides infinite devices of our own not possible for me to remember. Of the potato, and such venerous roots as are brought out of Spain, Portingal [Portugal], and the Indies to furnish up our banquets, I speak not, wherein our mures [husks of fruit], of no less force, and to be had about Crosby-Ravenswath, do now begin to have place . . .

I might here talk somewhat of the great silence that is used at the tables of the honourable and wiser sort generally over all the realm (albeit that too much deserveth no commendation, for it belongeth to guests neither to be *muti* nor *loquaces*), likewise of the moderate eating and drinking that is daily seen, and finally of the regard that each one hath to keep himself from the note of surfeiting and drunkenness (for which cause salt meat, except beef, bacon and pork, are not any whit esteemed, and yet these three may not be much powdered); but, as in rehearsal thereof I should commend the nobleman, merchant and frugal artificer, so I could not clear the meaner sort of husbandmen and country

40. The round Mostyn Salt, 1586, which is 'as richly and closely decorated with lion masks, fruit, flowers, birds, monkeys and dogs as any object can be, resembling in style the heavily carved screens and chimney pieces ... found in the greater houses.' Hugh Honour.

The most important piece of table plate at this time was the standing salt.

inhabitants of very much babbling (except it be here and there some odd yeoman), with whom he is thought to be the merriest that talketh of most ribaldry or the wisest man that speaketh fastest among them, and now and then surfeiting and drunkenness which they rather fall into for want of heed-taking than wilfully following or delighting in those errors of set mind and purpose. It may be that divers of them living at home, with hard and pinching diet, small drink, and some of them having scarce enough of that, are soonest overtaken when they come into such banquets; howbeit they take it generally as no small disgrace if they happen to be cupshotten [intoxicated], so that it is a grief unto them, though now sans remedy, sith the thing is done and past. If the friends also of the wealthier sort come to their houses from far, they are commonly so welcome till they depart as upon the first day of their coming; whereas in good towns and cities, as London, etc., men oftentimes complain of little room, and, in reward of a fat capon or plenty of beef and mutton bestowed upon them in the country, a cup of wine or beer with a napkin to wipe their lips, and 'You are heartily welcome!' is thought to be a great entertainment . . .

Heretofore there hath been much more time spent in eating and drinking than commonly is in these days; for whereas of old we had breakfasts in the forenoon, beverages or nunchions [snacks] after dinner, and thereto rear-suppers [light meal after supper] generally when it was time to go to rest . . . now these odd repasts, thanked be God, are very well left, and each one in manner (except here and there some young hungry stomach that cannot fast till dinner-time) contenteth himself with dinner and supper only . . .

With us the nobility, gentry and students do ordinarily go to dinner at eleven before noon, and to supper at five or between five and six at afternoon. The merchants dine and sup seldom before twelve at noon, and six at night, especially in London. The husbandmen dine also at high noon as they call it, and sup at seven or eight; but out of the term in our universities the scholars dine at ten. As for the poorest sort they generally dine and sup when they may, so that to talk of their order of repast it were but a needless matter. I might here take occasion also to set down the variety used by antiquity in their beginnings of their diets, wherein almost every nation had a several fashion, some beginning of custom (as we do in summer time) with salads at supper, and some ending with lettuce, some making their entry with eggs, and shutting up their tables with mulberries, as we do

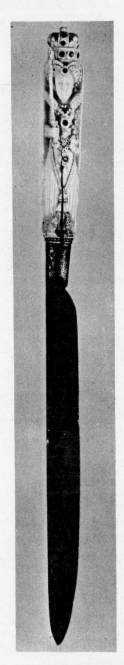

41. A sixteenth-century knife with a carved
ivory handle. These portrayed Queen or King
of England. This one shows Queen Elizabeth.

with fruit and conceits of all sorts. Divers (as the old Romans) began with a few crops of rue [shrub with bitter tasting leaves], as the Venetians did with the fish called *gobius*, the Belgies [Belgians] with butter, or (as we do yet also) with butter and eggs upon fish days. But whereas we commonly begin with the most gross food, and end with the most delicate, the Scot, thinking much to leave the best for his menial servants, maketh his entrance at the best, so that he is sure thereby to leave the worst. We use also our wines by degrees, so that the hottest cometh last to the table: but to stand upon such toys would spend much time and turn to small profit. Wherefore I will deal with other things more necessary for this turn.

William Harrison, *Description of England*, 1587

TO MAKE A PIPPEN PIE

Take a dozen of fair pippens, a pound of sugar in the crust and pie, half an ounce of cinnamon, two orange peels shred fine, two spoonfuls of rosewater, then heat your oven and let it stand in two hours or two and a half, and make a vent in the lid thereof: this pie is good when the quince is out of season.

The Good Hous-wives Treasurie, 1588

HOW TO MAKE AN EEL PIE

Take two pennyworth of very fat eels when they be flead [cut open] and very fair washed, steep them in a little fair water, and salt till they be half sodden, that they may slip from the bones, cut away the fins on every side, then slip them from the bones, and shred them somewhat fine with a knife and take two or three wardens [pears] and thread them very fine to put among them or pippins or other apples, if you do want wardens, then take a little salt, a little pepper, cinnamon, cloves, mace and sugar, and season it withal, put in a quarter of a pound of sweet butter, so put it in paste, and bake it not too rashly, you may put in the yolk of an egg and a little vergis [verjuice] when it is half baked if you will, but I think it is better without.

The Good Hous-wives Treasurie, 1588

TO MAKE MINCE PIES

Take your veal and perboil it a little, or mutton, then set it a cooling: and when it is cold, take three pound of suet to a leg of mutton, or four pound to a fillet of veal, and then mince them small by themselves, or together whether you will, then take to season them half an ounce of nutmegs, half an ounce of cloves and mace, half an ounce of cinnamon, a little pepper, as much

42. Sixteenth-century German stoneware jar mounted in silver gilt. It was probably decorated by English craftsmen.

salt as you think will season them, either to the mutton or to the
veal, take eight yolks of eggs when they are hard, half a pint of
rosewater full measure, half a pound of sugar, then strain the
yolks with the rosewater and the sugar and mingle it with your
meat, if you have any oranges or lemons you must take two of
them, and take peels very thin and mince them very small, and
put them in a pound of currants or dates, half a pound of
prunes, lay currants and dates upon the top of your meat, you
must take two or three pomewaters [juicy apples] or wardens
[pears] and mince with your meat, you may make them worse if
you will, if you will make good crust put in three or four yolks
of eggs, a little rosewater, and a good deal of sugar.

The Good Hous-wives Treasurie, 1588

HOW TO MAKE DAINTY BUTTER

In the month of May is very usual with us to eat some of the
smallest and youngest sage leaves with butter in a morning, and
I think the common use thereof doth sufficiently commend the
same to be wholesome; instead whereof all those which delight in
this herb may cause a few drops of the oil of sage to be well
wrought or tempered with the butter when it is new taken out of
the churn, until they find the same strong enough in taste to
their own liking; and this way I account more much wholesome
than the first, wherein you shall find a far more lively and
penetrative taste then can presently be had out of the green
herb.

. . . And it may be if you wash your butter thoroughly well
with rosewater before you dish it, and work up some fine sugar
in it, that the country people will go near to rob all Cockneys of
their breakfasts, unless the dairy be well looked unto.

Sir Hugh Platt, *A Jewell House of Art and Nature*, 1594

HOW TO PREVENT DRUNKENNESS

Drink first a good draught of sallet [salad] oil, for that will float
upon the wine which you shall drink, and suppress the spirits
from ascending into the brain. Also what quantity soever of new
milk you drink first, you may well drink thrice as much wine
after, without danger of being drunk. But how sick you shall be
with this prevention, I will not here determine, neither would I
have set down this experiment, but only for the help of such
modest drinkers as sometimes in company are drawn, or rather
forced to pledge in full bowls such quaffing companions as they

would be loth to offend, and will require reason at their hands
as they term it.

Sir Hugh Platt, A Jewell House of Art and Nature, 1594

TO STEW SPARROWS

Take good ale a pottle [tankard containing two quarts], or
after the quantities more or less by your discretion, and set it
over the fire to boil, and put in your sparrows and scum the
broth, then put therin onions, parsley, thyme, rosemary chopped
small, pepper and saffron, with cloves and mace a few. And
make sippets [diced toasted bread] as you do for fish, and lay the
sparrows upon with the said broth, and in the seething put in a
piece of sweet butter, and vergious [verjuice] if need be.

A.W., A Book of Cookerie, 1594

TO BOIL A CONY [RABBIT] WITH A PUDDING IN HIS BELLY

Take your cony and flay him, and leave on the ears, and wash it
fair, and take grated bread, sweet suet minced fine, corance
[currants] and some fine herbs, penerial [pennyroyal], winter
savoury, parsley, spinach or beets, sweet margerum [marjoram],
and chop your herbs fine, and season it with cloves, mace and
sugar, a little cream and salt, and yolks of eggs, and dates
minced fine. Then mingle all your stuff together, and put it in
your rabbits belly, and sew it up with thread: so: the broth take
mutton broth when it is boiled a little, and put it in a pot
whereas your rabbit may lie long-ways in it, and let your broth
boil or ever you put it in, then put in gooseberries or grapes,
corance and sweet butter, vergious [verjuice], salt, grated bread
and sugar a little, and when it is boiled, lay it in a dish with sops
[bread dipped in water or wine]. And so serve it in.

A.W., A Book of Cookerie, 1594

TAKE TWO QUINCES . . .

Take two quinces and two or three burr [burdock] roots and a
potato, and pare your potato, and scrape your roots, and put
them into a quart of wine, and let them boil till they be tender,
and put in an ounce of dates, and when they be boiled tender,
draw them through a strainer, wine and all; and then put in the
yolks of eight eggs and the brains of three or four
cock-sparrows, and strain them all with sugar, cinnammon and
ginger, and cloves and mace, and put in a little sweet butter, and

set it upon a chafing dish of coals between two platters, and so let it boil till it be something big.

Thomas Dawson, *The Good Huswifes Jewell*, 1596

TO BOIL A PIKE WITH ORANGES A BANQUET DISH

Take your pike, split him, and seeth him alone with water, butter, and salt; then take an earthen pot and put into it a pint of water, and another of wine, with two oranges or two lemons if you have them, if not, then take four or five oranges, the rinds being cut away, and sliced, and so put to the liquor, with five dates cut long ways, and season your broth with ginger, pepper and salt, and two dishes of sweet butter, boiling these together, and when you will serve him, lay your pike upon soppes [bread dipped in water or wine], casting your broth upon it, you must remember that you cut off your pikes head hard by the body and then his body to be split, cutting every side in two or three parts, and when it is enough, setting the body of the fish in order: then take his head and set it at the foremost part of the dish, standing upright with an orange in his mouth, and so serve him.

Thomas Dawson, *The Second Part of the Good Huswifes Jewell*, 1596

POTATOES

. . . the roots being roasted in the embers do loose much of their windiness especially being eaten sopped in wine.

John Gerard, *Herball or general Historie of Plantes*, 1597

DRESS

NICOLO DI FAVRI DESCRIBES WHAT WOMEN WORE, 1513

The usual vesture of the women is a cloth petticoat over the shift, lined with grey fur; over the petticoat they wear a long gown lined with some choice fur. The gentlewomen carry the train of their gown under the arm; the commonalty pin it behind or before. The sleeves of the gowns sit as close as possible, they are long and unslashed, the cuffs being lined with some choice fur. Their headgear is of various sorts of velvet, cap fashion, with lappets hanging down behind over their shoulders.

Others wear on their heads muslins. Some draw their hair from
under a kerchief and wear over the hair a cap, for the most part
white, round and seemly; but be the fashion as it may their hair
is never seen. Their stockings are black and their shoes double
soled.

Calendar of State Papers, Venice II

INVENTORY OF CLOTHES OF LONDON MERCHANT, WILLIAM POWNCETT, 1553

Item a worsted gown lined with black lamb and faced with lambskin	13s. 4d.
Item an old cloth gown faced with damask	10s. 0d.
Item an old coat of black velvet striped with lace	33s. 4d.
Item a torn velvet doublet	20s. 0d.
Item a coat of pink edged with lace	10s. 0d.
Item an old jacket and old doublet of worsted	3s. 4d.
Item a jacket of black velvet	33s. 4d.
Item a black cloth coat, old	6s. 8d.
Item a black cloth cap, a satin night cap, a girdle of velvet and a pair of martins	12s. 0d.
Item an old satin doublet	2s.(2)
Item a red mantle	4s. 0d.
Item a pair of new gloves and an old velvet purse	10d.
Item a gown of patterned damask with a border of velvet	60s. 0d.
Item a gown of black cloth lined with buckram and faced with satin	20s. 0d.
Item a gown lined with squirrel skins and faced with martins	60s. 0d.
Item a black cloth gown faced with damask	50s. 0d.

Essex Record Office

MEN'S HATS

. . . sometimes perking up like the spear or shaft of a steeple,
standing a quarter of a yard above the crown of their heads,
some more some less as pleased the fantasies of their inconstant
minds, some of velvet some of silk, some of wool and which is
more curious some of a certain kind of fine hair. These they
called beaver hats of xx, xxx, or xl shillings price, fetched from
beyond the seas from whence a great sort of other vanities do
come besides.

Philip Stubbes, *The Anatomie of Abuses,* 1583

SWADDLING CLOTHES

The Lady to the Nurse: How now, how doth the child? . . .
Unswaddle him, undo his swaddling bands, . . . wash him before
me . . . Pull off his shirt, thou art pretty and fat my little darling
. . . Now swaddle him again, but first put on his beggin [cap]
and his little band [collar] with an edge, where is his little
petticoat? Give him his coat of changeable [shot] taffeta and his
satin sleeves. Where is his bib? Let him have his gathered apron
with strings, and hang a muckinder [handerkerchief] to it. You
need not yet to give him his coral with the small golden chain,
for I believe it is better to let him sleep until the afternoon.

From *Dialogues* by Claudius Hollyband and
Peter Erondell, 1568

MEN'S MONSTROUS RUFFS

They have great and monstrous ruffs, made of cambric, holland,
or lawn, and a quarter of a yard or more deep. If the wind blow
and hit upon the crazy bark of their bruised ruffs then they go
flip-flap in the wind, like rags flying about, and lie upon their
shoulders like the dish-clout of a slut. But the devil, who first
invented ruffs, has invented also two mainstays or pillars for the
kingdom of ruffs, the one being the wire supportass, the other
starch. Starch is the devil's liquor, the starching houses are
consecrate to 'Belzebub and Cerberus, archdevils of great ruffs',
the ruffs themselves are the 'cartwheels of the devil's chariot of
pride, leading the direct way to the dungeon of hell.'

Philip Stubbes, *The Anatomie of Abuses,* 1583

BARBERS

Theodorus. What say you of the barbers and trimmers of
men? are they so neat, and so fine fellows as they are said
to be?

Amphilogus. There are no finer fellows under the sun, nor
experter in their noble science of barbing than they be. And
therefore in the fulness of their overflowing knowledge (oh
ingenious heads, and worthy to be dignified with the diadem of
folly and vain curiosity!) they have invented such strange
fashions and monstrous manners of cuttings, trimmings,
shavings and washings, that you would wonder to see. They have
one manner of cut called the French cut, another the Spanish
cut; one the Dutch cut, another the Italian; one the new cut,
another the old; one of the bravado fashion, another of the
mean fashion; one a gentleman's cut, another the common cut;

one cut of the court, another of the country, with infinite the like varieties, which I overpass. They have also other kinds of cuts innumerable; and therefore when you come to be trimmed, they will ask you whether you will be cut to look terrible to your enemy, or amiable to your friend, grim and stern in countenance, or pleasant and demure (for they have divers kinds of cuts for all these purposes, or else they lie). Then, when they have done all their feats, it is a world to consider, how their mustachios must be preserved and laid out, from one cheek to another, yea, almost from ear to another, and turned up like two horns towards the forehead. Besides that, when they come to the cutting of the hair, what snipping and snapping of the scissors is there, what tricking and trimming, what rubbing, what scratching, what combing and clawing, what trickling and toying, and all to tawe out [extort] money, you may be sure . . . You shall have also your orient perfumes for your nose, your fragrant waters for your face, wherewith you shall be all to besprinkled: your music again, and pleasant harmony, shall sound in your ears, and all to tickle the same with vain delight. And in the end your cloak shall be brushed, and 'God be with you, gentleman!'

Philip Stubbes, The Anatomie of Abuses, 1583

GOWNS

[Women's] gowns be no less famous than the rest, for some are of silk, some of velvet, some of grograin [coarse fabric of wool mixed with silk], some of taffeta, some of scarlet, and some of fine cloth, . . . If the whole gown be not silk or velvet, then the same shall be laid with lace, two or three fingers broad, all over the gown, or else the most part; or . . . garded [trimmed] with great gardes of velvet, every gard four or six fingers broad at the least, and edged with costly lace, . . . some [have] sleeves hanging down to their skirts, trailing on the ground, and cast over their shoulders like cow tails. Some have sleeves much shorter, cut up the arm, and pointed with silk ribbons very gallantly, tied with true loves knots . . . Then have they petticoats of the best cloth that can be bought, and of the fairest dye that can be made . . . they have kirtles [gowns] . . . either of silk, velvet, grograin . . . taffeta, satin, or scarlet, bordered with gardes, lace, fringe, and I can not tell what besides. So that, when they have all these goodly robes upon them, women seem to be the smallest part of themselves, not . . . women of flesh and blood, but rather puppets . . ., consisting of rags and clouts [patches] compact together.

Philip Stubbes, The Anatomie of Abuses, 1583

RUFFS

The women . . . use great ruffs and neckerchers of holland, lawn, cambric, and such cloth, as the greatest thread shall not be so big as the least hair that is; and lest they should fall down, they are smeared and starched in the devil's liquor, I mean starch — after that dried with great diligence, streaked, patted, and rubbed very nicely, and so applied to their goodly necks, and, withal, underpropped, with supportasses . . . beyond all this, . . . three or four degrees of minor ruffs, placed . . . one beneath another, and all under the master devilruff; . . . these great ruffs are . . . pleated, and crested full curiously, God wot. Then, last of all, they are either clogged with gold, silver, or silk lace of stately price, wrought all over with needle work, speckled and sparkled here and there with the sun, the moon, the stars, and many other antiques strange to behold. Some are wrought with open work down to the midst of the ruff and further; some with close work, some with purled lace so cloyed, and other gewgaws [baubles] so pestered, as the ruff is the least part of itself. Sometimes they are pinned up to their ears, sometimes they are suffered to hang over their shoulders, like windmill sails fluttering in the wind, and thus every one pleaseth herself in her foolish devices.

Philip Stubbes, The Anatomie of Abuses, 1583

WOMEN'S HAIR

. . . they are not simply content with their own hair, but buy other hair, either of horses, mares, or any other strange beasts, dying it of what colour they list themselves. And if there be any poor woman . . . that hath fair hair, these nice dames will not rest till they have bought it. Or if any children have fair hair, they will entice them into a secret place, and for a penny or two they will cut off their hair; as I heard that one did . . . of late, who, meeting a little child with very fair hair, inveigled her into a house, promised her a penny, and so cut off her hair.

Philip Stubbes, The Anatomie of Abuses, 1583

43. Lady in long gown and English
hood. Church brass, *c.* 1500, in
Rougham Church, Suffolk.

44. Man in a long gown, wearing wide
shoes. Church brass, 1507, in Great
Cressingham Church, Norfolk.

FASHIONS

The fantastical folly of our nation (even from the courtier to the carter), is such that no form of apparel liketh us longer than the first garment is in the wearing, if it continue so long, and be not laid aside to receive some other trinket newly devised by the fickle-headed tailors, who covet to have several tricks in cutting, thereby to draw fond customers to more expense of money. For my part, I can tell better how to inveigh against this enormity than describe any certainty of our attire; sithence such is our mutability, that to-day there is none to the Spanish guise, to-morrow the French toys are most fine and delectable, ere long no such apparel as that which is after the high Almain [German] fashion, by-and-bye the Turkish manner is generally best liked of, otherwise the Morisco gowns, the Barbarian fleeces, the mandilion [loose overcoat] worn to Colleyweston ward, and the short French breeches make a comely vesture that, except it were a dog in a doublet, you shall not see any so disguised as are my countrymen of England. And as these fashions are diverse, so likewise it is a world to see the costliness and the curiosity, the excess and the vanity, the pomp and the bravery, the change and the variety, and finally the fickleness and the folly, that is in all degrees, insomuch that nothing is more constant in England than inconstancy of attire. Oh, how much cost is bestowed nowadays upon our bodies, and how little upon our souls! How many suits of apparel hath the one, and how little furniture hath the other! How long time is asked in decking up of the first, and how little space left wherein to feed the latter! How curious, how nice also, are a number of men and women, and how hardly can the tailor please them in making it fit for their bodies! How many times must it be sent back again to him that made it! What chafing, what fretting, what reproachful language, doth the poor workman bear away! And many times when he doth nothing to it at all, yet when it is brought home again it is very fit and handsome. Then must we put it on, then must the long seams of our hose be set by a plumb-line, then we puff, then we blow, and finally sweat till we drop, that our clothes may stand well upon us. I will say nothing of our heads, which sometimes are polled, sometimes curled, or suffered to grow at length like woman's locks, many times cut off, above or under the ears, round as by a wooden dish. Neither will I meddle with our variety of beards, of which some are shaven from the chin like those of Turks, not a few cut short like to the beard of Marquess Otto, some made round like a rubbing-brush, others with a *pique de vant* (O! fine

45. Court dress of the Tudor period from Holbein's sketch-book.

fashion), or now and then suffered to grow long, the barbers being grown to be so cunning in this behalf as the tailors. And therefore if a man have a lean and straight face, a Marquess Otto's cut will make it broad and large; if it be platterlike, a long slender beard will make it seem the narrower; if he be weasel-beaked, then much hair left on the cheeks will make the owner look big like a bowdled hen, [with feathers ruffled], and so grim as a goose, if Cornelis of Chelmsford say true. Many old men do wear no beards at all. Some lusty courtiers also and gentlemen of courage do wear either rings of gold, stones, or pearl in their ears, whereby they imagine the workmanship of God not to be a little amended. But herein they rather disgrace than adorn their persons, as by their niceness in apparel, for which I say most nations do not unjustly deride us, as also for that we do seem to imitate all nations round about us, wherein we like to the polypus [cuttle-fish] or chameleon; and thereunto bestow most cost upon our rumps, and much more than upon all the rest of our bodies, as women do likewise upon their heads and shoulders. In women also, it is most to be lamented, that they do now far exceed the lightness of our men (who nevertheless are transformed from the cap even to the very shoe), and such staring attire, as in time past was supposed meet for none but light housewives only, is now become a habit for chaste and sober matrons. What should I say of their doublets with pendant codpieces [bags] on the breast, full of jags and cuts, and sleeves of sundry colours? Their galligaskins [loose skirts] to bear out their bums and make their attire to fit plum round (as they term it) about them. Their farthingales [hooped petticoats] and diversely coloured nether stocks of silk, jersey, and such like, whereby their bodies are rather deformed than commended? I have met with some of these trulls [slatterns] in London so disguised that it hath passed my skill to discern whether they were men or women.

Thus it is now come to pass, that women are become men, and men transformed into monsters.

William Harrison, *Description of England,* 1587

COSTLY CLOTHES

Neither was it ever merrier with England, than when an Englishman was known abroad by his own clothes, and contented himself at home with his fine carsie [kersey] hose, and a meane slop [loose jacket]; his coat, gown and cloak of brown, blue or puke [bluish black], with some pretty furniture of velvet or fur, and a doublet of sad tawnie [tan-coloured], or black velvet, or other comely silk, without such cuts and gawrish [garish] colours as are worn these days, and never brought in but by the consent of the French, who think themselves the gayest men, when they have most diversities of jagges [fringes], and change of colours, about them. Certes of all estates our merchants do least alter their attire, and therefore are most to be commended: for albeit that which they wear be very fine and costly, yet in form and colour it representeth a great piece of ancient gravity appertaining to citizens and burgesses, albeit the younger sort of their wives both in attire and costly housekeeping can not tell when and how to make an end, as being women indeed in whom all kind of curiosity is to be found and seen, and in far greater measure than in women of higher calling.

William Harrison, *Description of England,* 1587

THE QUEEN'S GLOVES

It was about the 15th year of the Queen's reign when the Right Honourable Edward de Vere, Earl of Oxford, came from Italy and brought with him gloves, sweet bags, a perfumed leather

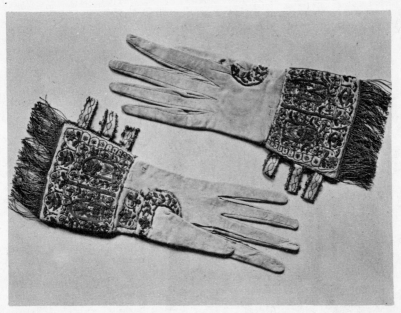

46. A fine pair of white kid gloves embroidered with silver, presented to Queen Elizabeth on a visit to Oxford. John Waterer suggests that they were made at Woodstock, a famous glove centre. The Queen's ban on the import of gloves lasted for 261 years.

jerkin, and other pleasant things; and that year the Queen had a pair of perfumed gloves, trimmed only with four tuffes or roses of coloured silks; the Queen took such pleasure in those gloves, that she was pictured with (them) on her hands, and for many years after it was called the Earl of Oxford's perfume.

John Stow, *A Survey of London*, 1598

FASHIONS

Now the women-folk of England, who have mostly blue-grey eyes and are fair and pretty, have far more liberty than in other lands, and know just how to make good use of it, for they often stroll out or drive by coach in very gorgeous clothes, and the men must put up with such ways, and may not punish them for it, indeed the good wives often beat their men, and if this is discovered, the nearest neighbour is placed on a cart and paraded through the whole town as a laughing-stock for the

47. About 1574 a Flemish traveller made this sketch of English women, showing the variety of costume, despite certain ordinances, controlling style.

victim, as a punishment — he is informed — for not having come to his neighbour's assistance when his wife was beating him. They lay great store by ruffs and starch them blue, so that their complexion shall appear the whiter, and some may well wear velvet for the street — quite common with them — who cannot afford a crust of dry bread at home I have been told. English burgher women usually wear high hats covered with velvet or silk for headgear, with cut-away kirtles when they go out, in old-fashioned style. Instead of whalebone they wear a broad circular piece of wood over the breast to keep the body straighter and more erect.

Thomas Platter, *Travels in England*, 1599

POMANDERS
Aromatic: Ward off Infection
Your only way to make a good pomander is this: Take an ounce of the finest garden mould, cleaned and steeped seven days in change of rosewater; then take the best labdanum [ladanum, a gum resin], benzoin, both storaxes, ambergris, civet, and musk; incorporate them together, and work them into what form you please. Then, if your breath be not too valiant, it will make you smell as sweet as any lady's dog.

POMATUM FOR THE SKIN

Wash Barrowes grease often times in May-dew that hath been
clarified in the sun, till it be exceeding white, then take
Marshmallow roots scraping off the outsides, then make thin
slices of them and mix them; set them to macerate [soften by
soaking] in a seething balneo [bath], and scum it well till it be
thoroughly clarified and will come to roap [be ropy], then strain
it, and put now and then a spoonful of May-dew therein, beating
it till it be thoroughly cold in often change of May-dew, then
throw away that dew, and put it in a glass covering it with
May-dew, and so reserve it for your use. Let the mallow roots be
two or three days dried in the shade before you use them . . .
This I had of a great professor of Art, and for a rare and dainty
Secret, as the best fucus [kind of seaweed] this day in use.

Sir Hugh Platt, *Delightes for Ladies to adorn*
their persons, 1602

Education

INSTRUCTIONS TO CHILDREN
> Arise betime out of thy bed,
> And bless thy breast and thy forehead,
> Then wash thy hands and thy face,
> Comb thy head, and ask God grace
> Thee to help in all thy works;
> Thou shall speed better what so thou carps*:
> Then go to the church, and hear a mass,
> There ask mercy for thy trespass.
> To whom thou meets come by the way
> Courteously 'good morn' thou say.
> When thou hast done, go break thy fast
> With meat and drink of good repast:
> Bless thy mouth or thou it eat,
> The better shall be thy diet.
> Before thy meat say thou thy grace,
> It occupies but little space:—
> Fore our meat, and drink, and us
> Thank we our Lord Jesus.

*Speaks

The Young Children's Book —
from the Ashmolean Museum MS.61, *c.* 1500

A LETTER BY LADY JANE GREY WHO IN HER TEENS KNEW GREEK, LATIN, HEBREW, FRENCH, ITALIAN

One of the greatest benefits that God gave me is that He sent me so sharp and severe parents and so gentle a schoolmaster, for when I am in the presence of either father or mother, whether I speak, keep silence, sit, stand, go, eat, drink, be merry, or sad (be sewing, playing, dancing or doing anything else) I must do it, as it were, in such weight, measure, and number even so

perfectly as God made the world, or else I am so sharply
taunted, so cruelly threatened, yea presented sometimes with
pinches, nips and bobs and other things (which I will not name
for the honour I bear them) so without measure that I think
myself in Hell till the time comes when I must go to Mr. Aylmer,
who teacheth me so gently, so pleasantly and with such pure
allurements to learn.

AN ELIZABETHAN SCHOOLBOY
(1) Getting up in the morning
[Francis the schoolboy, a late riser; Margaret, the maid.]

MARGARET: Ho Fraunces, rise and get you to school: you shall be
beaten, for it is past seven: make yourself readie quiclly, say
your prayers, then you shall have your breakfast.

FRANCIS: Margerite, geeve me my hosen: dispatche I pray you:
where is my doublet? bryng my garters, and my shooes:
geeve mee that shooyng horne.

MARGARET: Take first a cleane shirte, for yours is fowle.

FRANCIS: Make hast then, for I doo tarie too long.

MARGARET: It is moyst yet, tarry a little that I may drie it by the
fier.

FRANCIS: I had rather thou shouldst be shent, than I should be
either chid or beaten: where have you layde my girdle and
my inck-horne? Where is my gyrkin [jerkin] of Spanish
leather of Bouffe? Where be my sockes of linnen, of wollen,
of clothe? Where is my cap, my hat, my coate, my cloake, my
kaipe [cape or short coat], my gowne, my gloves, my
mittayns [mittens], my pumpes, my moyles [mules], my
slippers, my handkerchief, my pointes, my sachell, my
penknife and my books. Where is all my geare? I have
nothing ready: I will tell my father . . .

From Dialogues by Claudius Hollyband and
Peter Erondell, 1568

EDUCATION FOR A SIXTEENTH-CENTURY GENTLEMAN
To ride comely, to run fair at the tilt or ring, to play at all
weapons, to shoot fair in bow or surely in gun, to vault lustily, to
run, to leap, to wrestle, to swim, to dance comely, to sing and
play instruments cunningly, to hawk, to hunt, to play at tennis
and all pastimes containing either some fit exercise for war or
some pleasant pastime for peace; these be not only comely and
decent, but also very necessary for a courtly gentleman to use.

Roger Ascham, The Scholemaster, 1570

TO SEE WITH DILIGENCE YOUR MASTER TO BED

. . . when your master intendeth to bedward, see that you have
fire and candle sufficient. You must have clean water at night
and in the morning. If your master lie in fresh sheets, dry off
the moistness at the fire. If he lie in a strange place, see his
sheets be clean, then fold down his bed, and warm his night
kerchief, and see his house of office [privy] be clean. Help off
his clothes, and draw the curtains; make sure the fire and
candles, avoid [remove] the dogs, and shut the doors. And at
night or in the morning, your master being alone, if you have
anything to say, it is good knowing his pleasure. In the morning
if it be cold, make a fire, and have ready clean water, bring him
his petticoat warm, with his doublet, and all his apparel clean
brushed, and his shoes made clean, and help to array him, truss
[fasten] his points [tagged laces], strike up his hose, and see all
cleanly about him. Give him good attendance, and especially
among strangers, for attendance doth please masters very well.
Thus doing with diligence, God will prefer you to honour and
good fortune.

Hugh Rhodes, *The Boke of Nurture,*
or Schoole of good maners, 1577

THE EDUCATION OF ROBERT LANEHAM, 1575

Herewith meant I fully to bid ye farewell, had not this doubt
come to my mind, that here remains a doubt in you which I
ought (me thought) in any ways to clear: which is, ye marvel
perchance to see me so bookish. Let me tell you in a few words:
I went to school forsooth both at St Pauls' and also at Saint
Anthony's: in the fifth form, past Æsop's Fables I was, read
Terence: 'Vos istaec intro auferte': and began my Virgil: 'Tytire
tu patulae.' I knew my rules, could construe and parse with the
best of them. Since that, as partly ye know, have I traded the
feat of merchandise in sundry countries, and so got me
languages, which do so little hinder my Latin, as (I thank God)
have much increased it. I have leisure sometime, when I tend
not upon the council; whereby, now look I on one book, now on
another. Stories I delight in, the more ancient and rare, the
more likesome to me. If I told ye, I liked William of Malmesbury
so well, because of his diligence and antiquity, perchance ye
would construe it because I love Malmsey so well: but in faith! it
is not so, for sipped I no more sack and sugar (and yet never but
with company) than I do Malmsey, I should not blush so much a
days as I do: ye know my mind. Well now! thus fare ye heartily
well! i' faith! if with wishing it could have been, ye had had a

book or two this summer; but we shall come nearer shortly, and
then shall we merely meet; and grace a God! in the meantime
commend me, I beseech you, unto my good friends, almost most
of them your neighbours, Master Alderman Pullison, a special
friend of mine; and in any wise, to my good old friend Master
Smith, Customer [collector of Customs], by that same token, 'Set
my horse up to the rack and then let's have a cup of sack!' He
knows the token well enough and will laugh, I hold ye a groat.
To Master Thorogood, and to my merry companion (a Mercer,
ye wot, as we be) Master Denman, 'Mio fratello in Christo': he is
wont to summon me by the name of 'Ro. La. of the County
Nosingham [Lanehame had a red nose], Gentleman.' A good
companion, i' faith! Well once again, fare ye heartily well? From
the Court. At the City of Worcester, the XX of August 1575.

Your countryman, companion and friend assuredly: Mercer,
Merchant-adventurer, and Clerk of the Council-chamber door,
and also keeper of the same: El Principe Negro. Par me, R. L.
gent, Mercer.

Robert Laneham's Letter, as edited by Dr. Furnivall

TO TEACH GOOD MANNERS
There is few things to be understood more necessary than to
teach and govern children in learning and good manners, for it
is a high service to God, it getteth favour in the sight of men, it
multiplyeth goods, and increaseth thy good name, it also
provoketh to prayer by which God's grace is obtained, if thus
they be brought up in virtue, good manners and Godly learning.
The cause of the world being so evil of living as it is, is for the
lack of virtue, and Godly bringing up of youth. Which youth
showeth the dispositions and conditions of their parents or
masters, under whom they have been governed. For youth is
disposed to take such as they are accustomed in, good or evil.
For if the behaviour of the governor be evil, needs must the
child be evil.

It is also necessary for fathers and masters to cause their
children and servants to use fair and gentle speech, with
reverence and courtesy to their elders and betters, rebuking as
well their idle talk and stammering, as their uncomely gestures
in good or standing. And if you put them to school, see that
their masters be such as fear God, and live virtuously, such as
can punish sharply with patience, and not with rigour, for it
doth oft times make them to rebel and run away, whereof
chanceth oft times much harm. Also their parents must oft times

instruct them of God and of his laws, and virtuous instructions
of his word, and other good examples, and such like.

Hugh Rhodes, The Boke of Nurture,
or Schoole of good maners, 1577

OUR CALLING

Our calling creeps low and hath pain for a companion, still
thrust to the wall, though still confessed good. Our comfort
perforce is that these things be good things, which want no
praising, though they go a-cold for want of happing [covering].

Richard Mulcaster, Headmaster of St Paul's, 1582

DANGERS OF DANCING AND MUSIC

If you would have your son soft, womanish, unclean,
smooth-mouthed, affected to bawdry, scurrility, filthy rimes and
unseemly talking; briefly if you would have him, as it were,
transnatured into a woman or worse, and inclined to all kinds of
whoredom and abomination, set him to dancing school and to
learn Musick, and then you shall not fail of your purpose. And if
you would have your daughter riggish, bawdy and unclean and
a filthy speaker and suchlike, bring her up in music and dancing
and, my life for yours, you have won the goal.

Philip Stubbes, The Anatomie of Abuses, 1583

UNIVERSITIES AND SCHOOLS

Oxford (which lieth west and by north from London) standeth
most pleasantly, being environed in manner round about with
woods on the hills aloft, and goodly rivers in the bottoms and
valleys beneath, whose courses would breed no small commodity
to that city and country about, if such impediments were
removed as greatly annoy the same and hinder the carriage
which might be made thither also from London. That of
Cambridge is distant from London about forty and six miles
north and by east, and standeth very well, saving that it is
somewhat near unto the fens; whereby the wholesomeness of the
air is not a little corrupted. It is excellently well served with all
kinds of provision, but especially of fresh water fish and wild
fowl, by reason of the river that passeth thereby; and thereto the
Isle of Ely, which is so near at hand. Only wood is the chief want
to such as study there, wherefore this kind of provision is
brought them either from Essex and other places thereabouts, as
is also their coal, or otherwise the necessity thereof is supplied
with gall . . . and seacoal whereof they have great plenty led
thither by the Grant. . . .

The colleges of Oxford for curious workmanship and private commodities are much more stately, magnificent, and commodious than those of Cambridge: and thereunto the streets of the town for the most part are more large and comely. But for uniformity of building, orderly compaction and politic regiment the town of Cambridge, as the newer workmanship exceeds that of Oxford (which otherwise is, and hath been, the greater of the two) by many a fold (as I guess), although I know divers that are of the contrary opinion. . . .

In all other things there is so great equality between these two universities as no man can imagine how to set down any greater. . .

In some one college you shall have two hundred scholars, in others one hundred and fifty, in divers a hundred and forty, and in the rest less numbers, as the capacity of the said houses is able to receive: so that at this present, of one sort and other, there are about three thousand students nourished in them both. . .

48. An Elizabethan school. All the pupils are in one room. The clever boys received a good Latin education, sharing with others the benches and the floggings.

They were erected by their founders at the first only for poor men's sons, whose parents were not able to bring them up into learning; but now they have the least benefit of them by reason the rich do so encroach upon them. And so far has this inconvenience spread itself that it is in my time a hard matter for a poor man's child to come by a fellowship (though he be never so good a scholar and worthy of that room). . . .

In some grammar schools likewise which send scholars to these universities it is lamentable to see what bribery is used; for ere the scholar can be preferred, such bribage is made, that poor men's children are commonly shut out, and the richer sort received (who in time past thought it dishonour to live as it were upon alms), and yet being placed, most of them study little other than histories, tables, dice, and trifles. . . .

Everyone of these colleges have in like manner their professors and readers, that is to say, of divinity, of the civil law, Moreover, in the public schools of both the universities, there are found at the prince's charge (and that very largely) five provessors and readers, that is to say, of divinity, of the civil law, physic, the Hebrew and the Greek tongues. And for the other lectures, as of philosophy, logic, rhetoric, and the quadrivials (although the latter, I mean arithmetic, music, geometry, and astronomy, and with them all skill in the perspectives, are now smally regarded in either of them), the universities themselves do allow competent stipends to such as read the same, whereby they are sufficiently provided for, touching the maintenance of their estates and no less encouraged to be diligent in their functions. . . .

Thus we see that from our entrance into the university unto the last degree received is commonly eighteen or peradventure twenty years, in which time, if a student has not obtained sufficient learning thereby to serve his own turn and benefit his commonwealth, let him never look by tarrying longer to come by any more. . . .

To these two also we may in like sort add the third, which is at London (serving only for such as study the laws of the realm) where there are sundry famous houses, of which three are called by the name of Inns of the Court, the rest of the Chancery, and all built before time for the furtherance and commodity of such as apply their minds to our common laws. . . .

Besides these universities also there are great number of grammar schools throughout the realm, and those very liberally endowed, for the better relief of poor scholars, so that there are not many corporate towns now under the queen's domain that have not one grammar school at the least, with a sufficient living for a master and usher appointed to the same.

There are in like manner divers collegiate churches, as Windsor, Winchester, Eton, Westminster (in which I was some time an unprofitable grammarian under the reverend father Master Nowell, now dean of Paul's), and in those a great number of poor scholars, daily maintained by the liberality of the founders, with meat, books, and apparel, from whence, after they have been well entered in the knowledge of the Latin and Greek tongues and rules of versifying, they are sent to certain special houses in each university where they are received and trained up in the points of higher knowledge in their private halls. . . .

William Harrison, Description of England, 1587

TABLE OF PRECEPTS FOR CHILDREN
Do not speak till another has finished, and never interrupt.
Report the truth slowly and plainly.
Be chary of discussing matters not easily believed.
Never speak of yourself in praise or dispraise; one is
     arrogance, the other, folly.
Avoid too great brevity in speech or too much diffuseness
     or too many subjects or too much repetition.
Do not mock or scorn others; it is dangerous to scorn
     what is done ignorantly and even more dangerous
     to scorn physical defects.
Do not be too hasty in replying; answer slowly even
     about things you know perfectly.
Never stoop from your own dignity.

George Pettie, The Civile Conversation, a
translation of Stefano Guazzo's Civile Conversazione

WORDS BY A SCHOOLBOY IN HIS LATIN BOOK
John Slie his book 1589
John Slye is my name
And with my pen I write the same
God that made both sea and land
Give me grace to mend my hand

The rose is red, the leaves are green,
God save Elizabeth our noble Queen.

A. M. Bell, An Elizabethan Schoolboy and his Book, 1589

LEARNING THE ALPHABET

Cause 4 large dice of bone or wood to be made, and upon every square, one of the small letters of the cross row to be graven, but in some bigger shape, and the child using to play much with them, and being always told what letter chanceth, will soon gain his Alphabet, as it were by the way of sport or pastime. I have heard of a pair of cards, whereon most of the principle Grammar rules have been printed, and the School-Master hath found good sport thereat with his scholars.

Sir Hugh Platt, *A Jewell House of Art and Nature,* 1594

DOMESTIC TUTORS

A gentle squire would gladly entertain
Into his house some trencher-chaplain;
Some willing man that might instruct his sons,
And that would stand to good conditions.
First, that he lie upon the truckle-bed,
Whiles his young master lieth o'er his head.
Second, that he do, on no default,
Ever presume to sit above the salt.
Third, that he never change his trencher twice.
Fourth, that he use all common courtesies;
Sit bare at meals, and one half rise and wait.
Last, that he never his young master beat,
But he must ask his mother to define,
How many jerks* she would his breech should line.
All these observed, he could contented be,
To give five marks and winter livery.

Joseph Hall, *Satires,* 1597

*Blows, strokes

LONDON SCHOOLS, 1598

As divers schools, by suppressing of religious houses, whereof they were members, in the reign of Henry VIII., have been decayed, so again have some others been newly erected, and furnished for them; as namely *Paul's School,* in place of an old ruined house, was built in most ample manner, and largely endowed, in the year 1512, by John Colet, Doctor of Divinity, Dean of Paul's, for 153 poor men's children. . . . Again in the year 1553, after the erection of *Christ's Hospital* in the late dissolved house of the Gray Friars, a great number of poor children being taken in, a school was ordained there at the citizens' charges.

Also in the year 1561, the *Merchant Taylors* of London founded

one notable free grammar-school in the parish of St Laurence
Poultney. . . .

As for the meeting of the schoolmasters on festival days, at
festival churches, and the disputing of their scholars logically,
etc., the same was long since discontinued; but the arguing of
the schoolboys about the principles of grammar hath been
continued even till our time; for I myself, in my youth, have
yearly seen, on the eve of St Bartholomew the Apostle, the
scholars of divers grammar-schools repair unto the churchyard
of St Bartholomew, the priory in Smithfield, where upon a bank
boarded about under a tree, some one scholar hath stepped up,
and there both opposed and answered till he were by some
better scholar overcome and put down; and then the overcomer
taking the place, did like as the first; and in the end the best
opposers and answerers had rewards, which I observed not but it
made both good schoolmasters and also good scholars, diligently
against such times to prepare themselves for the obtaining of this
garland.

I remember there repaired to these exercises amongst others,
the masters and scholars of the free schools of St Paul's in
London, of St Peter's in Westminster, of St Thomas Acon's
Hospital, and of St Anthony's Hospital; whereof the last named
commonly presented the best scholars, and had the prize in
those days.

This priory of St Bartholomew being surrendered to Henry
VIII., those disputations . . . in that place surceased; and were
again, only for a year or twain, in the reign of Edward VI.,
revived in the cloister of Christ's Hospital, when the best
scholars, then still of St Anthony's School, were rewarded with
bows and arrows of silver, given to them by Sir Martin Bowes,
goldsmith.

Nevertheless, however, the encouragement failed, the scholars
of Paul's meetings with them of St Anthony's, would call them
"*Anthony's pigs,*" and they again would call the other, "*Pigeons of
Paul's,*" because many pigeons were bred in St Paul's church and
St Anthony was always figured with a pig following him; and
mindful of the former usage, did for a long season disorderly, in
the open street, provoke one another with: "*Salve tu quoque, placet
tibi mecum disputare?*" "*Placet.*" And so proceeding from this to
questions in grammar, they usually fell from words to blows with
their satchels full of books, many times in great heaps, that they
troubled the streets and passengers; so that finally they were
restrained, until the decay of St Anthony's school.

John Stow, *A Survey of London*

STUDENT LIFE AT OXFORD

These students lead a life almost monastic; for as the Monks had nothing in the world to do, but when they had said their prayers at stated hours, to employ themselves in instructive studies, no more have these. They are divided into three tables: the first is called the fellows table, to which are admitted earls, barons, gentlemen, doctors, and masters of arts, but very few of the latter; this is more plentifully and expensively served than the others: the second is for masters of arts, bachelors, some gentlemen, and eminent citizens: the third for people of low condition. While the rest are at dinner or supper in the great hall, where they are all assembled, one of the students reads aloud the bible, which is placed on a desk in the middle of the hall, and this office every one of them takes upon himself in his turn; as soon as grace is said after each meal, every one is at liberty either to retire to his own chambers, or to walk in the college garden, there being none that has not a delightful one. Their habit is almost the same as that of the jesuits, their gowns reaching down to their ankles, sometimes lined with fur; they wear square caps; the doctors, masters of arts, and professors, have another kind of gown that distinguishes them: every student of any considerable standing has a key to the college library, for no college is without one.

Paul Hentzner, *Travels in England*, 1598

CHRIST'S HOSPITAL

I saw Christ's Hospital . . ., founded by a great lady, and already in progress during her lifetime, which hospital finds food and drink and clothes for seven hundred young boys and girls, while reading and writing are taught in special schools in the same, and they are kept there until they are fit for some craft or service, when they are taken away and put out wherever they like, or opportunity offers, boys and girls alike; they are all fine children, taken from poor parents and put in here. They keep their hospital exceedingly clean — in the boys' long apartment are one hundred and forty beds in a row on either side, where they sleep two and two together, and by their beds they have low chests in which to keep their clothes, There are fewer girls in a smaller room.

Thomas Platter, *Travels in England*, 1599

TWO ACCOMPLISHED WOMEN, BORN, BRED AND EDUCATED IN THE TRUE ORTHODOX FAITH

The Earl of Bedford's house, in which Anne's father and mother were educated, was said to have been a 'very school of vertue', for the Earl was a great patron of letters. He was also a zealous supporter of the Reformation, and in prison for a time in Mary's reign for his religious opinions, afterwards living for a while in Geneva. Margaret, his third daughter and seventh child, was, until after the age of seven, brought up by a maternal aunt at Lilford, Northamptonshire, for her own mother had died soon after she was born. At the end of that period she returned to live with her father and his second wife in one of their many houses, Chenies in Buckinghamshire, Woburn in Bedfordshire, Exeter in Devon. How she was educated, or what she learned, is not definitely known, but both she and her sister Anne, who became Countess of Warwick, were accomplished women.

Margaret grew up into a woman of great acumen and determination. From her husband's death in 1605 to her own in 1616, she fought by law to win back, for her only daughter, the inheritance left by the will of her husband to a male heir in the person of his brother, and she caused to be prepared for this purpose great books of reference into which were copied all the family deeds.

In literature her interests would seem to have been predominantly religious. In 1591 Henry Peacham dedicated to her and to her sister, Anne, Countess of Warwick, *A Sermon on the last three verses of the first chapter of Job,* and William Perkins addressed to her one of his religious treatises. She employed Thomas Tymme, himself the author of a popular book of devotion, and a clever translator, to render into English, for her own edification, the Latin of Dudley Fenner's *Sacred Divinitie or the Truth which is according to Pietie, Described after the lawes of the onely and true methode and digested into ten bookes.* In her will she bequeathed two books, a Bible to Mr. Shute, 'preacher', and 'Duplesses booke of the Sacrament of the Masse' to her niece, Lady Herbert, who was Lady Hoby's sister-in-law.

Her letters reveal that the Countess of Cumberland possessed well-trained business instincts and an ability to administer her husband's estates while he was from home. She was a party with others in obtaining a patent from the Crown for obtaining sea-coal and using it in the smelting of iron. Many of her epistles the Countess herself wrote in 'a strange, cramped and irregular hand-writing', while she was no exception to the period in that she 'spelled as she liked', in various phonetic or partially phonetic forms, and thought nothing of varying the order of the letters in the spelling of the same word three or four times in one communication. In 1603 she wrote to the Countess of Shrewsbury, 'Madam I hope your ladyship will excuse that I answer not your letter with my own hand, but your ladyship knows how bad a Secretary I am which in these many lines would so much trouble you.'

Of her mother, Anne recorded that she 'had a great sharp Natural Wit, so as there was few worthy knowledge, but she had some insight into them, for tho she had no language but her own, yet was there few books of worth translated into English but she read them, whereby that excellent Mind of hers was much enriched . . . She was a lover of the Study and practice of Alchimy, by which she found out excellent Medicines, that did much good to many; she delighted in Distilling of waters, and other Chymical extractions, for she had some knowledge in most kind of Minerals, herbs, flowers and plants.' She was, wrote Anne, 'truly Religious, Devout and Conscientious, even from her very childhood, and did spend much time in reading the Scriptures and other good books, and in heavenly Meditations and in prayers fastings and Deeds of Charity.' The early death of her two sons did so much afflict her as that ever after 'the booke of Jobe was her dayly companion'.

Such was Anne's background. Her own education inevitably reflected it, since she was the only surviving child of her parents and much attached to both. How large a part Tudor ladies played in the practical education of their sons and daughters it is impossible, from the evidence available, to state with certainty: countless allusions in the correspondence of the period, however, evince their deep interest in the process. The Earl of Cumberland's last letter to his wife before his death was a reminder of that duty in which she did not fail: 'Before the presence of God, I command thee, and in the nearest love of my heart I desire thee, to take great care that sweet Nan, whom God bless, may be carefully brought up in the fear of God, not to delight in worldly vanities, which I too well know be but baits to draw her out of the heavenly kingdom.' In her will, Anne says she was 'borne, bred, and educated' by her 'blessed mother' in the 'true orthodox faith and religion established and maintained' by the Church of England. 'Bred up' for some time in her infancy by her great-aunt Mistress Alice Elmers of Lilford, Northamptonshire, she was there 'seasoned with the grounds of goodness and Religion', but her childhood was spent mostly with her mother, who did, 'with Singular ease and tenderness of affection, educate and bring her up, seasoning her youth with the grounds of true Religion and Moral Virtue, and all other qualities befitting her birth.'

Before Anne was twelve, she was learning to dance and was studying music, and, earlier than this, had been taught to read and write. For a brief period Samuel Daniel, the poet, was her tutor, but it is doubtful if she was at that time sufficiently precocious to derive from him that taste for poetry, history, and the classics which she later showed herself to possess. He exhorted her afterward, in one of his poems, to store 'that better part, the mansion of your mind' with

'the richest furniture of worth
To make ye highly good as highly born,
And set your virtues equal to your kind.'

In 1599 he dedicated his poem, *A General Defence of Learning*, to her mother. But Anne, like Grace Sherrington, and perhaps like Margaret Hoby, had a governess, one Mistress Anne Taylour, portrayed beside Daniel in Anne's Great Picture at Appleby Castle, and described beneath as 'Governesse to this Young Lady, a Religious and good Woman'. She was the daughter of one Mr. Cholmley, born in London, and the mother of many children who all died before her.

By her father's wishes, Anne was not, we learn from her own words, 'admitted to learn any language,' but 'for all other knowledge fit for her sex, none was bred up to greater perfection than herself.' In the Great Picture at Appleby she is certainly surrounded by books, and her will, made in 1676, mentioned specifically, as a valuable part of the property she left, her 'books' in her castles of Appleby, Brougham, Brough, and Pendragon, and in her castle of Skipton, and tower of Barden. Moreover, it was she who, in 1620, erected the first monument to the poet Spenser in Westminster Abbey.

Possessed apparently of a knowledge of law and politics, and fully capable of dealing with all the problems of estate management, with an indomitable spirit which bowed neither to King nor High Court Judges, Lady Anne became a great power in the north-west of England. In neither of her marriages was she ideally matched, and this seems to have guided her, when every-day duties had been performed, to find solace in literature and religion, and the compiling of family records.

The Diary of Lady Margaret Hoby, 1599-1605

The Arts

LITERATURE

SOME PROVERBS FROM TUDOR TIMES, *c.* 1486
A bow long bent at last waxeth weak.
A grunting horse and a groaning wife never fail their Master.
Age and wedlock tames man and beast.
An ill cook cannot lick his own fingers.
Better one bird in the hand than ten in the wood.
Beware the geese when the Fox preaches.
Children and chickens are always feeding.
Dinners cannot be long where dainties want.
God sends meat, the devil sends Cooks.
Ill putting a naked sword in a mad man's hand.
It is merry in hall when beards wag all.
Many kiss the child for the Nurse's sake.
Need hath no law.
Old men and far travellers may lie by authority.
Puff not against the wind.
Pouring oil into the fire is not the way to quench it.
Saying and doing are two things.
Somewhat is better than nothing.
Speak fair, and think what you will.
The Crow thinketh her own birds fairest.
Three may keep counsel if two be away.
You are as seasonable as Snow in Summer.
Young men may die, but old must die.

William Camden, *Remains concerning Britain*

GREAT DISORDERS
Sundry great disorders and inconveniences have been found to
ensue to this city by the inordinate haunting of great multitudes
of people, especially youth, to plays, interludes, and shows —
namely, occasion of frays and quarrels; evil practices of
incontinency in great inns having chambers and secret places

49. The Title-page woodcut of *Everyman*, 1530. The theme of this morality play is the summoning of Everyman by Death, depicted here.

adjoining to their open stages and galleries; inveigling and alluring of maids, specially orphans and good citizens' children under age, to privy and unmeet contracts; the publishing of unchaste, uncomely, and unshamefast speeches and doings; withdrawing of the queen's majesty's subjects from divine service on Sundays and holidays, at which times such plays were chiefly used; unthrifty waste of the money of the poor and fond persons; sundry robberies by picking and cutting of purses; uttering of popular, busy, and seditious matters; and many other corruptions of youth and other enormities — besides that also sundry slaughters and mayhemings [maiming] of the queen's subjects have happened by ruins of scaffolds, frames, and stages, and by engines, weapons, and powder used in plays.

from an act of the Common Council, 6 December 1574

'THE THEATRE' AND 'THE CURTAIN' ARE REPROVED

Satan hath not a more speedy way, and fitter school to work and teach his desire, to bring men and women into the snare of concupiscence and filthy lusts of wicked whoredom, than those

places, and plays, and theatres are . . . It hath stricken such a
blind zeal into the hearts of the people, that they shame not to
say, and affirm openly, that plays are as good as sermons, and
that they learn as much or more at a play, than they do at God's
word preached . . . Many can tarry at a vain play two or three
hours, whenas they will not abide scarce one hour at a sermon . . .
In their plays you shall learn all things that appertain to craft,
mischief, deceits and filthiness, etc. If you will learn how to be
false and deceive your husbands, or husbands their wives, how to
play the harlot, to obtain one's love, how to ravish, how to
beguile, how to betray, to flatter, lie, swear, forswear, how to
allure to whoredom, how to murder, how to poison, how to
disobey and rebel against princes, to consume treasures
prodigally, to move to lusts, to ransack and spoil cities and
towns, to be idle, to blaspheme, to sing filthy songs of love, to
speak filthily, to be proud, how to mock, scoff and deride any
nation . . . shall you not learn, then, at such interludes how to
practise them?

> John Northbrooke, *A Treatise wherein Dicing, Dauncing,*
> *vain Playes or Enterludes . . . are reproved . . .*, 1577

THE THEATRE THRICE DAMNED

Look upon the common plays in London, and see the multitude
that flocketh to them and followeth them: behold the sumptuous
Theatre houses, a continual monument of London's prodigality
and folly . . . Shall I reckon up the monstrous birds that breed in
this nest? without doubt I am ashamed, and I should surely
offend your chaste ears: but the old world is matched, and
Sodom overcome, for more horrible enormities, and swelling sins
are set out by those stages, than every man thinks for, or some
would believe, if I should paint them out in their colours;
without doubt you can scantly name me a sin, that by that sink
is not set a-gog: theft and whoredom; pride and prodigality;
villainy and blasphemy; these three couples of hellhounds never
cease barking there, and bite many, so as they are uncurable
ever after.

> Thomas White, *A Sermon Preached at Pawles Crosse,* 1578

'THE THEATRE EVIL'

Do these mockers and flouters of his Majesty, these dissembling
hipocrites, and flattering gnatoes, think to escape unpunished?
beware, therefore, you masking players, you painted repulchres,
you double dealing ambodexters, be warned betimes, and like
good computists, cast your accounts before, what will be the

reward thereof in the end, lest God destroy you in his wrath: abuse God no more, corrupt his people no longer with your dregs, and intermingle not his blessed word with such profane vanities . . . If their plays be of profane matters, then tend they to the dishonour of God, and nourishing of vice, both which are damnable. So that whether they be the one or the other, they are quite contrary to the word of grace, and sucked out of the Devil's teats to nourish us in idolatry, heathenry, and sin. And therefore they, carrying the note, or brand, of God his curse upon their backs which way soever they go, are to be hissed out of all Christian Kingdoms, if they will have Christ to dwell amongst them . . . For so often as they go to those houses where players frequent, they go to Venus' palace, and Satan's synagogue, to worship devils, and betray Jesus Christ . . . Do they not induce whoredom and uncleanness? nay, are they not rather plain devourers of maidenly virginity and chastity? For proof whereof, but mark the flocking and running to Theatres and Curtains, daily and hourly, night and day, time and tide, to see Plays and Interludes.

Philip Stubbes, The Anatomie of Abuses, 1583

DELIA DEDICATED TO THE COUNTESS OF PEMBROKE

I desire only to be graced by the countenance of your protection: whom the fortune of our time hath made the happy and judicial Patroness of the Muses (a glory hereditary to your house) to preserve them for those hideous Beasts, Oblivion and Barbarism.

Samuel Daniel, Delia, 1592

NOAH'S FLOOD AT CHESTER

Every company had his pageant or part, which pageants were a high scaffold with two rooms, and higher and a lower, upon four wheels. In the lower they apparelled themselves, and in the higher room they played, being all open on the top, that all beholders might hear and see them. The places where they played them was in every street. They began first at the abbey gates, and when the first pageant was played it was wheeled to the high cross before the mayor, and so to every street: and so every street had a pageant playing before them at one time, till all the pageants for the day appointed were played.

Archdeacon Rogers, 1594

OBJECTIONS TO STAGE PLAYS AND THEATRES
1. They are a special cause of corrupting their youth, containing nothing but unchaste matters, lascivious devices, shifts of cozenage, and other lewd and ungodly practices, being so that they impress the very quality and corruption of manners which they represent, contrary to the rules and art prescribed for the making of comedies even among the heathen, who used them seldom and at certain set times, and not all the year long as our manner is. Whereby such as frequent them, being of the base and refuse sort of people or such young gentlemen as have small regard of credit or conscience, draw the same into imitation and not to the avoiding the like vices which they represent.
2. They are the ordinary places for vagrant persons, masterless men, thieves, horse-stealers, whoremongers, cozeners, coney-catchers, contrivers of treason and other idle and dangerous persons to meet together and to make their matches to the great displeasure of Almighty God and the hurt and annoyance of her Majesty's people; which cannot be prevented nor discovered by the governors of the city for that they are out of the city's jurisdiction.
3. They maintain idleness in such persons as have no vocation, and draw apprentices and other servants from their ordinary works and all sorts of people from the resort unto sermons and other Christian exercises to the great hindrance of trades and profanation of religion established by her Highness within this realm.
4. In the time of sickness it is found by experience that many, having sores and yet not heart-sick, take occasion hereby to walk abroad and to recreate themselves by hearing a play. Whereby others are infected, and themselves also many things miscarry.

A letter from the Lord Mayor and Aldermem
of London to the Privy Council, 28 July 1597

A GOODLY HOCH-POCH
Now, lest such frightful shows of Fortune's fall,
And bloody Tyrant's rage, should chance appal
The dead stroke audience, midst the silent rout,
Comes leaping in a self-misformed lout,
And laughs, and grins, and frames his mimic face,
And jostles straight into the prince's place.
Then doth the theatre echo all aloud,
With gladsome noise of that applauding crowd.
A goodly hoch-poch; when vile russetings*

Are matched with monarchs and with mighty kings.
A goodly grace to sober tragic Muse,
When each base clown, his clumsy fist doth bruise†,
And show his teeth in double rotten row
For laughter at his self-resembled show.

Joseph Hall, Virgidemiarum, 1597

*Peasants
†Thumping benches to applaud

WILLIAM KEMP AND HIS FACE-PLAY DESCRIBED IN THE LAST SCENE OF A PLAY

Clowns have been thrust into plays by head and shoulders ever since Kemp could make a scurvy face . . . Why, if thou canst but draw thy mouth awry, lay thy leg over thy staff, saw a piece of cheese asunder with thy dagger, lap up drink on the earth, I warrant thee they'll laugh mightily.

The Pilgrimage to Parnassus, 1598

50. This illustration is from 'The Babes in the Wood', a ballad of 1595, which told a true tragic story of the day. A gentleman of Norfolk leaves his property to his young son and daughter. His brother hires two ruffians to kill them in a wood. One repents, kills the other, leaving the children in the wood, where they die. Two robins cover them with leaves.

STRUCTURE OF A PLAYHOUSE

. . . The frame of the said house to be set square and to contain four score foot of lawful assize every way square without, and fifty-five foot of like assize square every way within, with a good, sure and strong foundation of piles, brick, lime and sand both without and within to be wrought one foot of assize at the least above the ground. And the said frame to contain three storeys in height, the first or lower storey to contain twelve foot of lawful assize in height, the second storey eleven foot of lawful assize in height, and the third or upper storey to contain nine foot of lawful assize in height. All which storeys shall contain twelve foot and a half of lawful assize in breadth throughout, besides a jutty forwards in either of the said two upper storeys of ten inches of lawful assize, with four convenient divisions for gentlemen's rooms and other sufficient and convenient divisions for two-penny rooms, with necessary seats to be placed and set as well in those rooms as throughout all the rest of the galleries of the said house and with such-like stairs, conveyances and divisions without and within as are made and contrived in and to the late erected playhouse on the Bank, in the said parish of St. Saviour's, called the Globe; with a stage and tiring-house to be made, erected and set up within the said frame with a shadow or cover on the said stage. . . .

And which stage shall contain in length forty and three foot of lawful assize and in breadth to extend to the middle of the yard of the said house. The same stage to be paled in below with good, strong and sufficient new oaken boards, and likewise the lower storey of the said frame withinside; and the same lower storey to be also laid over and fenced with strong iron pikes. And the said stage to be in all other proportions contrived and fashioned like unto the stage of the said play-house called the Globe, with convenient windows and lights glazed to the said tiring-house, and the said frame, stage and staircases to be covered with tile and to have a sufficient gutter of lead to carry and convey the water from the covering of the said stage to fall backwards. And also all the said frame and the staircases thereof to be sufficiently enclosed without with lath, lime and hair, and the gentlemen's rooms and twopenny rooms to be sealed with lath, lime and hair, and all the floors of the said galleries, storeys and stage to be boarded with good and sufficient new deal boards of whole thickness where need shall be. And the said house, and other things before-mentioned, to be made and done, to be in all other contrivations, conveyances, fashions, thing and things effected, finished and done, according to the manner and fashion of the said house called the Globe, saving only that all the principal and main posts of the said frame and stage forward shall be square and wrought pilaster-wise with carved proportions called satyrs to be placed and set on the top of every of the same posts. . . .

Contract for building the Fortune Theatre
at the cost of £440 (dated 8 January, 1600)

MUSIC

ELIZABETH STRONGLY SUPPORTS THE CHAPEL CHOIR, 1559

Eliz. R: Whereas our Castle of Windsor hath of old been well furnished with singing-men and children. . . . We, willing that it should not be of less reputation in our days, but rather augmented and increased, declare that no singing-men or boys shall be taken out of the said Chapel, by virtue of any commission, not even for our household chapel. And we give power to the bearer of this to take any singing-men or boys from any chapel, our own household and St. Paul's only excepted. Given at Westminster, the 8th day of March, in the second year of our reign.

RICHARD FARRANT BECOMES MASTER OF THE CHORISTERS AT ST. GEORGE'S, 1564

The 24th of [April] in the 6th of Eliz. the Dean and Canons indented Richard Farrant, one of the Queen's Chapel, to be Master of the Choristers in this church, and to have a clerk's place and to be one of the organists in this Chapel: he to have the boarding, clothing, lodging and finding of the ten choristers: to enjoy the houses and emoluments of an organist, clerk and master. On condition of the premises to have £81 6s. 8d. per annum to be paid him monthly by the treasurer besides spur money and money given by strangers for singing of ballets, and the Master of the boys is to have power of placing and displacing the boys (except the present boys before their voice is broken which are not to be displaced without order of Chapter); he is also to find a sufficient service for those he displaces: he to be

51. An engraving of Thomas Tallis, an early Tudor composer, by Vandergucht.
From Wynkyn de Worde's collection of songs, 1530.

absent so far as the college statutes permit. The choristers to
have their chamber in the college to lie in still allowed them, but
the Master of the boys to provide them not only clothes and diet
but also bedding, and to leave them as well clothed as he finds
them: he to have the place for his life. After the displacing of
any boy he is to find another within a month or to be defaulted
18d. per week for default after the month is expired: he is not
to demand anything of the augmentation granted this year to
the clerks and choristers, nor be absent not above two months in
the year and that by leave of the Dean. . . .

E. H. Fellowes, *Windsor Historical Monographs*

SERIOUS MUSIC DECLINES
In times past, music was chiefly maintained by cathedral
churches, abbeys, colleges, parish churches, chantries, guilds,
fraternities, etc., but when the abbeys, . . . etc. were suppressed,
then went music into decay. To speak of music in houses, . . .
divers noblemen and women, in time past, imitating the prince,
would have organists and singingmen to serve God after the

manner of that time with music in their private chapels, but that imitation is also left. Then for such as served for private recreation in houses, these were no less esteemed than the others. . . . Now I will speak of the use of music in this time present. First for the church, ye do and shall see it so slenderly maintained in the cathedral churches and colleges and parish churches that when the old store of the musicians be worn out . . . ye shall have few or none remaining except it be a few singingmen and players on musical instruments. . . . There be another sort of musicians that be named speculators, that is to say, they that do become musicians by study without any practice thereof. There have been of such who have made songs and have pricked them out, and yet could not sing a part of them themselves. . . .

I being desirous to have and enrich myself with some more such exercises and qualities as young folk for the most part do delight in, went to the dancing school and fencing school and also learned to play on the gittern and cittern, which two instruments were then strange in England, and therefore the more desired and esteemed —

The Autobiography of Thomas Whythorne, c. 1576

A DESCRIPTION OF WINDSOR AND THE MUSIC THERE BY THE DUKE'S SECRETARY

The Castle stands upon a knoll or hill. In the outer court is a very beautiful, and spacious church, with a low flat roof covered with lead, as is common with all churches in England. In this church his highness listened for more than an hour to the beautiful music, the usual ceremonies, and the English sermon. The music, and especially the organ, was exquisite. At times could be heard cornets, then flutes, then recorders and other instruments. And there was a little boy who sang so sweetly, and lent such charm to the music with his little tongue, that it was really wonderful to listen to him. Their ceremonies indeed are very similar to those of the papists, with singing and so on. After the music, which lasted a long time, a minister or preacher ascended the pulpit for the sermon, and soon afterwards, it being noon, his highness went to dinner. . . .

Visit of Frederick, Duke of Würtemberg, 1592, quoted in Rye; *England as Seen by Foreigners*

LEARN TO SING

First, it is a knowledge easily taught, and quickly learned, where there is a good master, and an apt scholar.

2. The exercise of singing is delightful to Nature, and good to preserve the health of Man.

3. It doth strengthen all parts of the breast, and doth open the pipes.

4. It is a singular good remedy for a stuttering and stammering in the speech.

5. It is the best means to procure a perfect pronunciation, and to make a good orator.

6. It is the only way to know where Nature hath bestowed the benefit of a good voice: which gift is so rare, as there is not one among a thousand, that hath it: and in many, that excellent gift is lost, because they want Art to express Nature.

7. There is not any music of instruments whatsoever, comparable to that which is made of the voices of Men, where the voices are good, and the same well sorted and ordered.

8. The better the voice is, the meeter it is to honour and serve God therewith: and the voice of man is chiefly to be employed to that end.

Omnis spiritus laudet Dominum
    Since singing is so good a thing,
    I wish all men would learn to sing.

William Byrd, *Psalms, Sonnets and songs of sadness and pietie*, 1588

READING MUSICAL PART AT SIGHT

Philomathes to Polymathes about a 'banket':

. . . supper being ended, and music books being brought to the table, the mistress of the house presented me with a part, earnestly requesting me to sing; but when, after many excuses, I protested unfainedly that I could not, every one began to wonder! Yea, some whispered to others, demanding how I was brought up; so that upon shame of mine ignorance, I go now to seek out mine old friend Master Gnorimus to make myself his scholar.

Thomas Morley, *Plain and Easie Introduction to Practicall Musicke set down in the Form of a Dialogue*, 1597

THE DUKE OF STETTIN-POMERANIA SHOWS THE IMPORTANCE OF MUSIC IN HIS DESCRIPTION OF A CHOIRBOY PLAY IN 1602

The Queen keeps a number of young boys, who are taught to sing and to play on all sorts of musical instruments — they are also expected to continue their school studies at the same time. These boys have special instructors in the various arts, and especially in music. As part of their education in courtly manners they are required to put on a play once a week, and for this purpose the Queen has provided them with a theatre and with a great deal of rich apparel. Those who wish to see one of the performances must pay as much as eight shillings of our Pomeranian money [that is in English terms, the equivalent of a shilling — about four times the price of a normal theatre seat]. Yet there are always a good many people present, including ladies of the highest repute, since the plots are always well developed, and a suitably elevated character. All the performances are by candlelight and the effect is indeed spectacular. For a whole hour before the play begins there is a concert of music for organs, lutes, pandoras, citterns, viols and recorders. When we were there a boy 'cum voce tremula' [does this, perhaps, imply some kind of vibrato?] sang so charmingly to the accompaniment of a bass viol that with the possible exception of the Nuns at Milan, we heard nothing to equal him anywhere . . .

'The Diary of Philip Julius,
Duke of Stettin-Pomerania', G. von Bulow

52. Queen Elizabeth's virginals. This open view of a richly decorated small harpsichord bears the arms and device of Queen Elizabeth. It is Venetian mid-sixteenth century. The music written by Englishmen for this instrument had a highly individual national style.

JOHN WILLIAMS, DEAN OF WESTMINSTER ABBEY, ENTERTAINED FRENCH AMBASSADORS AT THE ABBEY, 1624

At their entrance, the organ was touched by the best finger of that age, Mr. Orlando Gibbons . . . and while a verse was played, The Lord Keeper presented the ambassadors and the rest of the noblest quality of their nation with [the] liturgy as it spake to them in their own language. The Lords ambassadors and their great train took up all the stalls, where they continued half an hour while the choirmen, vested in their rich copes, with their choristers, sang three several anthems, with most exquisite voices before them. . . .

J. Hacket, *Scrinia Reserata,* 1692

Sports – Pastimes

DANCING

Yet is there one, the most delightful king,
  A lofty jumping, or a leaping round,
When arm in arm two dancers are entwined
    And whirl themselves, with strict embracements
      bound,
    And still their feet an anapaest do sound —
An anapaest is all their music's song.
Whose two feet are short, and third is long.

Anonymous

REVELS AT KENILWORTH, 1575

Music and Dancing

On Sunday the forenoon occupied (as for the Sabbath day) in quiet and vacation from work, and in divine service and preaching at the parish church. The afternoon in excellent music of sundry sweet instruments, and in dancing of Lords and Ladies, and other worshipful degrees, uttered with such lively agility and commendable grace, as, whether it might be more strange to the eye, or pleasant to the mind, for my part indeed I could not discern: but excellently well was it (methought) in both.

Fireworks

At night late, as though Jupiter the last night had forgot for business, or forborn for courtesy and quiet, part of his welcome unto her highness (Queen Elizabeth) appointed: now entering at the first into his purpose moderately (as mortals do) with a warning piece or two, proceeding on with increase; at last the Altitonant displays me his main power: with blaze of burning darts, flying to and fro, leams of stars coruscant, streams and hails of fiery sparks, lightnings of wild fire on water and land, flight and shoot of thunderbolts; all with such countenance, terror, and vehemence, that the heavens thundered, the waters surged, the earth shook, and in such sort surely, as, had we not

53. An Elizabethan huntsman, from George Turberville's *The Noble Arte of Venerie or Hunting*, 1575.

been assured the thunderful deity was all hot in amity, and could not otherwise witness his welcoming unto her highness, it would have made me for my part, as hardy as I am, very vengeably afeard. This ado lasted while the midnight was past. . . .

Deer-hunting

Monday was hot; therefore her highness kept in till five o'clock in the evening: what time it pleased her to ride forth into the chase to hunt the Hart . . . which found anon, and after sore chase, and chafed by the hot pursuit of the hounds, was fain, of fine strength, at last to take soil [to run towards water]. There to behold the swift fleeting of the deer in front, with the stately carriage of his head in his swimming, spred (for the quantity) like the sail of a ship: the hounds harrowing after, as they had been a number of skiffs to the spoil of the carvel [a ship of about 140 tons]; the one no less eager in purchase of his prey, than was the other in safeguard of his life: so as the earning [baying] of the hounds in continuace of their cry, the swiftness of the Deer, the running of footmen, the galloping of horses, the blasting of horns, the halloing and shouts of the huntsmen, with the excellent echoes between whiles from the woods and waters in valleys resounding, moved pastime delightful to so high a degree, as for any person to take pleasure by most senses at once; in my opinion there can be no one way comparable to this, and especially in this place, that of nature is formed . . . for the purpose. . . . Well, the hart was killed, a goodly deer.

Bear-baiting

A great sort of bandogs [a kind of mastiff] were there tied in the outer court, and thirteen bears in the inner . . . the bears were brought forth into the court, the dogs set to them . . . very fierce both the one and the other and eager in argument. If the dog would pluck the bear by the throat, the bear would claw him again by the scalp. . . . Thus with plucking and tugging, scratching and biting, by plain tooth and nail on one side and the other, such expense of blood and leather was there between them, as a month's licking (I ween) will not recover. . . . It was a sport very pleasant, of these beasts: to see the bear with his pink eyes leering after his enemy's approach, the nimbleness and watch of the dog to take his advantage, and the force and experience of the bear again to avoid the assaults: if he were bitten in one place, how he would pinch in another to get free: that if he were taken once, then what shift with biting, with clawing, with roaring, tossing and tumbling, he would work to wind himself from them: and when he was loose, to shake his ears twice or thrice with the blood and the saliva about his face, was a matter of a goodly relief. . . .

An Italian Acrobat

In the meantime was there shown before her highness, by an Italian, such feats of agility in goings, turnings, tumblings, castings, hops, jumps, leaps, skips, springs, gambols, somersaults, capers, and flights: forward, backward, sideways, down, up, and with sundry windings, gyrings and circumflexions: also lightly and with such ease, as by me in few words it is not expressible by pen or speech, I tell you plain. I blessed me, by my faith, to behold him, and began to doubt whether he was a man or a spirit. . . .

Robert Laneham's Letter, as edited by Dr Furnivall

PREPARING FOR THE CHASE

Immediately after supper the huntsmen should go to his master's chamber, and, if he serve a king, then let him go to the Master of the Games' chamber, to know his pleasure in what

54. The Earl of Leicester's suit of armour used for tilting.

quarter he determineth to hunt the day following, that he may know his own quarter. That done, he may go to bed, to the end he may rise the earlier in the morning, according to the time and season, and according to the place where he must hunt. Then, when he is up and ready, let him drink a good draught and fetch his hound to make him break his fast a little. And let him not forget to fill his bottle with good wine. That done, let him take a little vinegar in the palm of his hand, and put it in the nostrils of his hound, for to make him snuff, to the end his scent may be the perfecter. Then let him to the wood. And if he chance by the way to find any hare, partridge, or any other beast or bird that is fearful, living upon seeds or pasturage, it is an evil sign or presage that he shall have but evil pastime that day. But if he find any beast of ravine, living upon prey, as wolf, fox, raven and such like, that is a token of good luck.

George Turberville, *The noble art of venerie or hunting*, 1576

BOWLING-ALLEYS

Common bowling alleys are privy [secret] moths, that eat up the credit of many idle citizens, whose gains at home are not able to weigh down their losses abroad, whose shops are so far from maintaining their play, that their wives and children cry out for bread, and go to bed supperless oft in the year.

Stephen Gosson, *Schoole of Abuse*, 1579

FOOTBALL

For as concerning football playing, I protest unto you it may rather be called a friendly kind of fight, than a play or recreation; a bloody and murdering practice, than a fellowly sport or pastime. For doth not every one lie in wait for his adversary, seeking to overthrow him and to pick [throw] him on his nose, though it be upon hard stones, in ditch or dale, in valley or hill, or what place soever it be he careth not, so he have him down. And he that can serve the most of this fashion, he is counted the only fellow, and who but he? So that by this means, sometimes their necks are broken, sometimes their backs, sometimes their legs, sometime their arms, sometime one part thrust out of joint, sometime another, sometime their noses gush out with blood, sometime their eyes start out, and sometimes hurt in one place, sometimes in another. But whosoever scapeth away the best goeth not scot-free, but is either sore wounded, and bruised, so as he dieth of it, or else scapeth very hardly.

And no marvel, for they have sleights to meet one betwixt two, to dash him against the heart with their elbows, to hit him under the short ribs with their gripped fists, and with their knees to catch him upon the hip, and to pick him on his neck, with an hundred such murdering devices. And hereof groweth envy, malice, rancour, choler, hatred, displeasure, enmity and what not else: and sometimes fighting, brawling, contention, quarrel picking, murder, homicide and great effusion of blood, as experience daily teacheth.

Philip Stubbes, *The Anatomie of Abuses*, 1583

MAY-DAY

Against May, Whitsunday, or some other time of the year, every parish, town and village assemble themselves together, both men, women and children, old and young, even all indifferently; and either going all together or dividing themselves into companies, they go some to the woods and groves, some to the hills and mountains, some to one place and some to another, where they spend all the night in pleasant pastimes; and in the morning they return, bring with them birch boughs and branches of trees, to deck their assemblies withal. And no marvel, for there is a great lord present amongst them, as superintendent and lord over their pastimes and sports, namely Sathan, prince of hell. But their chiefest jewel they bring from thence is their May-pole, which they bring home with great veneration, as thus, They have twenty or forty yoke of oxen, every ox having a sweet nose-gay of flowers placed on the tip of his horns; and these oxen draw home this May-pole (this stinking idol, rather) which is covered all over with flowers and herbs, bound round about with strings from the top to the bottom, and sometime painted with variable colours, with two or three hundred men, women and children following it with great devotion. And thus being reared up with handkerchiefs and flags streaming on the top, they straw the ground about, bind green boughs about it, set up summer-halls, bowers, and arbours hard by it; and then they fall to banquet and feast, to leap and dance about it, as the heathen people did at the dedication of their idols, whereof this is a perfect pattern, or rather the thing itself.

Philip Stubbes, *The Anatomie of Abuses*, 1583

'MY LORD OF MISRULE'

First, all the wild heads of the parish, conventing together, choose them a grand captain (of mischief), whom they ennoble with the title of my Lord of Misrule, and him they crown with great solemnity, and adopt for their king. This king anointed chooseth forth twenty, forty, threescore, or a hundred lusty-guts like to himself, to wait upon his lordly majesty, and to guard his noble person. Then, every one of these his men he investeth with his liveries of green, yellow, or some other light wanton colour. And, as though that were not gaudy enough, they bedeck themselves with scarfs, ribbons, and laces, hanged all over with gold rings, precious stones, and other jewels; this done, they tie about either leg twenty or forty bells, with rich handkershiefs in their hands, and sometimes laid across over their shoulders and necks, borrowed, for the most part, of their pretty Mopsies and loving Bessies, for bussing them in the dark. Thus, all things set in order, then have they their hobby-horses, dragons, and other antics, together with their pipers and thundering drummers, to strike up the devil's dance withal. Then march these heathen company towards the church and church-yard, their pipers piping, their drummers thundering, their stumps dancing, their bells jingling, their handkerchiefs swinging about their heads like madmen, their hobby-horses and other monsters skirmishing amongst the throng; and in this sort they go to the church (though the minister be at prayer or preaching), dancing and swinging their handkerchiefs over their heads in the church like devils incarnate, with such a confused noise that no man can hear his own voice. Then the foolish people, they look, they stare, they laugh, they fleer, and mount upon forms and pews to see these goodly pageants solemnized in this sort. Then, after this, about the church they go again and again, and so forth into the church-yard, where they have commonly their summer halls, their bowers, arbours, and banqueting-houses set up, wherein they feast, banquet and dance all that day, and peradventure all that night too. And thus these terrestrial furies spend the Sabbath-day. Then, for the further ennobling of this honourable lurdan (lord, I should say), they have also certain papers, wherein is painted some babblery, or other of imagery work, and these they call my Lord of Misrule's badges; these they give to every one that will give money for them, to maintain them in this their heathenry, devilry, drunkenness, pride and what not. And who will not show himself buxom to them, and give them money for these the devil's cognizances, they shall be mocked and flouted at shamefully; yea, and many times carried upon a coulstaff, and dived over head and ears in water, or otherwise most horribly abused. . . . Another sort of fantastical fools bring to these hell-hounds (the Lord of Misrule and his complices), some bread, some good ale, some new cheese, some cakes, some flauns, some tarts, some cream, some meat, some one thing, some another.

Philip Stubbes, *The Anatomie of Abuses*, 1583

BEAR-BAITING

. . . the baiting of a bear, besides that it is filthy, stinking, and loathsome game, is it not a dangerous and a perilous exercise, wherein a man is in danger of his life every minute of an hour? What Christian heart can take pleasure to see one poor beast to rent, tear, and kill another, and all for his foolish pleasure? And although they be bloody beasts to mankind, and seek his destruction, yet we are not to abuse them, for his sake who made them and whose creatures they are. For notwithstanding that they be evil to us, and thirst after our blood, yet are they good creatures in their own nature and kind, and made to set forth the glory, power, and magnificence of our God, and for our use, and therefore . . . we ought not to abuse them.

Philip Stubbes, *The Anatomie of Abuses*, 1583

TABLE GAMES

In the morning, perhaps, at chess, and after his belly is full then at cards, . . . then for some exercise of his arms at dice, and for a little motion of his body, to tennis; . . . and then, to cool himself a little, play at tables; and being disquieted in his patience . . . or missing two or three foul blots, then to an interlude, and so, like to a mill horse, treading always in the same steps.

Sir John Harington, *A Treatise on Playe*, 1597

SLIDING

When the great fen or moor, which watereth of the city on the north side is frozen, many young men play upon the ice, some striding as wide as they may, do slide swiftly: others make themselves seats of ice as great as millstones: one sits down, many hand in hand do draw him, and one slipping on a sudden, all fall together: some tie bones to their feet, and under their heels, and shoving themselves, by a little picked staff, do slide as swiftly as a bird flieth in the air, or an arrow out of a crossbow.

John Stow, *A Survey of London*, 1598

ENGLISH THEATRES AND BEAR-GARDENS

Without the city are some theatres, where English actors represent almost every day comedies and tragedies to very numerous audiences; these are concluded with variety of dances, accompanied by excellent music and the excessive applause of those that are present. Not far from one of these theatres, which are all built of wood, lies the royal barge, close to the river Thames. It has two splendid cabins, beautifully ornamented with glass windows, painting and gilding; it is kept upon dry ground, and sheltered from the weather.

There is still another place, built in the form of a theatre, which serves for the baiting of bears and bulls, They are fastened behind, and then worried by those great English dogs and mastiffs, but not without great risk to the dogs from the teeth of the one and the horns of the other; and it sometimes happens they are killed upon the spot. Fresh ones are immediately supplied in the places of those that are wounded or tired. To this entertainment there often follows that of whipping a blinded bear, which is performed by five or six men, standing in a circle with whips, which they exercise upon him without any mercy. Although he cannot escape from them because of his chain, he nevertheless defends himself, vigorously throwing down all who come within his reach and are not active enough to get out of it, and tearing the whips out of their hands and breaking them. At these spectacles and everywhere else, the English are constantly smoking the Nicotian weed which in America is called *Tobaca* — others call it *Paetum* — and generally in this manner: they have pipes on purpose made of clay, into the farther end of which they put the herb, so dry that it may be rubbed into powder, and lighting it, they draw the smoke into their mouths, which they puff out again through their nostrils, like funnels, along with it plenty of phlegm and defluxion [discharge] from the head. In these theatres, fruits, such as apples, pears and nuts, according to the season, are carried about to be sold, as well as wine and ale.

Paul Hentzner, *Travels in England,* 1598

COCK-FIGHTING

. . . in the city of London . . . cock-fights are held annually throughout three-quarters of the year (for in the remaining quarter they told me it was impossible since the feathers are full of blood) and I saw the place which is built like a theatre. In the centre on the floor stands a circular table covered with straw an with ledges round it, where the cocks are teased and incited to fly

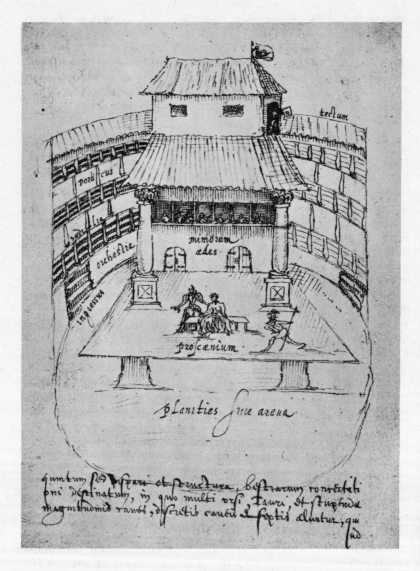

55. A drawing of the Swan Theatre in London about 1596, by Johann deWitt. One of the few uncontested bits of contemporary evidence regarding the form of the Elizabethan playhouse.

at one another, while those with wagers as to which cock will win, sit closest around the circular disk, but the Spectators who are merely present on their entrance penny sit around higher up, watching with eager pleasure the fierce and angry fight between the cocks, as these wound each other to death with spurs and beaks. And the party whose cock surrenders or dies loses the wager; I am told that stakes on a cock often amount to many thousands of crowns . . .

Thomas Platter, Travels in England, 1599

GAMES AND PASTIMES

Man, I dare challenge thee to throw the sledge,
To jump or leap over a ditch or hedge;
To wrestle, play at stoolball, or to run,
To pitch the bar, or to shoot off a gun;
To play at loggets, nineholes, or ten pins,
To try it out at football, by the shins;
At Ticktack, Irish, Noddie, Maw, and Ruff:
At hot-cockles, leap-frog, or blindman-buff.
To drink half pots, or deal at the whole can:
To play at base, or pen-and-ink-horn Sir Ihan (John):
To dance the Morris, play at barley-break,
At all exploits a man can think or speak;
At shove-groat, venter point, or cross and pile,
At 'beshrow him that's last at yonder stile';
At leaping o'er a Midsummer bon-fire,
Or at the drawing Dun out of the mire;
At 'shoot-cock, Gregory', stoolball and what not,
Pick-point, top and scourge, to make him hot.

Samuel Rowlands, The Letting of Humours
Blood in the Head-Vaine, 1600

CORNISH WRESTLING ON HALVAGER MOOR

. . . the two champions set forth stripped into their doublets and hosen, and untrussed, that they may so the better command the use of their limbs; and first shaking hands, in token of friendship, they fall presently to the effect of anger: for each striveth how to take hold of the other with his best advantage, and to bear his adverse party down; wherein whosoever overthroweth his mate, in such sort as that either his back, or the one shoulder and contrary heel do touch the ground, is accounted to give the fall. If he be only endangered and make a narrow escape, it is called a foyle.

R. Carew, Survey of Cornwall, 1602

56. Queen Elizabeth at a hunting picnic from George Turberville's, *The Noble Art of Venerie or Hunting*, 1575. This book deals with everything concerning hunting from the care of hounds to 'the place where and how an assembly should be made, in the presence of a Prince or some honourable person'. Here the Queen and courtiers feast on wine and capons.

THE QUINTAIN

*A quintain was a post used for tilting. It was fixed in the ground, and
had a revolving cross-piece, on one end a shield, the mark, on the other a
heavy bag of sand which swung round and struck the tilter who did not
swerve away quickly.*

This exercise of running at the Quintain was practised by the
youthful citizens, as well in summer as in winter, especially, in
the feast of Christmas. I have seen a Quintain set upon Cornhill,
by the Leaden Hall, where the attendants on the Lords of merry
disport have run, and made great pastime; for he that hit not
the broad end of the Quintain, was of all men laughed to scorn,
and he that hit it full, if he rode not the faster, had a sound
blow in his neck, with a bag full of sand hanging on the other
end.

I have also in the summer season seen some upon the river of
Thames rowed in wherries, with staves in their hands, flat at the
fore end, running against one another, and, for the most part,
one or both overthrown, and well ducked.

John Stow, A Survey of London, 1603

Health

CARE OF THE EYES

These things be good for the eyes: Every thing that is green or black is good for a man to look upon it. Also to look upon gold is good for the sight and so is glass, cold water and every cold thing, except the wind, is good for the eyes, and no hot thing, nor warm thing is good for the eyes except woman's milk and the blood of a dove.

These things be evil for the eyes: Every thing that is hot is not for the eyes, the sun, the fire, the snow and every thing that is white is not good for the sight and smoke, weeping, the wind, sickness, rheum, reading in small printed books, specially Greek books, and onions, garlic, chibobs [Welsh onion] and such like be not good for the eyes.

To clarify the eyes and the sight: Take of the seeds of oculi christi [wild sage] and put into the eyes two, three or four seeds, or else take cold water and with a fine linen cloth wash the eyes divers times in a day, the ofter the better, and change the water oft that it may be fresh and cold.

Andrew Boorde, *Breviary of Helthe*, 1547

TREATMENT FOR BALDNESS

Shave the head and beard and anoint the head with the grease of a fox. Or else wash the head with the juice of beets five or six times or else stamp garlic and rub the head with it and after that wash it with vinegar, do this five or six times. Or else make ashes of garlic and temper it with honey and anoint the head . . . Anoint the head with the oils of bitter almonds, or with the oil of wormwood, or with such like oils. The oil of myrtle is good, or the oil of galls or the oil of walnuts or the oil of maidenhair.

Andrew Boorde, *Breviary of Helthe*, 1547

SLEEPLESSNESS

The cause. This impediment doth come through idleness or weakness of the brain, or else through sickness, anger or fasting, or else through solicitude or repletion, or extreme heat, or extreme cold in the feet or such like.

A remedy. Take of the oil of violets an ounce, of opium half an ounce, incorporate this together with woman's milk and with a fine linen cloth lay it to the temples, or else use to eat of lettuce seeds, of white poppy seeds, or mandragora seeds . . . Of each three drams, but above all things mirth is best to bedward.

Andrew Boorde, *Breviary of Helthe,* 1547

THE SWEATING SICKNESS

In the very end of May began in the city of London the sickness called the sweating sickness, and afterward went all the realm almost of the which many died within 5 or 6 hours. By reason of this sickness the term was adjourned and the circuits of Assize also. The King was sore troubled with this plague, for divers died in the Court, of whom one was Sir Frances Poynes which was Ambassador in Spain, and other, so that the King for a space removed almost every day, till at the last he came to Tittenhangar a place of the Abbot of St Alban's and there he with a few determined to bide the chance that God would send him, which place was so purged daily with fires and other preservatives, that neither he nor the Queen nor none of their company was infected with that disease, such was the pleasure of God. In this great plague died Sir William Compton knight and William Cary esquire which were of the King's privy chamber, and whom the King highly favoured and many other worshipful men and women in England.

Edward Hall, *Life of Henry VIII,* 1548

THE GOOD HOUSEWIFELY PHYSIC

Good housewives provide, ere a sickness do come,
Of sundry good things in her house to have some.
Good *aqua composita,* and vinegar tart,
Rosewater, and treacle, to comfort the heart.
Cold herbs in her garden, for agues that burn,
That over-strong heat to good temper may turn.
White endive, and succory, with spinach enow;
All such, with good pot-herbs, should follow the plough.
Get water of fumitory, liver to cool,
And others the like, or else go like a fool.

DES LVXATIONS.
475

Ie ne veux en ceſt endroit laiſſer en arrie-
re l'aſtuce & inuention du Chirurgien de
Monſeigneur le Duc de Lorraine, nommé
Nicolas Picart, lequel fut appelé en vn village pres Nancy, pour reduire vne luxation de
l'eſpaule d'vn païſan: en la maiſon duquel il
n'y auoit que luy & ſa femme. Il mit & atta-
cha ledit Païſan ſur vne eſchelle, cõme deſſus auõs dit, & print vn baſton entre ſes iam-
bes, & le poſa ſous l'vn des eſchelons, & atta-
cha vn lien au deſſus du coulde du bras luxé:
puis de toute ſa peſanteur & force preſſa ſur
le baſton, & commanda à la femme de tirer
la ſelle de deſſous les pieds : & tout à l'inſtant
remit l'os en ſon lieu, comme tu vois par ceſte figure.

Et par faute d'vne eſchelle on ſe peut ai-
der d'vne perche poſée en trauers de deux
colõnes, ou d'vne porte, cõme tu vois par
ceſte figure: en laquelle t'eſt monſtré vn bois
auec liés, qui te ſera declaré tout maintenãt.

Figure pout reduire l'eſpaule deſſus l'eſchelle.
    Autre figure pour reduire l'eſpaule ſus vne porte

R iiij

57. A page from one of Ambroise Pare's books showing how to reset a
dislocated shoulder.

Conserves of barberry, quinces and such,
With syrups, that easeth the sickly, so much.
Ask *Medicus* counsel, ere medicine ye make
And honour that man for necessity's sake.
Though thousands hate physic, because of the cost,
Yet thousands it helpeth, that else should be lost,
Good broth, and good keeping, do much now and then:
Good diet with wisdom, best comforteth man.
In health, to be stirring shall profit thee best;
In sickness hate troubles, seek quiet and rest.
Remember thy soul: let no fancy prevail;
Make ready to God-ward; let faith never quail
The sooner thyself thou submittest to God,
the sooner He ceaseth to scourge with His rod.

> Thomas Tusser, *Five Hundreth Pointes*
> *of Good Husbandrie*, 1551

TREATMENT OF LUNATICS

. . . it appeared of late days of a lunatic named Michael, the
which went many years at liberty, and at last he did kill his wife
and his wife's sister, and his own self, wherefore I do advertise
every man the which is mad . . . to be kept in saveguard, in some
close house or chamber, where there is little light. And that he
have a keeper the which the mad man do fear . . . Also the
chamber . . . that the mad man is in, let there be no painted
cloths, nor painted walls, nor pictures . . ., for such things make
them full of fantasies. And use few words to them, except it be
for reprehension, or gentle reformation if they have any wit to
understand.

> Andrew Boorde, *A Compendyous Regyment*, 1567

GLUTTONY

And nowadays, if the table be not covered from the one end to
the other, as thick as one dish can stand by another, with delicate
meat of sundry sorts, one clean different from another, and to
every dish a several sauce, appropriate to his kind, it is thought
. . . unworthy the name of a dinner! Yea, so many dishes shall you
have pestering the table at once, as the most devouring glutton,
or the greediest cormorant that ever was, can scarce eat of every
one a little. And these many shall you have at the first course, as
many at the second, and peradventure, more at the third;
besides other sweet condiments, and delicate confections of
spiceries, and I can not tell what! And to these dainties all kinds

of wines are not wanting, you may be sure . . . I have heard my
father say, that in his days one dish or two of good wholesome
meat was thought sufficient for a man of great worship to dine
withal, and if they had three or four kinds, it was reputed a
sumptuous feast. A good piece of beef was thought then good
meat, and able for the best, but now, it is thought too gross for
their tender stomachs to digest.

. . . every county, city, town, village, and other place, hath
abundance of ale-houses, taverns, and inns, which are so fraught
with maltworms, night and day, that you would wonder to see
them. You shall have them there sitting at the wine and good-ale
all the day long, yea, all the night too, peradventure a whole
week together, so long as any money is left, swilling, gulling, and
carousing, from one to another, till never a one can speak a
ready word.

Philip Stubbes, *Anatomie of Abuses*, 1585

THE BOASTING OF A QUACK

And now here he did begin to brag and boast as though all the
keys of knowledge did hang at his girdle. For he said he had
attained unto the deep knowledge of the making of a certain
quintessence which he learned beyond the seas of his master one
Bornelious, a great magician. This shameless beast letted not to
say that if a man did drink of his quintessence continually every
day a certain quantity, the virtue thereof was such that a man
should not die before the day of the great Judgement, and that
it would preserve in the state he was in at thirty years of age,
and in the same strength and force of will although a man were
a hundred or six score years of age. Moreover his plaister was
answerable unto this, and forsooth he called it the only plaister
of the world, and that he attained unto it by his great travail,
cost, and charge, and that it was first sent from God by an angel
unto a red hill in Almayne, where was in times past a holy man
which wrought great marvels only with this plaister, and he
never used any other medicine but only this. His precious balm
or oil he said no man had, but only he, and that it was as rare a
thing to be had or found, as to see a black swan or a winter
swallow, and he called it the secret of the world, which is his
common vaunting phrase: but God knows the medicines were no
such things, but only shadowed under the vizard of deceit, and a
bait to steal fame and credit and to catch or scrape up money or
ware, for all is fish that cometh unto his net. Then this gaudy
fellow with his peerless speeches said that he had done more

The Vertue and Operation of this Balsame.

 Hat this *Balsame* may bee vsed to the health and profit of the buyers, it must bee alwaies kept close, and the vessell wherein it is, must be very wel stopt, or else it will consume and waste away.

Any person which hath his sight beginning to faile him, let him continually smell vnto this *Balsame*, and hee shall be holpen, and his sight shall be preserued.

Make this *Balsame* warme, and rub therewith the Nose within and without, of all those that haue a moyst and cold braine, so shall they be preserued in great health thereby.

And whosoeuer hath a cold Rheume descending from the braine, let them rubbe their Nostrils with this *Balsam* three times a day, morning, noone, and night, and it helpeth them.

Such as are heauy headed, dull witted, or forgetfull, let all those vse to anoint the hinder part of their head with this *Balsam*, and it comforteth the wit, and refresheth a man exceedingly well.

Giue sixe drops of this *Balsame* in a spoonefull of wine, beere, or ale fasting, to all those that haue no appetite, and it helpeth : also those that vse to drinke of it, are long preserued in young liking.

If any person haue a flegmy stomacke, let them vse euery morning fasting, to take sixe drops of this *Balsam* in wine, beere, or ale, and it expelleth the flegme, and comforteth the stomacke : also whosoeuer hath abundance of corruption in their stomacke, which is the cause of great feeblenesse, let them vse it as aforesaid, and euery twelfth, or fourteenth day purge themselues, so may they shortly be holpen, which might their life-time liue and suffer great paines.

Being taken euery morning sixe drops in a spoonefull of wine, beere, or ale, it preserueth one from poyson all the day a' ter: also it preserueth a man from all corrupt and poisoning ayre, and specially good to bee vsed in time of pestilence.

Such as are poysoned, let them instantly take sixe drops of this *Balsam* in a spoonefull of water, and so continue in taing of it twelue houres after, that is, euery houre sixe drops, so shall they be holpen.

Any person which by chance falleth, and is bruised on any part of his body, let him straightway anoynt the same place therewith, and it swageth the swelling, and putteth away the blackenesse of the sore : also when a man hath a stitch in the side, anoynt it therewith, and it helpeth.

Neyther any olde or young folke that haue a stinking breath, so that the stinke come from the stomacke, but it helpeth, if it be receiued euery morning fasting, fixe drops with a spoonefull of wine the space of fourteene daies, and fast two houres after they haue taken it.

Six drops of this *Balsame* put into a Fistel euery day the space of twenty dayes, healeth and stoppeth the Fistel: also it healeth all wounds old or new, laid vnto them twice a day according to the quantitie of the wound.

Sixe drops of this *Balsam* put into a broad Pustell, which commeth of cold and grosse humers, in the space of twelue daies it will be made whole.

Many which are sicke by occasion of cold and dry humors which causeth consumption, may drinke euery morning and euening six drops of this *Balsam* with wine, and they shall recouer their health againe.

Any body which hath a Postumation, which commeth of winde and moisture that would settle it selfe in any place of the body, anoint the same place with this *Balsam* three times a day, and in the space of eight daies it shall be healed.

Readily doth this *Balsam* heale all sores which chance in hands, legs, or armes, or any part of the body, if it be anointed with it three times a day.

Peaceably and very quickly this *Balsam* swageth swellings, which is not of the Dropsie, if the swelling bee anointed three times a day with it, and linnen clothes laid vpon them wet with the said *Balsam*.

Euery person that is taken with the palsey, let them morning and euening drinke six drops of this *Balsam* in a spoonefull of wine, and also anoint the party which is taken with the said palsey twice a day, and they shall be healed, and it comforteth all the parts of the body marueilously.

This *Balsam* healeth all paines in the ioynts, so that you wash the ioynts therewith ; and also plaister the said ioynts with linnen cloth wet in the said *Balsam* : this must be done twice a day.

He, or they which haue their sinewes drawn together, let them wash them with this *Balsam*, and they shalbe restored to their former health and strength.

Also it helpeth the Hemerods when they are very grieuous : also it is good for sicknesse, which chanceth in the hinder part which is named Tenasmos, if a linnen cloth wet with the said *Balsam* be put therein. Also this *Balsam* being mixed with sweet Ciuet, and layd vpon a little black wooll, and put into the eares, restoreth hearing.

This Balsam, made by N.P. *Master of Arts, and Minister of Gods word, is to be sold in Maiden Lane, at the signe of the Crowne ouer against Goldsmiths Hall, where it hath beene sold, and the premisses approued these fourescore yeares.* Viuat Rex.

good cures with his said quintessence, his only plaister and his precious balm than any one surgeon in England had done or could do with all the best medicines and remedies they have. And moreover said that he had spoken nothing but that which he would stand to and prove it. And that he did know that it was not necessary for us common surgeons (as it pleased the bragger to call us) to use such a number of medicines as we do.

William Clowes, *A Prooved Practise for all young Chirurgians concerning Burning with Gunpowder,* 1591

SWEET AND DELICATE DENTIFRICES OR RUBBERS FOR THE TEETH

Dissolue in foure ounces of warme water, three or foure drams of gumme Dragagant, and in one night this wil become a thicke substance like gellie, mingle the same with the powder of Alabaster finely ground and searsed, then make vp this substance into little round rowles of 4. or 5. inches in length. Also if you temper roset or some other colour that is not hurtfull with them, they will shew full of pleasing veines. These you may sweeten either with rosewater, ciuet, or muske. But if your teeth be verie scalie, let som expert Barber first take off the scales with his instrument, and then you may keepe them cleane with the aforesaid rowles. And heer by those miserable examples that I have seene in some of my nearest friendes, I am enforced to admonish all men to bee carefull, how they suffer their teeth to be made white with any *Aqua fortis,* which is the Barbars vsuall water, for vnlesse the same be both well delaied, and carefullie applied, a man within a few dressings, may be driven to borrow a ranke of teeth to eate his dinner with, vnlesse his gums doe helpe him the better.

Sir Hugh Platt, *The Jewell House of Art and Nature,* 1594

REMEDIES AGAINST POISON

Six things that heere in order shall insue
Against all poysons have a secret poure
Peares, Garlicke, Reddish-roots, Nuts, Rape, and Rew,
But *Garlicke* cheefe, for they that it devoure,
May drink, and care not who their drink do brew,
May walke in ayres infected every houre:
Sith Garlicke then hath poure to save from death:
Beare with it though it make unsavoury breath:
And scorne not Garlicke like to some, that think
It only makes men winke, and drinke, and stink.

Regimen Sanitatis of the School of Salerno. In Latin from the twelfth century. The English translation made in 1607 by Sir John Harington, who also invented the water-closet.

THE PLAGUE
The purple whip of vengeance, the plague, having beaten many thousands of men, women, and children to death, and still marking the people of this city every week by hundreds for the grave, is the only cause that all her inhabitants walk up and down like mourners at some great solemn funeral, the City herself being the chief mourners. The poison of this lingering infection strikes so deep into all men's hearts that their cheeks, like cowardly soldiers, have lost their colours; their eyes, as if they were in debt and durst not long abroad, do scarce peep out of their heads; and their tongues, like physicians illpaid, give but cold comfort. By the power of their pestilent charms all merry meetings are cut off, all frolic assemblies dissolved, and in their circles are raised up the black, sullen, and dogged spirits of sadness, of melancholy, and so, consequently, of mischief. Mirth is departed and lies dead and buried in men's bosoms; laughter dares not look a man in the face; jests are, like music to the deaf, not regarded; pleasure itself finds now no pleasure but in sighing and bewailing the miseries of the time. For, alack! What string is there now to be played upon whose touch can make us merry? Playhouses stand like taverns that have cast out their masters, the doors locked up, the flags, like their bushes [ivy-bush outside a tavern], taken down — or rather like houses lately infected, from whence the affrighted dwellers are fled, in hope to live better in the country.

Thomas Dekker, Work for Armourers, 1609

Work – Wages

THE OATH ADMINISTERED TO A GUILD APPRENTICE, 1504

Ye shall swear that ye shall be true unto our liege lord, the King, and to his heirs, Kings. Also ye shall swear that well and truly to your power ye shall serve your Master during the term of your apprenticeship. And ye shall hold and form the covenants in your indenture of apprenticeship contained. Also ye shall hold steadfastly, secretly and for counsel all and every the lawful ordinances, whatsoever they be, to the Craft or occupation of the Mercery belonging, and, as much as in you is, every of them, ye shall observe, hold and keep, and not to break, discover, open or show any of them to any person, but unto such as unto the fellowship of the Mercery is here according to this oath sworn. And that ye shall not depart out and from the said fellowship for to serve, not to be accompanied with any manner of person of any other company, fellowship, occupation or craft, whereby any prejudice, hurt, or harm may grow to be unto the fellowship of the Mercery or any of the secrets thereof thereby to be discovered or known. So help you God, and all the Saints, and by this Book.

Records of the Mercers' Company

HOURS OF WORK

Every craftsman and labourer shall be at work between the middle of the month of March and the middle of the month of September, before 5 of the clock in the morning. And that he have but half an hour for his breakfast and an hour and a half for his dinner at such time as he hath season for sleep appointed to him. And at such time as it is herein appointed that he shall not sleep then he is to have but an hour for his dinner and half an hour for his noon-meat. And that he depart not from his work till between 7 and 8 of the clock in the evening. And for

59. Metal Workers. 'The Tudor home . . . depended for much of its newly-won
comfort upon the accessories and utensils created by craftsmen in metal. Most
important was the ironwork forged by the blacksmith; the tableware of the
pewterer and tin caster; the lead cisterns and outside water-leeds of the plumber
The majority (of metal accessories) was to be found in the living-room and
kitchen.' G. Bernard Hughes.

the rest of the year they shall be at their work in the springing
of the day and depart not till night of the same day.
                        Statutes of the Realm, 6 Henry VIII C.4, 1515

FROM THE STATUTE OF ARTIFICERS, 1563

That no manner of person shall be hired or taken into service to
work for any less term than for one whole year, in any of the
skills of clothiers, woollen cloth weavers, hosiers, tailors,
shoemakers, tanners, pewterers, bakers, brewers, glovers, cutlers,
smiths, farriers, cappers, hat-makers, bowyers [bow-makers],
fletchers [arrow-makers], arrowhead-makers, butchers, cooks, or
millers.

That every person between the age of twelve years and the age
of threescore years, not being lawfully retained, nor apprentice,
nor being gentleman born, nor being a student in any of the
Universities, shall be compelled to serve in husbandry by the
year if required.

That the Justices of the Peace of every Shire shall yearly assemble themselves together and conferring together respecting the plenty or scarcity of the time shall have authority to rate and appoint the wages of all labourers, artificers, etc.

That it shall not be lawful to any person to set up any Craft, except he shall have been brought up therein seven years at the least.

Statutes of the Realm, 5 Elizabeth C.4, 1563

GUILDS

This extract from the Court Book shows how strictly the conditions of work were supervised, and how the quality of goods was maintained.

November 29, 1567. There shall be eight or ten persons elected and chosen by the wardens and assistants, to have the view of all the merchants' cloths hereafter to be made within the company. The cloths so by them seen and found truly made, they are to set the common seal of the house to every such cloth, in token of true workmanship done upon the same. And every such cloth as shall be by the said searchers found faulty in workmanship, or be delivered before it be viewed and sealed, every workman of such cloth to pay a fine of every such cloth, 20*s.*

London Clothworker's Court Book, 1567

60. Printing in the sixteenth century. An ordinary book would come from the printer in flat sheets. The binder would fold them and sew in quires. Many books were covered in paper. Normal binding would be in vellum, fastened with tapes. Those who could afford it had books bound in leather. Queen Elizabeth liked her books to be bound in embroidered velvet.

HUSBANDRY AND ENCLOSURE

In Norfolk behold the despair
   Of tillage too much to be born,
By drovers from fair unto fair,
   And others destroying the corn;
By custom and covetous pates,
   By gaps and opening gates.

What speak I of commoners by,
   With drawing all after a line,
So noying the corn as it lie,
   With cattle, with conies and swine?
When thou hast bestowed this cost,
   Look half of the same to be lost.

The flocks of the lords of the soil,
   Do yearly the winter corn wrong,
The same in a manner they spoil,
   With feeding so low and so long.
And therefore that champion field,
   Doth seldom good winter corn yield.

By Cambridge a town I do know,
   Where many a good husband do dwell,
Where losses by Lossels doth show
   More here than is needful to tell:
Determine at Court what they shall,
   Performed is nothing at all.

The champion robbeth by night,
   And prowleth and filcheth by day,
Himself and his beasts out of sight,
   Both spoileth and maketh away,
Not only thy grass but thy corn,
   Both after and ere it be shorn.

Pease-bolt with thy pease he will have,
   His household to feed and his hog:
Now stealeth he, now will he crave,
   And now will he cozen and cog.
In Bridewell a number be stript,
   Less worthy than thief to be whipt.

Thomas Tusser, *Five Hundreth Pointes*
of Good Husbandrie, 1573

DOMESTIC CHARGES IN THE SIXTEENTH CENTURY

(1) *Travelling Expenses and Carriage.*

Charges to London [from Littlecote, Wiltshire] for three, 5s. 4d. Charges there in dressing trouts, 2s. 8d. Boat to Barne Elmes and back, 2s. 8d. Charges from London for two, 2s. 8d. Mending a saddle at London, 4d. ... Carriage of garden-tools from London, 2s. ... A messenger for Mr Webb to go to London, 6d. ... J. Horseman when he sought Mr Stubbs' mare, 4s. ... Our charges at Wallingford when we did fetch the mare, 18d. Our horsemeat there, 12d. Mr Molyns for keeping the mare and colt, 13s. 4d. R. Phillips seeking for the mare, 15d. T. Lazenby to London and home, 9s. 4d.

(2) *Wages of Farm Labourers at Littlecote.*

Osmond, 2 days' work, 6d., and 4 days' work, 16d. Osmond, for hedging and felling the coppice, 38s., Walter Eyres, Parker and Edney for helping with the Rick, 9d. ... A Thatcher for 5 days' work. 2s. ... A woman 'yelming' [arranging straw for thatching]10 days, 20d. Mowing the Wearmead, 17s. 6d. Sandes, 3 days' threshing, 9d.

61. Building in the sixteenth century, with scaffolding, ladders, hoists, wheelbarrow, carpenters, masons, hod-carriers, mortar-mixers. From R. Holinshed. *The Chronicles of England, Scotlande and Irelande,* 1577.

(3) *Miscellaneous.*
Garden seeds, 3s. 3d. Rosemary seeds, 10d. Rosemary, 6d. Strawberries, 9d. Brand-iron, 20d. 2 bottles of vinegar, 8d. Pair of hose and shoes for Anthony Swayte, 2s. 4d. Two pheasant-nets, 15d.

(4) *Wages of Skilled Labourers at Littlecote.*
Lionel Pearce, for making 15 dozen hurdles, 12s. 6d. The Taskers at Littlecote . . . for threshing 37 quarters [of wheat], 18s. 6d. Dressing a mangy mare and a colt, 2s. 10d. Setting 3 horse-shoes, 9d. The rat-catcher, 2s. 6d. J. Mitchell and Harry Cook for fishing, 16d.

(5) *Washing* (3 months).
5 shirts, handkerchiefs, night kerchiefs, and socks, 18d. Anthony's clothes, 12d. 6 shirts, 18 handkerchiefs, and a waistcoat, 2s. 6 shirts, handkerchiefs, night kerchiefs, socks and collars, 20d. 5 shirts, 8 handkerchiefs, a night kerchief, a collar and socks, 20d. Anthony's clothes, 10d. 4 shirts, 12d. 4 shirts, 6 handkerchiefs, socks and night kerchiefs, 14d. 3 shirts, 4 handkerchiefs, and socks, 10d. 3 shirts, 5 handkerchiefs, 10d. 2 shirts, 4 handkerchiefs, 1 pair socks, and 5 sheets, 13d. 6 shirts, 6 handkerchiefs, and 1 pair socks, 19d. 4 shirts, 5 handkerchiefs, and 1 pair socks, 13d. 1 tablecloth, and 14 napkins, 14d.

Total, £0, 17s. 5d.

(6) *Dress*
Mending Anthony's shoes, 6d. Pair of shoes for him and mending his hose, 20d. Mr More for a pair of gloves when he went to Ratcliff, 18d. Twelve Badges (besides 16s. which his Worship paid), 20s. Pair of shoes for his Worship, 2s. 9d. 4 shirts, 6 bands, 6 pair cuffs (besides 6s. which his Worship paid), £4.

6¾ yds. murry satin, at 12s., £4 1s. (whereof Cornelius the tailor, paid 41s., namely, of Mrs Biggs, 20s., and this accountant, 20s.). . . . 4¼ ells murry taffeta sarsnet to line a doublet and canions, 15s. . . . Three dozen of buttons, 12d. Silk to make button holes, 6d. A canopy embroidered with a train of changeable taffeta, £8. Cornelius the tailor in his bill, 30s. His man Humphrey, 12d. 3½ yards of black satin at 12s. 6d. . . . Pair of shoes, 2s. 6d. Raising a pair of shoes, 1d. . . . Mending a pair of shoes, 5d.

(7) *Furniture and Household Stuff.*
His worship when he bought table-boards. £4. Two glass bottles, 2s. . . . Two chairs covered with grene, 22s. . . . Three

136 EVERY ONE A WITNESS

dozen of trenchers, 15d. Long table cloths, 5s. Percy which he paid for cloth for a pair of sheets; two diaper cloths; 3 table napkins, etc., 40s. Three brooms, 2d. Sope, 3d. Nails for the carpenter, 4d. Taps, 1d. ... Hazelden for the curtains of Wedmoll lace, rings, curtain rods and making, 18s. 1 lb. of candles, 4d. A dozen of Pewter trencher plates, 5s. 6 spoons, 5d. An earthen salt pot, 2d. Salt, 3d. Sand to scour the pewter, 1d. Hazelden for mats and matting the great chamber and middle chamber, 4s. 6d. Looking glass, 5s. The carpenter for sawing the end of a form, 2d.

(8) *Sundries.*

¼ oz. of tobacco, 10d. ... Four tobacco pipes, 2s. Ink and a glass, 2d. The Apothecary upon his bill, 8s. Gardening stuff for Cornelius the gardener, 23s. 3d. Quire of Paper, 2d. Sweetmeats at Mistress West's, 21s. 2½ oz. dates, 5d. ... Percy which he paid for a book, 6d. Paper and parchment, 8d. A basket, 2s. 6d.

(9) *Hotel Bill.*

Friday dyner Juny 20.

Butter	iiijd.
A pece of bief	xiiijd.
A legg of mutton	xviijd.
A loyne of veale	xxijd.
2 peckes of pescodes	viij.
3 rabbettes	ijs.
A quart of creame	vjd.
3 quarts of strawberries	xvjd.
2 li. of cheries	xxd.
Di : li. of muske confectes	xd.
Di : li. of violett confectes	xjd.
Orenges	iiijd.
2 Lemans	vjd.
Bred	viijd.
Beare	ixd.

0 . 14 . 11

The Darrell Papers, as quoted in Hall's
Society in the Elizabethan Age

62. Casting type for printing beside a charcoal fire. Ruari McLean says that the sources of the types were all of continental origin. Further information, 'Higden's Polychronicon, 1495, was the first book in which music was printed from type in England; and his song-book of 1530, the first actual music-book printed in England . . . Venus and Adonis, 1593, the first known printing of Shakespeare, was set wholly in roman.'

A BOOKSELLER

If I were to paint Sloth . . . by Saint John the Evangelist I swear, I would draw it like a stationer that I know, with his thumb under his girdle, who if a man comes to his stall and ask him for a book, never stirs his head, or looks upon him, but stands stone still, and speaks not a word: only with his little finger points backwards to his boy, who must be his interpreter, and so all the day, gaping like a dumb image, he sits without motion, except at such times as he goes to dinner or supper: for then he is as quick as other three, eating six times every day.

Thomas Nashe, *Pierce Penilesse*, 1592

A WEAVING FACTORY

Within one room being large and long,
There stood two hundred looms full strong:
Two hundred men the truth is so,
Wrought in these looms all in a row.

And in another place hard by
An hundred women merrily,
Were carding hard with joyful cheer,
Who singing sat, with voices clear.
And in a chamber close beside,
Two hundred maidens did abide
In petticoats of stammell red
And milk-white kerchers on their head.

These pretty maids did never lin
But in that place all day did spin:
And spinning so with voices meet,
Like nightingales they sung full sweet.
Then to another room came they,
Where children were in poor array:
And everyone sat picking wool,
The finest from the coarse to cull.

A dye-house likewise had he then,
Wherein he kept full forty men;
And likewise in his fulling mill,
Full twenty persons kept he still.

Thomas Deloney, *The Pleasant History*
of Jack of Newbury, 1596

LONDON APPRENTICES

The ancient habit of the apprentices of London was a flat round
cap, hair close cut, narrow falling bands, coarse side coats,
close hose, cloth stockings, and other such severe apparel
When this garb had been urged by some to the disparagement
of apprentices, as a token of servitude, one, many a year ago,
undertaking the defence of these apprentices, wrote thus, that
this imported the commendable thrift of the citizens, and was
only the mark of an apprentice's vocation and calling (and which
anciently, no question, was the ordinary habit of a citizen), which
point of ancient discipline, he said, the grave common lawyers
do still retain in their profession; for the professors of that
learning, we see, do at this present retain the parti-coloured
coats of serving-men at their serjeants feasts; and he wished, that
the remembrance of this ancient livery might be preserved by
the grave citizens, in setting apart a particular time or day for
the feast of their apprenticeship, when they should wear their

former apprentice's garb; making profession in this way, that they gloried in the ensigns of their honest apprenticeship.

In the time of Queen Mary, the beginning of Queen Elizabeth, as well as many years before, all apprentices wore blue cloaks in the summer, and blue gowns in the winter. But it was not lawful for any man, either servant or other, to wear their gowns lower than the calves of their legs, except they were above threescore years of age; but, the length of the cloaks being not limited, they made them down to their shoes. Their breeches and stockings were usually of white broad cloath, viz. round slops, and their stockings sewed up close thereto, as if they were all but one piece. They also wore flat caps both then and many years after, as well apprentices as journeymen and others, both at home and abroad; whom the pages of the court in derision called flat-caps.

When apprentices and journeymen attended upon their masters

63. A sixteenth-century spinning wheel. It shows the distaff (a stick holding the raw wool) and spindle (the wooden implement used in drawing out the thread). The wheel revolves the spindle.

64. Making wool.

65. Making clothes.

and mistresses in the night they went before them carrying a lanthorn and candle in their hands and a great long club on their necks; and many well-grown sturdy apprentices used to wear long daggers in the day time on their backs or sides.

Anciently it was the general use and custom of all apprentices in London (mercers only excepted, being commonly merchants, and of better rank, as it seems) to carry water tankards, to serve their masters' houses with water, fetched either from the Thames, or the common conduits of London.

It was a great matter in former times to give £10 to bind a youth apprentice; but in King James the First's time, they gave £20, £40, £60 and sometimes £100 with an apprentice; but now these prices are vastly enhanced, to £500, £600, or £800.

John Stow, *A Survey of London*, 1598

PORTRAIT OF A USURER
The first of them is Usury (a devil of good credit in the city) who having privily stolen a sufficient stock from the old miser his father, hath lately set up for himself, and hath four of his brothers his apprentices. The first of them is Hardness-of-Heart, who bringing into his bank contempt-of-the-poor, is set by him to beat beggars from his door, and arrest his debtors by latitats, The second is, Unmeasurable-Care-and-Trouble-of-Mind, who hath brought this portion to be employed: destruction-of-the-mind, neglect-of-God's-service, want-of-faith, jealousy-of-loss: he keeps the cash, and suffers not a mouse to enter, but he scores him. The third is Violence, and for him he hath bought a sergeant's office, who hath so many eyes like Argus to watch that no poor creditor can escape him: his stock is a bunch of writs, and a hanger, and ordinarily he wears his mace at his back instead of a dagger. The fourth is Rapine, and he jets about the streets to steal for him: he is a passing good hooker and picklock; and for a short knife and a horn thimble, turn him loose to all the fraternity: his stock is false keys, engines, and sword-and-buckler: him he employs to rob from them he hath lent money to, to the end they may be the fitter to commit a forfeiture.

This Usury is jump of the complexion of the baboon his father; he is haired like a great ape, and swart like a tawny Indian, his horns are sometimes hidden in a button cap (as Th. Nashe described him), but now he is fallen to his flat cap, because he is chief warden of his company: he is narrow-browed, and squirrel-eyed, and the chiefest ornament of his face is, that his nose sticks in the midst like an embossment in terrace work, here and there embellished and decked with *verucæ* for want of purging with agaric; some authors have compared it to a rutter's cod-piece, but I like not the allusion so well, by reason the tyings have no correspondence. His mouth is always mumbling, as if he were at his matins: and his beard is bristled here and there like a sow that had the lousy. Double-chinned he is, and over his throat hangs a bunch of skin like a money-bag. Band wears he none, but a welt of coarse holland, and if you see it stitched with blue thread, it is no workaday wearing. His truss is the piece of an old packcloth, the mark washed out; and if you spy a pair of Bridget's satin sleeves to it, you may be assured it is a holiday. His points are the edging of some cast packsaddle, cut out sparingly (I warrant you) to serve him and his household for trussing leather. His jacket forsooth is faced with moth-eaten budge, and it is no less than Lisle grogram of the worst. It is bound to his body with a cordelier's girdle, dyed black for comeliness sake: and in his bosom he bears his handkerchief made of the reversion of his old tablecloth. His spectacles hang beating over his codpiece like the flag in the top of a maypole. His breeches and stockings are of one piece I warrant you,

66. Ruff making. The monkeys pretend to be workers and so ridicule the fashions of the time.

67. The Arms of the Mines Royal Company, granted by Elizabeth I, 1568. At the top, holding a wedge and a compass, is the 'Schicht Master', in charge of prospecting and mining. On the right is a smelter, holding a fork; on the left stands the hammer-man. Below is a miner with two hammers and a lamp. From Sir J. Pettus, *Fodinae Regales*, 1670.

which, having served him in pure kersey for the tester of a bed some twenty years, is by the frugality of a dyer and the courtesy of a tailor for this present made a sconce for his buttocks. His shoes of the old cut, broad at the toes and cross-buckled with brass, and have loop-holes like a sconce for his toes to shoot out at. His gown is suitable, and as seemly as the rest, full of threads I warrant you, wheresoever the wool is employed, welted on the back with the clipping of a bare cast velvet hood, and faced with foins that had kept a widow's tail warm twenty winters before his time.

Thus attired, he walks Paul's, coughing at every step as if he were broken-winded, grunting sometime for the pain of the stone and strangury: and continually thus old, and seeming ready to die, he notwithstanding lives to confound many families. If you come to borrow money, he will take no usury, no marry will he not: but if you require ten pound, you shall pay him forty shillings for an old cap, and the rest is yours in ready money; the man loves good dealing. If you desire commodities at his hand, why sir you shall have them, but how? not (as the caterpillars wont to sell) at high prices, but at the best and easiest pennyworth, as in conscience you can desire them: only this, at the insealing of the assurance, if you help him away with a chest of glass for ten pound of ten shillings price, you shall command his warehouse another time. Tut he is for you at casual marts, commodities of proclamations and hobby-horses, you shall have all that you please, so he receive what he desires, It is a common custom of his to buy up cracked angels at nine shillings the piece. Now sir if a gentleman (on good assurance of land) request him of money, 'Good sir,' saith he, with a counterfeit sigh 'I would be glad to please your worship, but my good money is abroad, and that I have, I dare not put in your hands.' The gentleman thinking this conscience, where it is subtlety, and being beside that in some necessity, ventures on the cracked angels, some of which cannot fly for soldering, and pays double interest to the miser, under the cloak of honesty. If he fails his

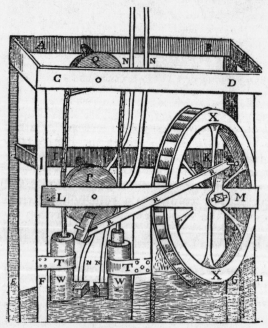

68. The water-powered pumping engine erected by Peter Morris, a German or Dutch engineer, in 1582. J. Bate describes it: 'Water-mill or Engin near the North end of Lundon Brid [g] e; which Engin by the Ebbing and Flowing of the Thames, doth mount the sayd water unto the top of a Turret, and by that means it is conveyed above two miles in compass, for the use and service of that City'. From *Mysteries of Nature and Art*, by J. Bate, *c.* 1654.

day, God forbid he should take the forfeiture, he will not thrive
by other men's curses, but because men must live, and we are
infidels if we provide not for our families, he is content with this
his own; only a leaf, a toy of this or that manor, worth both his
principal and ten times the interest; this is easy for the
gentleman to pay, and reasonable in him to receive. If a citizen
come to borrow, 'My friend' quoth he, 'you must keep day, I am
glad to help young men without harming myself': then paying
him out the money and receiving his assurance, he casts Jolly
Robins in his head how to cozen the simple fellow. If he have a
shop well furnished, a stock to receive out of the Chamber,
possibility after the death of his father, all this he hearkens after:
and if he fail of his day, 'Well,' saith he, 'for charity sake I will
forbear you, mine interest paid': meanwhile (unknown to the
wretch) he sues him upon the original to an outlawry, and if the
second time he fail (as by some slight encouragement he causes
him to do) he turns him out a doors like a careless young man,
yet for Christianity sake, he lets him at liberty, and will in charity
content him with his goods.

Thomas Lodge, *Wits Miserie and Worlds Madnesse,* 1596

WARNING TO MONEY-MAKERS

Because of the great dearth of corn this year proclamation is
made against those ingrossers, forestallers, and ingraters of corn
that increase the price of corn by spreading a false report that
much quantity of corn is being carried out of the realm by sea
and thereby occasion given of want. Likewise it is straitly
forbidden to carry any corn by sea out of the realm. Moreover
sundry persons of ability that had intended to save their charges
by living privately in London or towns corporate, thereby leaving
their hospitality and the relief of their poor neighbours, are
charged not to break up their households; and all others that
have of late time broken up their households to return to their
houses again without delay.

Royal Proclamation, 1596

VARIOUS PAYMENTS, 1596

MR TREASURER. He hath for his entertainment 130 pounds 16
shillings 8 pence a year, and 10 dishes of meat to his first mess,
and 6 dishes to his second, every meal. He and Mr Comptroller
(there being no Lord Steward) have the government of the
whole household, and placing of all Her Majesty's servants. They

are likewise to be counselled and assisted by the officers of the board; but they two together are absolute of themselves.

GROOMS. These have 4 marks a year apiece, and meat as aforesaid; they have for fee a penny out of the yeomen's fee, and they have also the drippings of all the meats roasted throughout the year for their fee.

CHILDREN. These have 40 shillings yearly apiece, and 6 pence a day boardwages.

from The Book of Household of Queen Elizabeth,
as it was ordained in the 43^d year of her Reign

MEN OF TRADES

Men of trades and sellers of wares in this City have oftentimes changed their places, as they have found their best advantage. For where as Mercers, and Haberdashers used to keep their shops in West Cheape, of later time they held them on London Bridge, where partly they yet remain. The Goldsmiths of Gutherons lane, the old Exchange, are now for the most part removed into the Southside of West Cheape, the Peperers and Grocers of Sopers lane, are now in Bucklesberrie, and other places dispersed. The Drapers of Lombardstreete and of Cornehill, are seated in Candlewickstreet, and Watheling street: the Skinners from Saint Marie Pellipers or at the Axe, into Budge row, and Walbrooke: The Stock-fishmongers in Thames street: wet Fishmongers in Knight-riders street, and Bridge street; The Ironmongers of Ironmongers lane, and old Jurie, into Thames street; the Vinteners from the Vinetree into divers places. But the Brewers for the more part remain neare to the friendly waters of Thames.

John Stow, *A Survey of London,* 1603

Agriculture

ENCLOSURE

'Your sheep', said I, 'which are usually so tame and so cheaply fed, are now, it is said, so greedy and wild, that they devour men, and lay waste and depopulate fields, houses and towns. For in those parts of the realm where the finest and therefore most costly wool is produced, these nobles and gentlemen, and even holy Abbots, not satisfied with the revenues and annual profits derived from their estates, and not content with leading an idle life and doing no good to the country, but rather doing it harm, leave no ground to be tilled, but enclose every bit of land for pasture, pull down houses, and destroy towns, leaving only the church to pen the sheep in. And, as if enough English land were not wasted on parks and preserves of game, these holy men turn all human habitations and cultivated land into a wilderness. Thus in order that one insatiable glutton and plague of his native land may join field to field and surround many thousand acres with one ring fence, many tenants are ejected and, either through fraud or violence, are deprived of their goods, or else wearied by oppression are driven to sell. Thus by hook or by crook the poor wretches are compelled to leave their homes — men, women, husbands, wives, orphans, widows, parents with little children and a family not rich but numerous, for farm work requires many hands: away they must go, I say, from their familiar and accustomed homes, and find no shelter to go to. All their household furniture, which would not fetch a great price if it could wait for a purchaser, as it must be thrust out, they sell for a trifle: and soon, when they have spent that in moving from place to place, what remains for them but to steal, and be hung, justly forsooth, or wander about and beg? And yet even then they are put in prison as vagrants, for going about idle, when, though they eagerly offer their labour, there is no one to hire them. For there is no farm work, to which they had been bred, to be had, when there is no plough land left. For one shepherd

147

or herdsman is sufficient for eating up with stock land for whose cultivation many hands were once required, that it might raise crops. And so it is that the price of food has risen in many parts. Nay, the price of wool has grown so high that the poor, who used to make cloth in England, cannot buy it, and so are driven from work to idleness.'

Sir Thomas More, Utopia, 1516

LIMITATION OF SHEEP FARMING, 1534
From Thomas Cromwell to Henry VIII

Please it your most royal Majesty to be advertised how that according to your most high pleasure and commandment I have made search for such patents and grants as your Highness and also the most famous King your father — whose soul our Lord pardon — have granted unto Sir Richard Weston, knight, your under treasurer of your exchequer, and the same have sent to your Highness herein closed. It may also please your most royal Majesty to know how that yesterday there passed your Commons a bill that no person within this your realm shall hereafter keep and nourish above the number of 2,000 sheep, and also that the eighth part of every man's land, being a farmer, shall for every hereafter be put in tillage yearly; which bill, if by the great wisdom, virtue, goodness and zeal that your Highness beareth towards this your realm, might have good success and take good effect among your lords above, I do conjecture and suppose in my poor simple and unworthy judgment, that your Highness shall do the most noble, profitable and most beneficial thing that ever was done to the commonwealth of this your realm, and shall thereby increase such wealth in the same amongst the great number and multitude for your most loving and obedient subjects as never was seen in this realm since Brutus' time. Most humbly prostrate at the feet of your magnificence, I beseech your Highness to pardon my boldness in this writing to your grace; which only proceedeth for the truth, duty, allegiance and love I do bear to your Majesty and the commonwealth of this your realm, as our Lord knoweth unto whom I shall, as I am most bounded, incessantly pray for the countenance and prosperous conservation of your most excellent, most royal and imperial estate long to endure.

Record Office Calendar

SOIL AND PRODUCE
The soil of Britain is such as by the testimonies and reports both

Hulbondape

69. Ploughing with oxen. The title-page of Fitzherbert's *The Boke of Husbandrie*, 1523.

of the old and new writers, and experience also of such as now inhabit the same, is very fruitful, and such indeed as bringeth forth many commodities, whereof other countries have need. . . . Nevertheless it is more inclined to feeding and grazing than profitable for tillage and bearing of corn, by reason whereof the country is wonderfully replenished with meat and all kind of cattle; and such store is there also of the same in every place that the fourth part of the land is scarcely manured for the provision and maintenance of grain. . . .

There are also in this island great plenty of fresh rivers and streams, as you have heard already, and these thoroughly fraught with all kinds of delicate fish accustomed to be found in rivers. . . .

The pasture of this island is according to the nature and bounty of the soil, whereby in most places it is plentiful, very fine, batable, and such as either fatteth our cattle with speed or yieldeth great abundance of milk and cream whereof the yellowest butter and finest cheese are made. . . .

The yield of our corn-ground is also much after this rate following. Throughout the land (if you please to make an estimate thereof by the acre) in mean and indifferent years, wherein each acre of rye or wheat, well tilled and dressed will yield commonly sixteen or twenty bushels, an acre of barley six and thirty bushels, of oats and such like four or five quarters, which proportion is notwithstanding oft abated toward the north, as it is oftentimes surmounted in the south. Of mixed corn, as peas and beans sown together, tares and oats (which they call bulmong), rye and wheat (named miscelin) . . . their yield is nevertheless much after this proportion. . . .

Of late years also we have found and taken up a great trade in planting of hops, whereof our moory hitherto and unprofitable grounds do yield such plenty and increase that there are few farmers or occupiers in the country which have not gardens and hops growing of their own, and these far better than do come from Flanders unto us. . . .

The cattle which we breed are commonly such as for greatness of bone, sweetness of flesh, and other benefits to be reaped by the same, give place unto none other; as may appear first by our oxen, whose largeness, height, weight, tallow, hides and horns are such as none of any other nation do commonly or may easily exceed them. Our sheep likewise, for good taste of flesh, quantity of limbs, fineness of fleece, give no place unto any, more than do our goats . . . and our deer not come behind. As for our conies, I have seen them so fat in some soils . . . that the grease of one being weighed hath very near six or seven ounces. . . .

I touch in this place one benefit which our nation wanteth, and that is wine, the fault whereof is not in our soil, but the negligence of our countrymen. . . . I muse not a little wherefore the planting of vines should be neglected in England.

Now our soil either will not, or at the leastwise may not, bear either woad or madder. . . . The like I may say of flax, which by law ought to be sown in every country town in England, more or less. . . .

Glass also hath been made here in great plenty before, and in the time of the Romans, and the said stuff also, beside fine scissors, shears, collars of gold and silver for women's neck's, cruises and cups of amber, were a parcel of the tribute which Augustus in his days laid upon this island. . . .

We have in England great plenty of quicksilver, antimony, sulphur, blacklead, and orpiment red and yellow. We have also the finest alum . . . the natural cinnabarium or vermilion, the sulphurous glebe called bitumen in old time for mortar, and yet burned in lamps where oil is scant . . . the chrysocolla, copperas, and mineral stone, whereof petriolum is made, and that which is most strange, the mineral pearl. . . .

Of coal mines we have such plenty in the north and western parts of our island as may suffice for all the realm of England, and so must they do hereafter indeed, if wood be not better cherished than it is at this present. . . . Besides our coal mines, we have pits in like sort of white plaster and of fat and white and other coloured marl. . . . We have saltpetre for our ordinance and salt soda for our glass. . . .

Tin and lead . . . are very plentiful with us, the one in Cornwall, Devonshire and elsewhere in the north, the other in Derbyshire, Weredale and sundry places of this island.

Copper is lately not found, but rather restored again to light. . . .

As for our steel, it is not so good for edge-tools as that of Cologne, and yet the one is often sold for the other.

William Harrison, *Description of England,* 1587

YEOMANRY DECAYED
There is no life more pleasant than a yeoman's life, but nowadays yeomanry is decayed, hospitality gone to wrack, and husbandry almost quite fallen. The reason is because landlords, not contented with such revenues as their predecessors received, nor yet satisfied that they live like swinish epicures quietly at their ease, doing no good to the commonwealth, do leave no ground for tillage, but do enclose for pasture many thousand acres of ground within one hedge, the husbandmen are thrust out of their own, or else by deceit constrained to sell all that they have.

William Vaughan, *Golden Grove,* 1600

Religion

HERETICS

28th April, 1494. Also this year, the 28th day of April was burnt
in Smithfield an old woman, . . . called Johan Bowghton, which
was there burnt for many heresies to the number of nine
Articles of heresy. And never would turn from the said heresies
for no exhortation, but in the false and heretical opinions died.

May 1498. This year in the beginning of May, the King being at
Canterbury, was burnt a heretic, a priest, which by the King's
exhortation before his death was converted from his erroneous
opinions, and died a Christian man; whereof his Grace gave
great honour.

16th June, 1499. This year, the Sunday being the 16th day of
June, stood at the Cross of Pauls four heretics bearing faggots;
and upon the next Sunday following stood there eight heretics,
which were all burnt upon the left cheek, and upon their
garments or gowns was set a Red Cross and a Brawderid faggot,
which said cross and faggot they were enjoined to wear all the
time of their lives upon pain of going to the fire if they were
found without the same conysaunce.

Kingsford's *Chronicles of London*

EASTER

This day is called in many places, God's Sunday; you know well
that it is the manner at this day to do the fire out of the hall,
and the black winter brands, and all things that is foul with fume
and smoke shall be done away, and there the fire was shall be
gaily arrayed with fair flowers, and strewed with green rushes all
about.

The Festival, 1511

A PILGRIMAGE SHRINE

St Mary of Walsingham in Norfolk was, for English people, a most popular medieval pilgrimage-place. Erasmus (speaking as Ogygius) in a dialogue with Menedemus describes his own visit to the place just before 1514, when he left England.

MENEDEMUS. But what wind carried you to England?

OGYGIUS. A very favourable wind, and I had made half a promise to the beyond-sea she-saint [our Lady of Walsingham] to pay her another visit within two or three years.

MENEDEMUS. What did you go to ask for of her?

OGYGIUS. Nothing new but those common matters, the health of my family, the increase of my fortune, a long and happy life in this world, and eternal happiness in the next.

MENEDEMUS. But could not our Virgin Mary have done as much for you here? She has at Antwerp a temple much more magnificent than that beyond sea.

OGYGIUS. I will not deny that she is able, but one thing is bestowed in one place and another thing in another.

MENEDEMUS. . . . Give me some account of that beyond-sea lady.

OGYGIUS. I will do it as briefly as I can. Her name is very famous all over England, and you shall scarce find anybody in that island who thinks his affairs can be prosperous unless he every year makes some present to that lady, greater or smaller, according as his circumstances are in the world.

MENEDEMUS. Whereabouts does she dwell?

OGYGIUS. Near the coast, upon the furthest part between the west and the north, about three miles from the sea. It is a town that depends chiefly upon the resort of strangers.

PART OF THE EARLIEST TRUE PAMPHLET, 1529

Into less than eleven pages Simon Fish packs 'a brilliant piece of violent and outspoken anti-clerical propaganda, calling for the dissolution of the monasteries'. Either through Anne Boleyn or some royal servant it reached Henry VIII, who it is said, studied it 'carefully and long kept it by him'.

Who is she that will set her hands to work to get threepence a day and may have at least twenty pence a day to sleep an hour with a friar, a monk, or a priest? What is he that would labour for a groat a day and may have at least twelve pence a day to be bawd to a priest, a monk, or a friar? What a sort are there of them that marry priests' sovereign ladies but to cloak the priest's incontinency and that they may have a living of the priest themselves for their labour? How many thousands doth such lubricity bring to beggary, theft and idleness, which should have kept their good name and have set themselves to work had not been this excess treasure of the spirituality? What honest man dare take any man or woman in his service that hath been at such a school with a spiritual man? Oh, the grievous shipwreck of the commonwealth, which in ancient time before the coming in of these ravenous wolves was so prosperous: that then there were but few thieves: yea, theft was at that time so rare that Cæsar was not compelled to make penalty of death upon felony, as your grace may well perceive in his institutes. There was also at that time but few poor people and yet they did not beg, but there was given them enough unasked, for there was at that time none of these ravenous wolves to ask it from them as it appeareth in the Acts of the Apostles. Is it any marvel though there be now so many beggars, thieves and idle people? Nay truly.

Simon Fish, *The Supplication for the Beggars*, 1529

DEED OF SURRENDER OF FURNESS ABBEY, 1537

We the said Abbot and convent ... have freely given, granted, and surrendered up into the hands of the Lord and King, that now is, Henry VIII, by the grace of God, King of England and France, defender of the Faith, Lord of Ireland, and head upon earth of the Anglican Church, have surrendered our monastery of Furness aforesaid, and also the site and foundation of the same, and all the goods, chattels, jewels, and church ornaments of the same, and also the debts, actions, and other things whatsoever, unto us, or any of us, or unto the said monastery, appertaining, belonging or owing, and also all manner of domains, castles, manors, lands, tenements, advowsons of churches and chantries, knights' fees, rents, reversions, liberties, and services, with all our hereditaments whatsoever, in the counties of York and Lancaster, or elsewhere in the realm of England and Ireland and in the Isle of Man, to have and to hold. . . .

In witness whereof we have, with our unanimous and full assent and consent, affixed our common seal to these presents. Given in the Chapter House of our said monastery, the ninth day of April, in the twenty-eighth year of the reign of our said lord the King, and in the year of our Lord and Saviour, 1537.

By me, Roger, Abbot of Furness. By me, Brian Garner, Prior. By me, John Thornton, etc. etc.

Translation from *Guide-book to Furness Abbey*

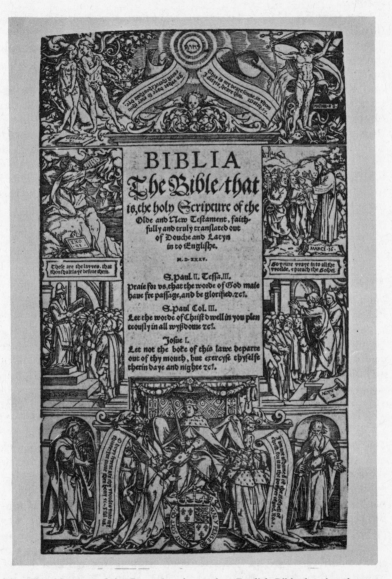

70. The title page of the first printed complete English Bible, bearing the name of Miles Coverdale, which appeared in 1535. It came probably from Luther's version and the Vulgate, with help from Tyndale's translation of the New Testament.

IDOLATRY

A letter from Elis Price to Lord Cromwell telling him about the Image of Darvell Gathern in 1538.

That there is an Image of Darvellgadern, in whom the people have so great confidence, hope, and trust, that they come daily a pilgrimage unto him, some with kine, other with oxen or horses, and the rest with money: in so much that there was five or six hundred pilgrims . . . that offered to the said Image the fifth day of this present month of April. The innocent people hath been sore allured and enticed to worship the said Image, in so much that there is a common saying as yet amongst them that who so ever will offer any thing to the said Image of Darvellgadern, he hath power to fetch him or them that so offers out of Hell when they be damned . . . Written in North Wales the sixth day of this present April.

> Your bedman and daily
> orator by duty
> Elis Price

THE DISSOLUTION OF THE MONASTERIES

The Commissioners' Report on Glastonbury to Thomas Cromwell, 1539

Please it your Lordship to be advertised, that we came to Glastonbury on Friday last past, about ten of the clock in the forenoon; and for that the Abbot was then at Sharpham, a place of his a mile and somewhat more from the abbey, we, without any delay, went into the same place, and there examined him upon certain articles. And for that his answer was not then to our purpose, we advised him to call to his remembrance that which he had then forgotten, and so declare the truth, and then came with him the same day to the abbey, and there anew proceeded that night to search his study for letters and books; and found in his study secretly laid, as well a written book or arguments against the divorce of the King's Majesty and the lady dowager, which we take to be a great matter, as also divers pardons, copies of bulls, and the counterfeit life of Thomas Becket in print; but we could not find any letter that was material. And so we proceeded again to his examination concerning the articles we received from your Lordship, in the anwers whereof, as we take it, shall appear his cankered and traitorous heart and mind against the King's Majesty and his succession. And so with fair words as we could, we have conveyed him from hence into the tower, being but a very weak man and sickly. And as yet we have neither discharged servant nor monk; but now the Abbot being gone, we will, with as much celerity as we may, proceed to the despatching of them. We have in money £300 and above; but the certainty of plate and other stuff there as yet we know not, for we have not had opportunity for the same, but shortly we intend — God willing — to proceed to the same; whereof we shall ascertain your Lordship as shortly as we may.

This is also to advertise your Lordship, that we have found a fair chalice of gold, and divers other parcels of plate, which the Abbot had hid secretly from all such commissioners as have been there in times past; and as yet he knoweth not that we have found the same. It may please your Lordship to advertise us of the King's pleasure by this bearer, to whom we shall deliver the custody and keeping of the house, with such stuff as we intend to leave there convenient to the King's use. We assure your Lordship it is the goodliest house of that sort that ever we have seen. We would that your Lordship did know it as we do; then we doubt not but your Lordship would judge it a house meet for the King's Majesty and for no man else: which is to our great comfort; and we trust verily that there shall never come any double hood within that house again.

Also this is advertise your Lordship, that there is never a doctor within that house; but there be three bachelors of divinity, which be but meanly learned, as we can perceive. And thus Our Lord preserve your good Lordship.

From Glastonbury, the 22nd day of September, 1539

Yours to command,
Richard Pollard
Thomas Mayle
Richard Layton

To the right honourable
and their singular good
lord, my Lord Privy Seal,
this be delivered

Letters relating to Suppression of Monasteries

THE LITANY IN ENGLISH

1544. Upon the 18 of October, the Litany in the English tongue is, by the King's commandment, sung openly in Paul's at London; and Commandment given that it should be sung in the same tongue throughout all England. It was used in London, in some parish church, even since June in the year expired; and the children of Paul's school, whereof I was one at that time, enforced to buy those books, wherewith we went in general procession, as it was then appointed, before the King went to Boulogne.

William Harrison, *Chronologie*

THE WESTERN REBELLION, 1549
Here is reaction to the changes of the first Act of Uniformity, 1549
The articles of the commons of Devonshire and Cornwall, sent to the King. . . .

FIRST, forsomuch as man, except he be born of water, and the Holy Ghost, can not enter into the kingdom of God, and forsomuch as the gates of heaven be not open without this blessed sacrament of baptism; therefore we will that our curates shall minister this sacrament at all times of need, as well on the week days, as on the holy days.

II. Item, we will have our children confirmed of the Bishop, whensoever we shall within the diocese resort unto him.

III. Item, forsomuch as we constantly believe, that after the priest hath spoken the words of consecration being at mass, there celebrating and consecrating the same, there is [in very reality] the body and blood of our Saviour Jesus Christ God and man, and that no substance of bread and wine remaineth after, but the very self same body that was born of the virgin Mary, and was given upon the cross for our redemption: therefore we will have mass celebrated as it hath been in times past, without any man communicating with the priests, forsomuch as many rudely presuming unworthily to receive the same, put no difference between the Lord's body and other kind of meat; some saying that it is bread before and after, some saying that it is profitable to no man except he receive it: with many other abused terms.

IV. Item, we will have in our churches reservation.

V. Item, we will have holy bread and holy water in the remembrance of Christ's precious body and blood.

VI. Item, we will have that our priests shall sing or say with an audible voice, God's service in the quire of the parish churches, and not God's service to be set forth like a Christmas play.

VII. Item, forsomuch as priests be men dedicated to God for ministering and celebrating the blessed sacraments, and preaching of God's word, we will that they shall live chaste without marriage, as Saint Paul did, being the elect and chosen vessel of God, saying unto all honest priests: Be you followers of me.

VIII. Item, we will that the six articles which our sovereign Lord King Henry the Eighth set forth in his latter days, shall be used and so taken as they were at that time.

IX. Item, we pray God save King Edward, for we be his both body and goods.

Raphael Holinshed, Chronicles, 1577

SUNDAY OBSERVANCE

It is lamentable to see the wicked boldness of those that will be counted God's people, who pass nothing at all of keeping and hallowing the Sunday. And these people are of two sorts. The one sort, if they have any business to do, though there be no extreme need, they must not spare for the Sunday, they must ride and journey on the Sunday; they must drive and carry on the Sunday; they must row and ferry on the Sunday; they must buy and sell on the Sunday; they must keep markets and fairs on the Sunday. Finally, they use all days alike, work-days and holy days all are one. The other sort is worse. For although they will not travel nor labour on the Sunday, as they do on the weekday; yet they will not rest in holiness, as God commandeth; but they rest in ungodliness and filthiness, prancing in their pride, pranking and pricking, pointing and painting themselves, to be gorgeous and gay; they rest in excess and superfluity, in gluttony and drunkenness, like rats and swine; they rest in brawling and railing, in quarrelling and fighting: they rest in wantonness, in toyish talking, in filthy fleshliness; so that it doth too evidently appear that God is more dishonoured, and the devil better served on the Sunday than upon all the days in the week beside.

Homily of the Place and Time of Prayer, 1574

THE SEVEN TEMPTERS

. . . concerning the tempters, the Devils I mean who will not omit anything that may work unto man's destruction, it is not one devil only that doth it, but it is divers and especially seven of them. They be accounted and named the seven principal or captain devils, because they have always borne a great sway among men. The first is called Lucifer, the devil of pride and presumption. The second is called Belzebub, the lord of envy and malice. The third is called Sathan, the master of wrath and disdain. The fourth is called Abadan, who is the patron of sloth and idleness. The fifth is named Mammon, who is the father of Covetousness and snudgery [miserliness]. The sixth is named Belphegor, the God of gluttony and drunkenness. And the seventh is called

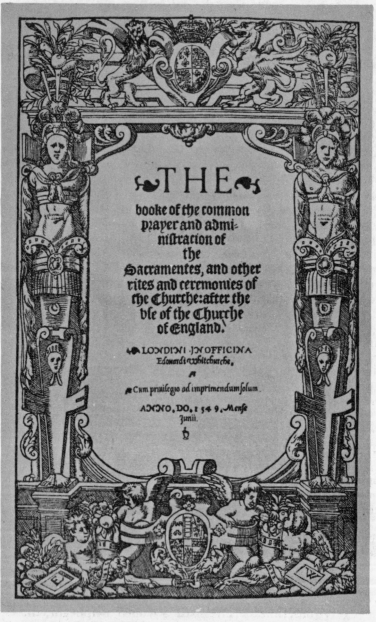

71. Title page of the first prayer-book, 1549.

Asmodius, the ruler of lechery and whoredom. And whosoever is infected with any of the said vices, be sure he is possessed with a great captain devil, which must of necessity be cast out, or else of force the man must perish. These in the time of our trouble, grief or sickness, and especially Sathan, ∴.. will put into our minds all that he may, to have a mistrust in our good God, and that we be not of the number of those that be predestinate and elect to be saved, so will be present unto us whatsoever we have done and committed against the commandments of God, and will put into our minds huge mountains, as it were, of sins, that by the outrageousness and greatness of them he may bring us into desparation, which do stagger and doubt of God's mercy and pardon.

The Autobiography of Thomas Whythorne, c. 1576

THE PRIEST HOLE

A house where I used secretly to be given hospitality was visited once by certain Catholics, who gave a satisfactory account of themselves, both to me and to the head of the family, and said that they wished to hear Mass. After the end of Mass, when the people had left, I stayed on as usual and went upstairs to the room where I kept my books and resumed my work. Not quite two hours later the house was surrounded by a large mob of men. Whether they came on information or on chance, I do not know. But the servant rushed up to my room — I was still there — and warned me of the danger. She made me come downstairs at once and showed me a hiding-place underground; Catholic houses have several places like this, otherwise there would be no security. I got down into it, taking my breviary with me — it was all I had near me at the time, and to loiter would have been dangerous. Meantime the heretics had already made their way into the house and were examining the remoter parts. From my cave-like hide I could follow their movements by the noise and uproar they raised. Step by step they drew closer, and when they entered my room the sight of my books was an added incentive to their search. In that room also there was a secret passage-way for which they demanded the key, and as they opened the door giving on to it they were standing immediately above my head. I could hear practically every word they said. 'Here! Look!' they called out, 'A chalice! And a missal!' The things were, in fact, there. There had been no time to hide them, and, in any case, it would have been impossible. Then they demanded a hammer and other tools, to break through the wall and panelling. They were certain now that I could not be far away.

Meanwhile I was praying fervently to God that He would avert the danger. At the same time I reflected that it would be better to surrender myself into the enemy's hands than be dragged out ignominiously. I believed that some Judas had given information and betrayed me, but, to cover up the traitor, they wanted my discovery to appear accidental, and not the result of treachery.

While I was reflecting in this way, one of the men, either by mistake or on purpose or at the prompting of a good angel, shouted out: 'Why waste time getting hammers and hatchets? There's not enough space here for a man. Look at the corners. You can see where everything leads to. There can't be a hiding-place here.'

They took the fellow's word for it, and the party abandoned their plan of search and destruction. It was God's design, I think, that they should lose all the common sense they possessed, for it was astonishing that men like this, skilled in their task, should fail to find a place that was constructed with no particular cunning or ingenuity. And so they gave up, tired after their search, and went away, taking with them everything they found — the silver chalice, the missal, several books, and I don't know what else.

Fr. William Weston, Autobiography, c. 1585

FATHER JOHN GERARD DESCRIBES HIS TORTURE, 1597

On the third day the warder came to my room straight from his dinner. Looking sorry for himself, he said the Lords Commissioners had arrived with the Queen's Attorney-General and that I had to go down to them at once.

'I am ready,' I said, 'but just let me say an *Our Father* and *Hail Mary* downstairs.'

He let me go, and then we went off together to the Lieutenant's lodgings inside the walls of the Tower. Five men were there waiting for me, none of whom, except Wade, had examined me before. He was there to direct the charges against me. . . .

'You say,' said the Attorney-General, 'you have no wish to obstruct the Government. Tell us, then, where Father Garnet is. He is an enemy of the state, and you are bound to report on all such men.'

'He isn't an enemy of the state,' I said. . . . 'But I don't know where he lives, and if I did, I would not not tell you.'

'Then we'll see to it that you tell us before we leave this place.'

'Please God you won't,' I answered.

Then they produced a warrant for putting me to torture. They had it ready by them and handed it to me to read. (In this prison a special warrant is required for torture.)

I saw the warrant was properly made out and signed, and then I answered: 'With God's help I shall never do anything which is unjust or act against my conscience or the Catholic faith, you have me in your power. You can do with me what God allows you to do — more you cannot do.'

Then they began to implore me not to force them to take steps they were loath to take. They said they would have to put me to torture every day, as long as my life lasted, until I gave them the information they wanted.

'I trust in God's goodness,' I answered, 'that He will prevent me from ever committing a sin such as this — the sin of accusing innocent people. We are all in God's hands and therefore I have no fear of anything you can do to me.'

72. The tomb of the Southampton family by Gerard Johnson the Elder, 1592. Below the effigy of his father, is the kneeling figure of the third Earl, who was the patron of William Shakespeare.

This was the sense of my answers, as far as I can recall them now.

We went to the torture-room in a kind of solemn procession, the attendants walking ahead with lighted candles.

The chamber was underground and dark, particularly near the entrance. It was a vast place and every device and instrument of human torture was there. They pointed out some of them to me and said I would try them all. Then they asked me again whether I would confess.

'I cannot,' I said.

I fell on my knees for a moment's prayer. Then they took me to a big upright pillar, one of the wooden posts which held the roof of this huge underground chamber. Driven into the top of it were iron staples for supporting heavy weights. Then they put my wrists into iron gauntlets and ordered me to climb two or three wicker steps. My arms were then lifted up and an iron bar was passed through the rings of one gauntlet, then through the staple and rings of the second gauntlet. This done, they fastened the bar with a pin to prevent it slipping, and then, removing the wicker steps one by one from under my feet, they left me hanging by my hands and arms fastened above my head. The tips of my toes, however, still touched the ground, and they had to dig away the earth from under them. They had hung me up from the highest staple in the pillar and could not raise me any higher, without driving in another staple.

Hanging like this I began to pray. The gentlemen standing around asked me whether I was willing to confess now.

'I cannot and I will not,' I answered.

But I could hardly utter the words, such a gripping pain came over me, It was worst in my chest and belly, my hands and arms. All the blood in my body seemed to rush up into my arms and hands and I thought that blood was oozing from the ends of my fingers and pores of my skin. But it was only a sensation caused by my flesh swelling above the irons holding them. The pain was so intense that I thought I could not possibly endure it, and added to it, I had an interior temptation. Yet I did not feel any inclination or wish to give them the information they wanted. The Lord saw my weakness with the eyes of His mercy, and did not permit me to be tempted beyond my strength. With the temptation He sent me relief. Seeing my agony and the struggle going on in my mind, He gave me this most merciful thought: the utmost and worst they can do is to kill you, and you have often wanted to give your life for your Lord God. The Lord

God sees all you are enduring — He can do all things. You are in God's keeping. With these thoughts, God in His infinite goodness and mercy gave me the grace of resignation, and with a desire to die and a hope (I admit) that I would, I offered Him myself to do with me as He wished. From that moment the conflict in my soul ceased, and even the physical pain seemed much more bearable than before, though it must, in fact, I am sure, have been greater with the growing strain and weariness of my body. . . .

Sometime after one o'clock, I think, I fell into a faint. How long I was unconscious I don't know, but I think it was long, for the men held my body up or put the wicker steps under my feet until I came to. Then they heard me pray and immediately let me down again. And they did this every time I fainted — eight or nine times that day — before it struck five. . . .

A little later they took me down. My legs and feet were not damaged, but it was a great effort to stand upright. . . .

John Gerard, *Autobiography*, 1609

LESS RELIGIOUS DEVOTION

And for my parishioners, they are a kind of people that love a pot of ale better than a pulpit, and a corn rick better than a church door, who, coming to divine service more for fashion than devotion, are contented after a little capping and kneeling, coughing and spitting, to help me to sing out a psalm, and sleep at the second lesson, or awake to stand up at the gospel, and say 'Amen' at the peace of God, and stay till the banns of matrimony be asked, or till the clerk have cried a pied stray bullock, a black sheep or a gray mare, and then, for that some dwell far off, be glad to be gotten home to dinner.

Nicholas Breton, *A merrie dialogue betwixt the taker and mistaker*

Witchcraft

ST OSYTH WITCHES, 1582

*In most of the English trials a woman was accused of witchcraft for some
simple annoyance. These irritations in everyday life led to more
contention than the very serious charge of bewitching to death. The
testimony of children was as eagerly received as that of neighbours.
Nothing was excluded, as we find in the trial of the witches of St Osyth
at the county sessions at Chelmsford in 1582.*

*The evidence at the long-drawn-out trial included losses among cattle
and sheep, butter that would not churn and beer that would not brew, a
cart bewitched so that it would not move for an hour, a man bewitched to
death for refusing to sell milk. Judge Darcy felt that he was dealing with
a 'nest of witches'. Two were not indicted; two were discharged; four
were acquitted; four were convicted but were reprieved; two were hanged
— these were Elizabeth Bennet, indicted for killing four people, and
Ursula Kempe for causing three deaths.*

*Agnes Heard was charged with a number of trivial happenings —
affecting sheep, cattle, butter and beer; but these culminated in the
charge of bewitching to death the wife of a minister:*

Richard Harrison, cleric, parson of Beaumont, saith that he and
his late wife did dwell in Little Oakley in a house of his said wife,
and that he, the said Richard Harrison, had also the parsonage
of Oakley in farm. And about summer twelve-month, he being at
London, his wife had a duck sitting on certain eggs under a
cherry tree in a hedge. And when the said duck had hatched, his
said wife did suspect one Agnes Heard, a light woman and a
common harlot, to have stolen her ducklings; and that his said
wife went unto the said Agnes Heard and rated her and all-to
[soundly] chid her. But she could get no knowledge of her
ducklings, and so came home, and was very angry against the
said Agnes.

And within a short time after, the said Richard Harrison went
into a chamber and there did read on his books for the space of
two or three hours, bidding his wife to go to bed with the

166

children, and that he would come to her. And she so did. And
being awhile laid down in her bed, his wife did cry out, 'Oh,
Lord, Lord, help me and keep me!' And he running to her
asked her what she ailed. And she said, 'Oh, Lord! I am sore
afraid, and have been divers times, but that I will not tell you.'
And said, 'I am in doubt, husband, that yonder wicked harlot,
Agnes Heard, doth bewitch me.' And the said Richard Harrison
said to his wife, 'I pray you be content and think not so, but
trust in God, and put your trust in him only, and he will defend
you from her, and from the Devil himself also.' And [he] said
moreover, 'What will the people say, that I, being a preacher,
should have my wife so weak in faith?'

This examinate [person being examined] saith that within two
months after, his said wife said unto him, 'I pray you, as ever
there was love between us (as I hope there hath been, for I have
five pretty children by you, I thank God), seek some remedy for
me against yonder wicked beast (meaning the same Agnes
Heard). And if you will not, I will complain to my father, and I
think he will see some remedy for me. For,' said she, 'if I have
no remedy, she will utterly consume me.' Whereupon this
examinate did exhort his wife as he did before, and desired her
to pray to God, and that he would hang her, the same Agnes
Heard, if he could prove any such matter.

And after, he went to the parsonage, and there he saith he
gathered plums. And the said Agnes Heard then came to the
hedge side, and Anwick's wife with her, and said unto him. 'I
pray you give me some plums, sir.' And this examinate saith
unto her, 'I am glad you are here, you vile strumpet!' Saying, 'I
do think you have bewitched my wife, and, as truly as God doth
live, if I can perceive that she be troubled any more as she hath
been, I will not leave a whole bone about thee. And besides, I
will seek to have thee hanged!' And [he] saith he said unto her
that his wife would make her father privy unto it, and that
'Then, I warrant thee, he will have you hanged, for he will make
good friends, and is a stout man of himself.' And [he] saith that
then he did rehearse divers things to her that were thought she
had bewitched, as geese and hogs. And as he was coming down
of the tree, she, the said Agnes, did depart suddenly from him
without having any plums.

This examinate saith (after which speeches so by him used
unto her, and before Christmas) his said wife was taken sore
sick, and was at many times afraid both sleeping and waking.
And [she] did call this examinate, her husband, unto her not

above two days before her death and said unto him: 'Husband, God bless you and your children, for I am now utterly consumed with yonder wicked creature' (naming the said Agnes Heard). Which words, he saith, were spoken by her in the presence of John Pollin and Mother Poppe. And within two days after, his said wife departed out of this world in a perfect faith, repeating these words, 'Oh, Agnes Heard, Agnes Heard! She hath consumed me!'

Agnes Heard was found Not Guilty by the jury, and acquitted.

SUPERSTITIONS

In our childhood our mother's maids have so terrified us with an ugly devil having horns on his head, fire in his mouth, and a tail in his breech, eyes like a basin, fangs like a dog, claws like a bear, a skin like a nigger, and a voice roaring like a lion, whereby we start and are afraid when we hear one cry Boo: and they have so affrayed us with bull beggars, spirits, witches, elves, hags, fairies, satyrs, fauns, tritons, centaurs, dwarfs, giants, imps, conjurors, nymphs, changelings, Incubus, Robin Goodfellow, the mare, the man in the oak, the hellwain, the firedrake, Tom Thumb, hobgoblin, Tom tumbler, and such other bugs, that we were afraid of our own shadows: in so much as some never fear the devil, but in a dark night; and then a polled [hornless] sheep is a perilous beast, and many times is taken for our father's soul, specially in a churchyard, where a right hardy man heretofore scarce dare pass by night, but this hair would stand upright.

Reginald Scot, *The Discoverie of Witchcraft*, 1584

EXORCISM

If a soul wander in the likeness of a man or woman by night, molestine men, with bewailing their torments in purgatory, by reason of tithes forgotten, &c.: and neither masses nor conjurations can help; the exorcist in his ceremonial apparel must go to the tomb of that body, and spurn thereat with his foot, saying: '*Vade ad gehennam*, Get thee packing to hell': and by and by the soul goeth thither, and there remaineth for ever.

Reginald Scot, *The Discoverie of Witchcraft*, 1584

EVIDENCE IN WITCH TRIALS

Reginald Scot in 1584 gives this as typical evidence against one accused of witchery:

She was at my house of late, she would have had a pot of milk. She departed in a [rage] because she had it not. She railed, she cursed, she mumbled and whispered, and finally she said she would be even with me. And soon after, my child, my sow, or my pullet died, or was strangely taken. Nay, if it please your worship, I have further proof: I was with a wise woman and she told me I had an ill neighbour, and that she would come to my house yet it were long, and so she did. And that she had a mark above her waist, and so had she; and God forgive me, my stomach hath gone against her a great while. Her mother before her was counted a witch. She hath been beaten and scratched by the face till blood was drawn upon her, because she hath been suspected and afterwards some of these persons were said to amend.

THE WITCHES' CAULDRON

Then he (the Devil) teacheth them to make ointments of the bowels and members of children, whereby they ride in the air, and accomplish all their desires. So as, if there be any children unbaptised, or not guarded with the sign of the cross, or orisons; then the witches may and do catch them from their mothers' sides in the night, or out of their cradles, or otherwise kill them with their ceremonies; and after burial steal them out of their graves, and seethe them in a cauldron, until their flesh be made potable. Of the thickest whereof they make ointments, whereby they ride in the air; but the thinner potion they put into flagons, whereof whosoever drinketh, observing certain ceremonies, immediately becometh a master or rather a mistress in that practice and faculty. . . .

It shall not be amiss here in this place to repeat an ointment greatly to this purpose. . . . The receipt is as followeth. R. the fat of young children, and seethe it with water in a brazen vessel, reserving the thickest of that which remaineth boiled in the bottom, which they lay up and keep, until occasion serveth to use it. They put hereunto *eleoselinum, aconitum, frondes populeas,* and soot. Another receipt to the same purpose. R. *Sium, acarum vulgare, pentaphyllon,* the blood of a flitter-mouse, *solanum somniferum, et oleum.* They stamp all these together, and then they rub all parts of their bodies exceedingly, till they look red, and be very hot, so as the pores may be opened, and their flesh soluble and loose. They join herewithal either fat, or oil instead whereof, that the force of the ointment may the rather pierce inwardly, and so be more effectual. By this means in a moonlight night they seem to be carried in the air, to feasting, singing, dancing, kissing, culling, and other acts of venery, with such youths as they love and desire most: for the force of their imagination is so vehement, that almost all that part of the brain, wherein the memory consisteth, is full of such conceits. And whereas they are naturally prone to believe any thing; so do they receive such impressions and steadfast imaginations into their minds, as even their spirits are altered thereby; not thinking upon any thing else, either by day or by night. And this helpeth them forward in their imaginations, that their usual food is none other commonly but beets, roots, nuts, beans, peas, &c.

Reginald Scot, *The Discoverie of Witchcraft*, 1584

A STRANGE TRANSFORMATION

It happened in the city of Salamin, in the kingdom of Cyprus (wherein is a good haven) that a ship loaden with merchandize stayed there for a short space. In the mean time many of the soldiers and mariners went to shore, to provide fresh victuals. Among which number, a certain Englishman, being a sturdy young fellow, went to a woman's house, a little way out of the city, and not far from the sea side, to see whether she had any eggs to sell. Who perceiving him to be a lusty young fellow, a stranger, and far from his country (so as upon the loss of him there would be the less miss or inquiry) she considered with herself how to destroy him; and willed him to stay there a while, whilst she went to fetch a few eggs for him. But she tarried long, so as the young man called unto her, desiring her to make haste: for he told her that the tide would be spent, and by that means his ship would be gone, and leave him behind. Howbeit, after some detracting of time, she brought him a few eggs, willing him to return to her, if his ship were gone when he came. The young fellow returned towards his ship: but before he went aboard, he would needs eat an egg or twain to satisfy his hunger, and within short space he became dumb and out of his wits (as he afterwards said). When he would have entered into the ship, the mariners beat him back with a cudgel, saying: 'What a murrain lacks the ass? Whither the devil will this ass?' The ass or young man (I cannot tell by which name I should term him) being many times repelled, and understanding their words that called him ass, considering that he could speak never a word, and yet could understand every body; he thought that he was bewitched by the woman, at whose house he was. And therefore, when by no means he could get into the boat, but was driven to tarry and see her departure, being also beaten from place to place as an ass, he remembered the witch's words, and the words of his own fellows that called him ass, and returned to the witch's house, in whose service he remained by the space of three years, doing nothing with his hands all that while, but carried such burdens as she laid on his back; having only this comfort, that although he were reputed an ass among strangers and beasts, yet that both this witch, and all other witches knew him to be a man.

After three years were passed over, in a morning betimes he went to town before his dame, who upon some occasion (of like to make water) stayed a little behind. In the meantime being near to church, he heard a little sacring bell ring to the elevation of a morrow mass, and not daring to go into the church, lest he should have been beaten and driven out with cudgels, in great devotion he fell down in the churchyard upon the knees of his hinder legs, and did lift his forefeet over his head, as the priest doth hold the sacrament at the elevation. Which prodigious sight when certain merchants of Genoa espied and with wonder beheld, anon cometh the witch with a cudgel in her hand, beating forth the ass. And because (as it hath been said) such kinds of witchcrafts are very usual in those parts, the merchants aforesaid made such means, as both the ass and the witch were attached by the judge. And she being examined and set upon the rack, confessed the whole matter, and promised, that if she might have liberty to go home, she would restore him to his old shape: and being dismissed, she did accordingly. So as notwithstanding, they apprehended again, and burned her: and the young man returned into his country with a joyful and merry heart.

Reginald Scot, *The Discoverie of Witchcraft*, 1584

WHAT IS A WITCH?

[The witch is] one that worketh by the Devil, or by some devilish curious art, either hurting or healing, revealing things secret or foretelling things to come, which the Devil hath devised to entangle and snare men's sails withal unto damnation.

George Gifford, *Discourse of the Subtle Practices
of Devils by Witches and Sorcerers*, 1587

AGNES SAMPSON AND OTHER WITCHES, 1591

Within the town of Trenent, in the kingdom of Scotland, there dwelleth one David Seaton, who, being deputy bailiff in the said town, had a maid called Geillis Duncane, who used secretly to absent and lie forth of her master's house every other night.

This Geillis Duncane took in hand to help all such as were troubled or grieved with any kind of sickness or infirmity, and in short space did perform many matters most miraculous; which things, for as much as she began to do them upon a sudden, having never done the like before, made her master and others to be in great admiration, and wondered thereat: by means whereof, the said David Seaton had his maid in great suspicion that she did not those things by natural and lawful ways, but rather supposed it to be done by some extraordinary and unlawful means. Whereupon, her master began to grow very inquisitive, and examined her which way and by what means she was able to perform matters of so great importance; whereat she gave him no answer. Nevertheless, her master, to the intent that he might the better try and find out the truth of the same, did with the help of others torment her with the torture of the pilliwinks upon her fingers, which is a grievous torture; and binding or wrenching her head with a cord or rope, which is a most cruel torment also; yet would she not confess anything; whereupon, they suspecting that she had been marked by the devil, (as commonly witches are,) made diligent search about her, and found the enemy's mark to be in her fore crag, or fore part of her throat; which being found, she confessed that all her doings were done by the wicked allurements and enticements of the devil, and that she did them by witchcraft. After this her confession, she was committed to prison, where she continued a season, where immediately she accused these persons following to be notorious witches, and caused them forthwith to be apprehended, one after another, viz. Agnes Sampson, the eldest witch of them all, dwelling in Haddington; Agnes Tompson of Edinburgh; Doctor Fian alias John Cuningham, master of the school at Saltpans in Lothian. . . .

The said Agnes Sampson was after brought again before the King's Majesty and his Council, and being examined of the meetings and detestable dealings of those witches, she confessed, that upon the night of All-hallow Even last, she was accompanied, as well with the persons aforesaid, as also with a great many other witches, to the number of two hundred, and that all they together went to sea, each one in a riddle or sieve, and went into the same very substantially, with flagons of wine, making merry and drinking by the way in the same riddles or sieves, to the kirk of North Berwick in Lothian; and that after they had landed, took hands on the land, and danced this reel or short dance, singing all with one voice,

Commer go ye before, commer go ye,
Gif ye will not go before, commer let me.

At which time she confessed, that this Geillis Duncane did go before them, playing this reel or dance, upon a small trump, called a Jew's trump, until they entered into the kirk of North Berwick.

These confessions made the King in a wonderful admiration, and he sent for the said Geillis Duncane, who upon the like trump did play the said dance before the King's Majesty, who in respect of the strangeness of these matters, took great delight to be present at their examinations.

The said Agnes Sampson confessed that the devil, being then at North Berwick kirk attending their coming, in the habit or likeness of a man, and seeing that they tarried over long, he at their coming enjoined them all to a penance, which was, that they should kiss his buttocks, in sign of duty to him; which being put over the pulpit bare, everyone did as he had enjoined them. And having made his ungodly exhortations, wherein he did greatly inveigh against the King of Scotland, he received their oaths for their good and true service towards him, and departed; which done, they returned to sea, and so home again. At which time, the witches demanded of the devil, 'Why he did bear such hatred to the King?' Who answered, 'By reason the King is the greatest enemy he hath in the world.' All which their confessions and depositions are still extant upon record.

The said Agnes Sampson confessed before the King's Majesty sundry things, which were so miraculous and strange, as that his Majesty said 'they were all extreme liars'; whereat she answered, 'she would not wish his Majesty to suppose her words to be false, but rather to believe them, in that she would discover such matter unto him as his Majesty should not anyway doubt of.' And thereupon taking his Majesty a little aside, she declared unto him the very words. which passed between the King's Majesty and his Queen at Upslo in Norway, the first night of marriage, with the answer each to other; whereat the King's Majesty wondered greatly, and swore, 'by the living God, that he believed all the devils in hell could not have discovered the same,' acknowledging her words to be most true; and therefore gave the more credit to the rest that is before declared.

Touching this Agnes Sampson, she is the only woman who, by the devil's persuasion, should have intended and put in execution the King's Majesty's death in this manner. She confessed that she took a black toad, and did hang the same up by the heels three days, and collected and gathered the venom as it dropped and fell from it in an oyster shell, and kept the same venom close covered, until she should obtain any part or piece of foul linen cloth that had appertained to the King's Majesty, as shirt, handkercher, napkin or any other thing, which she practised to obtain by means of one John Kers, who being attendant in his Majesty's chamber, desired him for old acquaintance between them, to help her to one, or a piece of such a cloth as is aforesaid; which thing the said John Kers denied to help her to saying he could not help her unto it. And the said Agnes Sampson, by her depositions since her apprehension, saith, that if she had obtained any one piece of linen cloth which the King had worn and fouled, she had bewitched him to death, and put him to such extraordinary pains, as if he had been lying upon sharp thorns and ends of needles. Moreover she confessed, that at the time when his Majesty was in Denmark, she being accompanied by the parties before specially named, took a cat and christened it, and afterward bound to each part of that cat, the chiefest part of a dead man, and several joints of his body: and that in the night following, the said cat was conveyed into the midst of the sea by all these witches, sailing in their riddles or sieves, as is aforesaid, and so left the said cat right before the town of Leith in Scotland. This done, there did arise such a tempest in the sea, as a greater hath not been seen; which tempest was the cause of the perishing of a boat or vessel coming from the town of Brunt Island to the town of Leith, wherein was sundry jewels and rich gifts, which should have been presented to the now Queen of Scotland, at her Majesty's coming to Leith. Again, it is confessed, that the said christened cat was the cause that the King's Majesty's ship, at his coming forth of Denmark, had a contrary wind to the rest of his ships then being in his company; which thing was most strange and true, as the King's Majesty acknowledgeth, for when the rest of the ships had a fair and good wind, then was the wind contrary and altogether against his Majesty; and further, the said witch declared, that his Majesty had never come safely from the sea, if his faith had not prevailed above their intentions.

Newes from Scotland, 1591

WARBOYS WITCHES
Robert Throckmorton was a squire living at Warboys in the county of Huntingdon. His daughter suffered from violent hysteria.
About the tenth of November which was in the year 1589,

Mistress Jane, one of the daughters of the said Master Throckmorton, being near the age of ten years, fell upon the sudden into a strange kind of sickness and distemperature of body, the manner whereof was as followeth. Sometimes she would neese [sneeze] very loud and thick for the space of half an hour together, and presently as one in a great trance and swoon lay quietly as long. Soon after she would begin to swell and heave up her belly, so as none was able to bend her, or keep her down. Sometime she would shake one leg and no other part of her, as if the palsy had been in it; sometimes the other. Presently she would shake one of her arms, and then the other, and soon after her head, as if she had been infected with the running palsy.

About this time, Mrs Alice Samuel, a neighbour who was seventy-six years old, came to pay her respects to the family. Jane turned against this woman and cried 'Look where the old witch sitteth . . . Did you ever see one more like a witch than she is? Take off her black thrumbed [fringed] cap, for I cannot abide to look on her.' The parents ignored this outburst. But within two months, Jane's four sisters, ranging in age from nine to fifteen, began to show similar symptoms. They all said, and the servants also, that Mrs Samuel was a witch.

Dr Philip Barrow of Cambridge University, the family physician, told the Throckmortons that he himself 'had some experience of the malice of some witches, and he verily thought that there was some kind of sorcery and witchcraft wrought toward [their] child.' At last the parents agreed and confronted Mrs Samuel with the children.

The girls at once fell to the ground 'strangely tormented'. Mrs Samuel denied that she was a witch. The whole family now accused her, and forced the unhappy woman to live with them. The children now took pleasure in tormenting her.

Many times also as she sat talking with these children, being in their fits by the fire side, they would say unto her: Look you here, Mother Samuel, do you not see this thing that sitteth here by us? She would answer no, not she. Why, they would say again, I marvell that you do not see it. Look how it leapeth, skippeth, and playeth up and down, pointing at it with their fingers here and there as it leaped.

In September, 1590, Lady Cromwell, wife of Sir Henry, the richest commoner in England, grandfather of Oliver Cromwell, called on the Throckmortons. She saw Mrs Samuel, who was one of her tenants, and scolded her, knocked off her bonnet and tugged her hair. The old lady cried out, 'Madam, why do you use me thus? I never did you any harm, as yet.'

After this unhappy encounter, Lady Cromwell had bad dreams, her health declined, and she died fifteen months later, in July 1592.

Mrs Samuel was so often called a witch that she almost believed it. 'O Sir, I have been the cause of all this trouble to your children . . . Good master, forgive me.' Dr Dorrington, the local parson, persuaded her to confess. On the next day, however, she withdrew her confession.

She was immediately arrested and taken before William Wickham, the Bishop of Lincoln. Extremely frightened she added to her first confession and gave the names of her familiars: three brown chickens, Pluck, Catch and White. She was brought back to Huntingdon, imprisoned for the assizes with her husband John and her daughter Agnes.

The five children now accused the three of them, and, continuing their fits, declared that Mrs Samuel had caused the death of Lady Cromwell. The three Samuels were tried at Huntingdon on 5 April 1593 for the witch murder of Lady Cromwell.

The story of the children was given as evidence, and contained the words said to be spoken by Mrs Samuel, 'Even as I am a witch and consented to the death of Lady Cromwell . . .'

The jury took five hours to find all three Guilty on the count of [bewitching of the five daughters of Robert Throckmorton Esquire, and divers other persons, with sundry devilish and grievous torments: and also for the bewitching to death of the Lady Cromwell, the like hath not been heard of in this age.] *They were executed.*

KINDS OF WITCHES
Magicians

Magicians be those which by uttering of certain superstitious words conceived, adventure to attempt things above the course of nature, by bringing forth dead men's ghosts, as they falsely pretend, in showing things either secret or in places far off, and in showing them in any shape or likeness.

Soothsaying wizards

Soothsayers or wizards . . . divine and fortell things to come, and raise up evil spirits by certain superstitions and conceived forms of words. And unto such words as he demanded of them, do answer by voice, or else set before their eyes in glasses, crystal stones or rings, the pictures or images of things sought for.

Divinators

The professors of the art of divination which be puffed up

with prophesying spirits. And can manifest who hath stolen things and tell where things lost or stolen be.

Jugglers

Jugglers and flighty curers of diseases, which for the curing of all sicknesses and sores of man and beast, use either certain superstitious words or writings called charms or spells hanged about the neck or some other part of the body.

Enchanters and charmers

Enchanters or charmers, through certain words pronounced and characters or images, herbs or other things applied, think they can do what they list, the devil so deceiveth them, or in very deed dispatcheth those things which the enchanters would have done. From these somewhat differ witches or hags, and augurers or soothsayers by birds, diviners by seeing the entrails of beasts sacrificed.

Witches

A witch or hag is she which being deluded by a league made with the devil through his persuasion, inspiration and piggling, thinketh she can design what manner of evil things soever, either by thought or imprecation, as to shake the air with lightnings and thunder, to cause hail and tempests, to remove green corn or trees to another place, to be carried of her familiar (which hath taken upon him the deceitful shape of a goat, swine, or calf, etc.) into some mountain far distant, in a wonderful short space of time, and sometimes to fly upon a staff or fork, or some other instrument, and to spend all the night after with her sweetheart, in playing, sporting, banqueting, dancing, dalliance, and divers other devilish lusts and lewd disports, and to show a thousand such monstrous mockeries.

William West, *Simboleography*, 1594

WITCHCRAFT, 1597

The fearful abounding at this time and in this country of these detestable slaves of the devil, the witches or enchanters, hath moved me, beloved reader, to despatch in post this following treatise of mine, not in any wise, as I protest, to serve for a show of mine own learning and ingene [ingenuity], but only (moved of conscience) to press thereby, so far as I can, to resolve the doubting hearts of many, both that such assaults of Satan are most certainly practised, and that the instrument thereof merits most severely to be punished, against the damnable opinions of two, principally in our age; whereof the one called Scot, an Englishman, is not ashamed in public print to deny that there can be such thing as witchcraft, and so maintains the old error of the Sadducees in denying of spirits. The other, called Wierus, a German physician, sets out a public apology for all these crafts-folks, whereby procuring for them impunity, he plainly betrays himself to have been one of that profession . . .

Witches ought to be put to death, according to the law of God, the civil and imperial law, and the municipal law of all Christian nations: yea, to spare the life, and not strike whom God bids strike, and so severely punish in so odious a treason against God, is not only unlawful, but doubtless as great a sin in the magistrate as was Saul's sparing Agag.

[Lest the innocent should be accused of witchcraft ordeals should be resorted to.]

Two good helps may be used: the one is the finding of their mark, and the trying the insensibleness thereof; the other is their floating on the water, — for, as in a secret murder, if the dead carcass be at any time thereafter handled by the murderer, it will gush out of blood, as if the blood were crying to Heaven for the revenge of the murderer (God having appointed that secret supernatural sign for trial of that secret unnatural crime), so that it appears that God hath appointed (for a supernatural sign of the monstrous impiety of witches) that the water shall refuse to receive them in her bosom that have shaken off them the sacred water of baptism, and wilfully refused the benefit thereof; — no, not so much as their eyes are able to shed tears (threaten and torture them as you please), while first they repent (God not permitting them to dissemble their obstinacy in so horrible a crime); albeit, the women-kind especially, be able otherwise to shed tears at every light occasion when they will, yea, although it were dissembling like the crocodiles.

James VI of Scotland, *Demonologie*, 1597

LOOK ABOUT YE, MY NEIGHBOURS

Out of these [impostures] is shaped [for] us the idea of a witch — an old, weather-beaten crone, having the chin and her knees meeting for age, walking like a bow, leaning on a staff; hollow-eyed, untoothed, furrowed on her face, having her limbs trembling with the palsy, going mumbling in the streets; one that hath forgotten her paternoster, and yet hath a shrewd tongue to call a drab a drab.

If she hath learned of an old wife, in a chimney end, 'Pax, Max, Fax,' for a spell, or can say Sir John Grantham's curse for the miller's eels —

All ye that have stolen the miller's eels,
Laudate dominum de coelis;
And all they that have consented thereto,
Benedicamus domino.

— why then, beware. Look about ye, my neighbours. If any of you have a sheep sick of the giddies, or a hog of the mumps, or a horse of the staggers, or a knavish boy of the school, or an idle girl of the wheel, or a young drab of the sullens, and hath not fat enough for her porridge or butter enough for her bread, and she hath a little help of the epilepsy or cramp to teach her to roll her eyes, wry her mouth, gnash her teeth, startle with her body, hold her arms and hands stiff, and then, when an old Mother Nobs hath by chance called her an idle young housewife, or bid the devil scratch her, then no doubt but Mother Nobs is the witch, and the young girl is owl-blasted.

Samuel Harsnett (who became Archbishop of York),
Declaration of Popish Impostures, 1599

Travel

ONE DANGER OF TRAVELLING

TRAVELLER: I pray you set me a little in my right way out of the village.

PLOUGHMAN: Keep still to the right hand until you come to the corner of a wood, then turn at the left hand.

TRAVELLER: Have we no thieves in that forest?

PLOUGHMAN: No sir, for the provost-marshal hung the other day half a dozen at the gallows which you see before you at the top of that hill.

TRAVELLER: Truly I fear lest we be here robbed. We shall spur a little harder for it waxeth night.

Claudius Hollyband, French Littleton, 1576

PRIVATE OR 'BYE LETTERS'

These, delivered at some distant place, were recognized first in Articles *drawn up by Randolph in 1584, and prescribe:*

'That no Posts servant or boy, riding with the Packet shall deliver any bye letters or private packets before he have first discharged himself of the Packet for her Majesty's affairs, he delivering the same unto the hands of the next standing Post. Unto whom also he shall commit and deliver all the bye letters and private packets as well as the other, upon pain of the forfeiture of ten shillings to the Post offended, and the displeasure of the Master of the Posts.

That no post's servant or boy, riding with the Packet and having bye letters or private packets or other kind of carriage commited unto them, shall adventure to open or break up or any other ways directly or indirectly shall fraudulently embezzle or convey the same wilfully, but shall safely deliver the same unto the hands of the next Post, as is aforesaid. And whatsoever he be that shall be found to be faulty herein, he shall lose his

Master's service, and the Master shall underlie such punishment as the Master of the Posts shall find him worthy of'.

THE STATE OF THE ROADS

Now to speak generally of our common highways through the English part of the isle (for of the rest I can say nothing), you shall understand that in the clay or cledgy soil they are often very deep and troublesome in the winter half. Wherefore by authority of parliament an order is taken for their yearly amendment, whereby all sorts of the common people do employ their travail for six days in summer upon the same. And albeit that the intent of the statute is very profitable for the reparations of the decayed places, yet the rich do so cancel their portions, and the poor so loiter in their labours, that of all the six, scarcely two good days' work are well performed and accomplished in a parish on these so necessary affairs. Besides this, such as have land lying upon the sides of the ways do utterly neglect to ditch and scour their drains and water-courses for better avoidance of the winter waters (except it may be set off or cut from the meaning of the statute), whereby the streets do grow to be much more gulled than before, and thereby very noisome for such as travel by the same. Sometimes also, and that very often, these days' works are not employed upon those ways that lead from market to market, but each surveyor amendeth such by-plots and lanes as seem best for his own commodity and more easy passage unto his fields and pastures. And whereas in some places there is such want of stones, as thereby the inhabitants are driven to seek them far off in other soils, the owners of the lands wherein those stones are to be had, and which hitherto have given money to have them borne away, do now reap no small commodity by raising the same to excessive prices, whereby their neighbours are driven to grievous charges, which is another cause wherefore the meaning of that good law is very much defrauded. Finally, this is another thing likewise to be considered of, that the trees and bushes growing by the streets' sides do not a little keep off the force of the sun in summer for drying up of the lanes. Wherefore if order were taken that their boughs should continually be kept short, and the bushes not suffered to spread so far into the narrow paths, that inconvenience would also be remedied, and many a slough prove hard ground that yet is deep and hollow. Of the daily encroaching of the covetous upon the highways I speak not. But this I know by experience, that whereas some streets within these five and twenty years have been in most places fifty foot broad according to the law, whereby the traveller might either escape the thief, or shift the mire, or pass by the loaden cart without danger of himself and his horse; now they are brought unto twelve, or twenty, or six and twenty at the most, which is another cause also whereby the ways be the worse, and many an honest man encumbered in his journey. But what speak I of these things whereof I do not think to hear a just redress, because the error is so common, and the benefit thereby so sweet and profitable to many by such houses and cottages as are raised upon the same.

William Harrison, *Description of England,* 1587

ENGLISH INNS

Each comer is sure to lie in clean sheets, wherein no man hath been lodged since they came from the laundress or out of the water wherein they were last washed. If the traveller have an horse, his bed doth cost him nothing, but if he go on foot he is sure to pay a penny for the same: but whether he be horseman or footman if his chamber be once appointed he may carry the key with him, as of his own house, so long as he lodgeth there. If he lose ought whilst he abideth in the inn, the host is bound by a general custom to restore the damage, so that there is no greater security anywhere for travellers than in the greatest inns of England.

Their horses in like sort are walked, dressed and looked unto by certain hostlers or hired servants, appointed at the charges of the goodman of the house, who in hope of extraordinary reward will deal very diligently, after outward appearance, in this their function and calling.

Herein nevertheless are many of them blame-worthy, in that they do not only deceive the beast oftentimes of his allowance by sundry means, except their owners look well to them; but also make such packs [evil confederacies] with slipper merchants [slippery customers] which hunt after prey (for what place is sure from evil and wicked persons?) that many an honest man is spoiled of his goods as he travelleth to and fro, in which feat also the counsel of the tapsters or drawers of drink, and chamberlains is not seldom behind or wanting. Certes I believe that not a chapman or traveller in England is robbed by the way without the knowledge of some of them; for when he cometh into the inn, and alighteth from his horse, the hostler forthwith is very busy to take down his budget [leathern bag] or capcase [bag or wallet] in the yard from his saddle-bow, which he peiseth [weighs] slyly in his hand to feel the weight thereof: or if he miss of this pitch [aim], when the guest hath taken up his chamber, the chamberlain that looketh to the making of the beds will be sure to remove it from the place where the owner hath set it, as if it were to set it more conveniently somewhere else, whereby he getteth an inkling whether it be money or other sort wares, and thereof giveth warning to such odd guests as haunt the house and are of his confederacy, to the utter undoing of many an honest yeoman as he journeyeth by the way. The tapster in like sort for his part doth mark his behaviour, and what plenty of money he draweth when he payeth the shot [bill], to the like end: so that it shall be an hard matter to escape all their subtle practices. Some think it a gay matter to commit their budgets at their coming to the goodman of the house: but thereby they oft bewray themselves. For albeit their money be safe for the time that it is in his hands (for you shall not hear that a man is robbed in his inn) yet after their departure the host can make no warrantise [promise] of the same, sith their protection extendeth no further than the gate of his own house: and there cannot be a surer token unto such as pry and watch for those booties, than to see any guest deliver his capcase in such manner.

In all our inns we have plenty of ale, beer and sundry kinds of wine, and such is the capacity of some of them that they are able to lodge two hundred or three hundred persons and their horses at ease, and thereto with a very short warning make such provision for their diet, as to him that is unacquainted withal may seem to be incredible. Howbeit of all in England there are no worse inns than in London, and yet many are there far better than the best that I have heard of in any foreign country, if all the circumstances be duly considered . . . And it is a world to see how each owner of them contendeth with other for goodness of entertainment of their guests, as about fineness and change of linen, furniture of bedding, beauty of rooms, service at table, costliness of plate, strength of drink, variety of wines, or well using of horses. Finally there is not so much omitted among them as the gorgeousness of their very signs at their doors, wherein some do consume thirty or forty pounds, a mere vanity in mine opinion; but so vain will they needs be, and that not only to give some outward token of innkeeper's wealth, but also to procure good guests to the frequenting of their houses in hope there to be well used.

William Harrison, Description of England, 1587

THE LONDON TO CAMBRIDGE ROAD

On the road we passed through a villainous boggy and wild country and several times missed our way because the country thereabouts is very little inhabited and is nearly a waste; and there is one spot in particular where the mud is so deep that in my opinion it would scarcely be possible to pass with a coach in winter or in rainy weather.

Visit of Frederick, Duke of Würtemberg, 1592, Rye:
England as Seen by Foreigners

Law – Crime

ABUSES

. . . make a law that they which plucked down farms and towns of husbandry shall re-edify them, or else yield and uprender the possession thereof to such as will go to the cost of building anew. Suffer not these rich men to buy up all to engross and forestall, and with their monopoly to keep the market alone as please them. Let not so many be brought up in idleness; let husbandry and tillage be restored; let clothworking be renewed, that there may be honest labours for this idle sort to pass their time in profitably, which hitherto either poverty hath caused to be thieves, or else now be either vagabonds or idle serving men, and shortly will be thieves.

Sir Thomas More, *Utopia*, 1516

ROGUES AND VAGABONDS

A Ruffler goeth with a weapon to seek service, saying he hath been a servitor in the wars, and beggeth for his relief. But his chiefest trade is to rob poor wayfaring men and market women.

A Prigman goeth with a stick in his hand like an idle person. His property is to steal clothes off the hedge, which they call 'storing of the rogueman'.

A Whipjack is one that, by colour of a counterfeit licence (which they call a 'gibe', and the seals they call 'jarks'), doth use to beg like a mariner; but his chiefest trade is to rob booths in a fair, or to pilfer ware from stalls, which they call 'heaving of the booth'.

A Frater goeth with a like licence to beg for some spittal-house or hospital. Their prey is commonly upon poor women as they go and come to the markets.

185

A Quire Bird is one that came lately out of prison, and goeth to seek service. He is commonly a stealer of horses, which they term a 'prigger of palfreys'.

An Upright Man is one that goeth with the truncheon of a staff, which staff they call a 'filchman'. This man is of so much authority that, meeting with any of his profession, he may call them to account and command a sharp or 'snap' unto himself of all that they have gained by their trade in one month. And if he do them wrong, they have no remedy against him — no, though he beat them, as he useth commonly to do. He may also command any of their women, which they call 'doxies', to serve his turn. He hath the chief place at any market walk and other assemblies, and is not of any to be controlled.

John Awdeley, *Fraternitye of Vacabondes*, 1561

A COURTESY MAN

A courtesy man is one that walketh about the back lanes in London in the day time, and sometimes in the broad streets in the night season, and when he meeteth some handsome young man cleanly apparelled or some other honest citizen, he maketh humble salutations and low courtesy, and sheweth him that he hath a word or two to speak with his mastership. This child can behave himself mannerly, for he will desire him that talketh withal to take the upper hand, and shew him much reverence, and at last like his familiar acquaintance will put on his cap, and walk side by side and talk on this fashion: 'Oh sir, you seem to be a man and one that favoureth men, and therefore I am the more bolder to break my mind unto your good mastership. Thus it is sir, there is a certain of us (though I say it, both tall and handsome men of their hands) which have come lately from the wars, and as God knoweth have nothing to take to, being both masterless and moneyless, and knowing no way whereby to earn one penny. And further, whereas we have been wealthily brought up and we also have been had in good estimation, we are ashamed now to declare our misery and to fall a-craving as common beggars, and as for to steal and rob (God is our record) it striketh us to the heart to think of such a mischief, that ever any handsome man should fall into such a danger for this worldly trash . . . 'Alas sir, it is not a groat or twelvepence I speak for, being such a company of servitors as we have been: yet nevertheless God forbid I should not receive your gentle offer at this time . . .'

These kind of idle vagabonds will go commonly well-apparelled, without any weapon, and in place where they meet together, as at their hostelries or other places, they will bear the part of right good gentlemen, and some are the more trusted, but commonly they pay them with stealing a pair of sheets or coverlet, and so take their farewell early in the morning, before the master or dame be stirring.

John Awdeley, *The Fraternitye of Vacabondes*, 1561

RUFFLERS ON SHOOTER'S HILL

Now these rufflers, the outcasts of serving-men, when begging or craving fails, then they pick [knock down] and pilfer from other inferior beggars that they meet by the way, as rogues, palliards, morts and doxies. Yea, if they meet with a woman alone riding to the market either old man or boy that he knoweth will not resist, such they filch and spoil. These rufflers, after a year or two at the farthest, become uprightmen, unless they be prevented by twined hemp.

I had of late years an old man to my tenant, who customably a great time went twice in a week to London, either with fruit or with peascods, when time served therefore. And as he was coming homewards on Blackheath, at the end thereof next to Shooter's Hill, he overtook two rufflers, the one mannerly waiting on the other, as one had been the master, and the other the man or servant carrying his master's cloak. This old man was very glad that he might have their company over the hill, because that day he had made a good market; for he had seven shillings in his purse, and an old angel [gold coin worth ten shillings], which this poor man had thought had not been in his purse, for he willed his wife over night to take out the same angel and lay it up until his coming home again. And he verily thought that his wife had so done, which indeed forgot to do it. Thus after salutations had, this master ruffler entered into communication with this simple old man, who, riding softly beside them, communed of many matters. Thus feeding this old man with pleasant talk, until they were on the top of the hill, where these rufflers might well behold the coast about them clear, quickly steps unto this poor man, and taketh hold of his horse bridle, and leadeth him into the wood, and demandeth of him what and how much money he had in his purse. 'Now, by my troth,' quoth this old man; 'you are a merry gentleman. I know you mean not to take away anything from me, but rather to give me some if I should ask it of you.' By and by, this servant thief casteth the cloak that he carried on his arm about this poor man's face, that he should not mark or view them, with sharp words to deliver quickly that he had, and to confess truly what was in his purse. This poor man, then all abashed, yielded and confessed that he had but just seven shillings in his purse; and the truth is he knew of no more. This old angel was fallen out of a little purse into the bottom of a great purse. Now, this seven shillings in white money they quickly found, thinking indeed that there had been no more; yet farther groping and searching found this old angel . . . 'This old knave told me that he had but seven shillings, and here is more by an angel: what an old knave and a false knave have we here!' Therewith they went on their way, and left the old man in the wood, doing him no more harm.

Thomas Harman, *A Caveat or Warening for Commen Cursetors*, 1567

A HOOKER OR ANGLER

These hookers, or anglers, be perilous and most wicked knaves, and be derived or proceed forth from the uprightmen. They commonly go in frieze jerkins and gally-slops [loose breeches], pointed beneath the knee. These when they practise their pilfering, it is all by night; for, as they walk a-day-times from house to house, to demand charity, they vigilantly mark where or in what place they may attain to their prey, casting their eyes up to every window, well noting what they see there, whether apparel or linen, hanging near unto the said windows, and that will they be sure to have the next night following. For they customably carry with them a staff of five or six foot long, in which, within one inch of the top thereof, is a little hole bored through, in which hole they put an iron hook, and with the same they will pluck unto them quickly anything that they may reach therewith, which hook in the daytime they covertly carry about them, and is never seen or taken out till they come to the place where they work their feat. Such have I seen at my house, and have oft talked with them and have handled their staves, not then understanding to what use or intent they served, although I had and perceived, by their talk and behaviour, great likelihood of evil suspicion in them. They will either lean upon their staff, to hide the hole thereof, when they talk with you, or hold their hand upon the hole; and what stuff, either woollen or linen, they thus hook out, they never carry the same forthwith to their stauling-kens [houses receiving stolen goods], but hide the same a three days in some secret corner, and after convey the same to their houses abovesaid, where their host or hostess giveth them money for the same, but half the value that it is worth, or else their doxies shall afar off sell the same at the like houses. I was credibly informed that a hooker came to a farmer's house in the dead of the night, and putting back a draw-window of a low chamber, the bed standing hard by the said window, in which lay three persons (a man and two big boys), this hooker with his staff plucked off their garments which lay upon them to keep them warm, with the coverlet and sheet, and left them lying asleep naked saving their shirts, and had away all clean, and never could understand where it became. I verily suppose that when they were well waked with cold, they surely thought that Robin Goodfellow (according to the old saying) had been with them that night.

Thomas Harman, *A Caveat or Warening for Commen Cursetors,*
1567

WATCHMEN AND CONSTABLES

Uxor. What number of men in harness are these? Some sleeping, and many of them seemeth to go whispering together, and behind them there appeareth other men putting forth their heads out of corners, wearing no harness.

Civis. These are not only the constables with the watchmen in London, but also almost through this realm, most falsely abusing the time, coming very late to the watch, sitting down in some common place of watching, wherein some falleth on sleep by the reason of labour or much drinking before, or else nature requireth rest in the night. These fellows think every hour a thousand until they go home, home, home, every man to bed. Good night, good night! God save the Queen! sayeth the constables, farewell, neighbours. Eftsoons after their departing creepeth forth the wild rogue and his fellows, having two or three other harlots for their turn, with picklocks, handsaws, long hooks, ladders, &c., to break into houses, rob, murder, steal, and do all mischief in the houses of true men, utterly undoing honest people to maintain their harlots. Great hoses, lined cloaks, long daggers, and feathers, these must be paid for, &c. This cometh for want of punishment by the day, and idle watch in the night. God grant that some of the watch be not the scouts to the thieves. Yes; God grant that some men have not conspirators of thieves in their own houses, which, like Judases, deceive their masters. If this watch be not better looked unto, good wife, in every place in this realm, and all the night long searching every

suspected corner, no man shall be able to keep a penny, no;
scant [scarcely] his own life in a while. For they that dare attempt
such matters in the city of London, what will they do in houses
smally guarded, or by the highway? Yet there is much execution,
but it helpeth not. It is the excess of apparel. Hose, hose, great
hose! too little wages, too many serving-men, too many
tippling-houses, too many drags, too many knaves, too little
labour, too much idleness.

William Bullein, A Dialogue against the Pestilence, 1573

PUNISHMENT

In cases of felony, manslaughter, robbery, murder, rape, piracy,
and such capital crimes as are not reputed for treason or hurt of
the estate, our sentence pronounced upon the offender is, to
hang till he be dead. ...

The greatest and most grievous punishment used in England
for such as offend against the State is drawing from the prison
to the place of execution upon a hurdle or sled, where they are
hanged till they be half dead and then taken down and
quartered alive. ...

And whensoever any of the nobility are convicted of high
treason by their peers, that is to say, equals, this manner of their
death is converted into the loss of their heads only.
notwithstanding that their sentence do run after the former
order. ...

If a woman poison her husband, she is burned alive; if a
servant kill his master, he is to be executed for petty treason; he
that poisoneth a man is to be boiled to death in water or lead ...
Perjury is punished by the pillory, burning in the forehead with
the letter P. ... Rogues are burned through the ears: carriers of
sheep out of the land by the loss of their hands. ...

Witches are hanged or sometimes burned; but thieves are
hanged ... generally on the gibbet or gallows, saving in Halifax,
where they are beheaded in a strange manner.

Rogues and vagabonds are often stocked and whipped; scolds
are ducked upon ducking-stools in the water. ...

William Harrison, Description of England, 1577

ROGUES, VAGRANTS AND THE LAW (STATUTE OF 1572)

With us the poor is commonly divided into three sorts, so that
some are poor by impotency, as the fatherless child, the aged,
blind and lame, and the diseased person that is judged to be

fforstaller and
regrat of markett
and bey res and
vittelars

73. In the pillory. From
Vetusta Monumenta, 1497.

incurable: the second are poor by casualty, as the wounded
soldier, the decayed householder, and the sick person visited
with grievous and painful diseases: the third consisteth of
thriftless poor, as the rioter that hath consumed all, the
vagabond that will abide nowhere but runneth up and down
from place to place, and finally the rogue and the strumpet. . . .
Such as are idle beggars through their own default are of two
sorts, and continue their estates either by casual or mere
voluntary means. Those that are such by casual means are in the
beginning justly to be referred either to the first or second sort
of poor aforementioned, but, degenerating into the thriftless
sort, they do what they can to continue their misery, and, with
such impediments as they have, to stray and wander about, as
creatures abhorring all labour and every honest exercise. Certes
I call these casual means, not in the respect of the original of
their poverty, but of the continuance of the same, from whence
they will not be delivered, such is their own ungracious lewdness
and froward disposition. The voluntary means proceed from
outward causes, as by making of corrosives and applying the
same to the more fleshy parts of their bodies, and also laying of
ratsbane, spearwort, crowfoot and such like unto their whole
members, thereby to raise pitiful and odious sores and move the

hearts of the goers by such places where they lie, to yearn at their misery, and thereupon bestow large alms upon them. How artificially they beg, what forcible speech, and how they select and choose out words of vehemency, whereby they do in manner conjure or adjure the goer-by to pity their cases, I pass over to remember, as judging the name of God and Christ to be more conversant in the mouths of none and yet the presence of the heavenly Majesty further off from no men than from this ungracious company. Which maketh me to think that punishment is far meeter for them than liberality or alms, and sith Christ willeth us chiefly to have a regard to himself and his poor members.

Unto this nest is another sort to be referred, more sturdy than the rest, which, having sound and perfect limbs, do yet notwithstanding sometime counterfeit the possession of all sorts of diseases. Divers times in their apparel also they will be like serving-men or labourers: oftentimes they can play the mariners and seek for ships which they never lost. But in fine they are all thieves and caterpillars [extortioners] in the commonwealth, and by the word of God not permitted to eat, sith they do but lick the sweat from the true labourer's brows, and bereave the godly poor of that which is due unto them, to maintain their excess, consuming the charity of well-disposed people bestowed upon them, after a most wicked and detestable manner.

It is not yet full threescore years since this trade began: but how it hath prospered since that time it is easy to judge, for they are now supposed, of one sex and another, to amount unto above 10,000 persons, as I have heard reported. Moreover, in counterfeiting the Egyptian rogues, they have devised a language among themselves, which they name 'canting', but others 'pedlar's French', a speech compact thirty years since of English and a great number of odd words of their own devising, without all order or reason, and yet such is it as none but themselves are able to understand. The first deviser thereof was hanged by the neck — a just reward, no doubt, for his deserts, and a common end to all of that profession.

A gentleman [Thomas Harman] also of late hath taken great pains to search out the secret practices of this ungracious rabble. And among other things he setteth down and describeth three and twenty sorts of them whose names it shall not be amiss to remember whereby each one may take occasion to read and know as also by his industry what wicked people they are, and what villainy remaineth in them.

The several disorders and degrees amongst our idle vagabonds.

1. Rufflers.
2. Uprightmen.
3. Hookers or anglers.
4. Rogues.
5. Wild rogues.
6. Priggers of prancers.
7. Palliards.
8. Fraters.
9. Abrams.
10. Freshwater mariners or whipjacks.
11. Dummerers.
12. Drunken tinkers.
13. Swadders or pedlars.
14. Jarkmen or patricoes.

Of the women kind.

1. Demanders for glimmer or fire.
2. Bawdy-baskets.
3. Morts.
4. Autem morts.
5. Walking morts.
6. Doxies.
7. Dells.
8. Kinching morts.
9. Kinching coes.

Palliards: beggars in patched cloaks.
Abrams: lunatic beggars licensed to beg by Bethlehem Hospital.
Dummerers: beggars pretending dumbness.
Swaddlers: pedlars.
Priggers of prancers: horse-thieves.
Fraters: men holding false licences to collect alms for 'spital-houses'.
Freshwater mariners: pretended shipwrecked sailors.
Drunken tinkers: thieves posing as tinkers.
Jarkmen: rogues like clerks making false licences in order to marry their comrades.
Demanders for glimmer: female beggars pretending to have lost their possessions in a fire.
Morts: female beggars not legally married.
Dells: female beggars still maidens.
Bawdy-baskets: female pedlars.
Autem morts: female rogues legally married.
Doxies: mistresses to rogues.
Kinching morts: young female rogues.
Kinching coes: young male rogues.

The punishment that is ordained for this kind of people is very sharp, and yet it cannot restrain them from their gadding: wherefore the end must needs be martial law, to be exercised upon them, as upon thieves, robbers, despisers of all laws, and

¶A Caueat or Warening,
FOR COMMEN CVRSE-
TORS VVLGARELY CALLED
Uagabones, set forth by Thomas Harman,
Esquiere, for the vtilite and proffyt of his naturall
Cuntrey. Augmented and inlarged by the fyrst author here of.
Anno Domini, M. D. LXVII.

¶ Vewed, examined and allowed, according vnto the
Queenes Maiestyes Iniunctions,

¶ Imprinted at London in Fleteſtrete at the signe of the
Falcon; by Wylliam Gryffith, and are to be sold at his shoppe in
Saynt Dunstones Churche yarde. in the West.
Anno Domini. 1 5 6 7.

74. Whipping at the Cart Tail, 1567.

enemies to the commonwealth and welfare of the land. What notable robberies, pilferies, murders, rapes and stealings of young children, burning, breaking and disfiguring their limbs to make them pitiful in the sight of the people. I need not to rehearse. But for their idle roguing about the country the law ordaineth this manner of correction. The rogue being apprehended, committed to prison, and tried in the next assizes (whether they be of gaol delivery or sessions of the peace), if he happen to be convicted for a vagabond, either by inquest of office or the testimony of two honest and credible witnesses upon their oaths, he is then immediately adjudged to be grievously whipped and burned through the gristle of the right ear with an hot iron of the compass of an inch about, as a manifestation of his wicked life, and due punishment received for the same. And this judgment is to be executed upon him except some honest person worth five pounds in the Queen's books in goods, or twenty shillings in land, or some rich householder to be allowed by the justices, will be bound in recognisance to retain him in his service for one whole year. If he be taken the second time, and proved to have forsaken his said service, he shall then be whipped again, bored likewise through the other ear, and set to service: from whence if he depart before a year be expired and happen afterward to be attached again, he is condemned to suffer pains of death as a felon (except before excepted) without benefit of clergy or sanctuary, as by the statute doth appear. Among rogues and idle persons, finally, we find to be comprised all proctors that go up and down with counterfeit licences, cozeners and such as gad about the country using unlawful games, practisers of physiognomy and palmistry, tellers of fortune, fencers, players, minstrels, jugglers, pedlars, tinkers, pretended scholars, shipmen, prisoners gathering for fees, and others, so oft as they be taken without sufficient licence. From among which company our bearwards are not excepted, and just cause: for I have read that they have, either voluntarily or for want of power to master their savage beasts, been occasion of the death and devouration of many children in sundry countries by which they have passed, whose parents never knew what was become of them. And for that cause there is and have been many sharp laws made for bearwards in Germany, whereof you may read in other. But to our rogues. Each one also that harboureth or aideth them with meat or money is taxed and compelled to fine with the queen's majesty for every time that he doth succour them as it shall please the justices of peace to assign, so that the taxation exceed not twenty shillings, as I have been informed.

William Harrison, *The Description of England,* 1587

CRIME AND PUNISHMENT

Thomas Botesworth is fined 4d because he is a common brawler and disturber of his neighbours and to give him warning to leave it or else he is to be carried in a dung cart about the town in an open assembly, and then to be put in the stocks and then to be banished out of the lordship.

Essex Record Office, 1588

PICKPOCKETS

An exquisite foist [pickpocket] must have three properties that a good surgeon should have, and that is an eagle's eye, a lady's hand, and a lion's heart: an eagle's eye to spy a purchase, to have a quick insight where the boung [purse] lies, and then a lion's heart not to fear what the end will be, and then a lady's hand to be little and nimble, and better to dive into the pocket.

Robert Greene, *Conny-catching,* 1591

COMMON SCOLDS

The wife of Walter Hycocks and the wife of Peter Philips do be common scolds and therefore it is ordered that they shall be admonished thereof in the church, to leave their scolding. But upon complaint made by their neighbours the second time they shall be punished by the ducking stool according to the discretion of the constable.

Essex Record Office, 1592

PICKPOCKETS, BARTHOLOMEW FAIR

While we were at this show, one of our company, Tobias Salander, Doctor of Physic, had his pocket picked of his purse, with nine crowns, which, without doubt, was so cleverly taken from him by an Englishman, who always kept very close to him, that the Doctor did not perceive it.

Paul Hentzner, *Travels in England,* 1598

FOR STEALING TWO FLAXEN SHEETS

Agnes Osier alias Beggar of Brook Street in South Weald, Spinster, for breaking into the house of William Reynolds of the same in the night-time, and stealing two flaxen sheets worth 4s 4d and 60s in money, belonging to the said William. Guilty; to be hanged.

Essex Record Office, 1599

VERY FOULLY ASSAULTED

28 June 1599. On Monday was sevennight Tom Compton and
MacWilliams went into the field upon an old quarrel, where
MacWilliams was left dead in the place and Compton came away
sore hurt. The Lady Cheke and her friends follow the matter
with great extremity and will not be persuaded but that he had
help, which for aught I hear will not be proved. The same day
in Nottinghamshire John Stanhope assaulted Sir Charles
Cavendish very foully, the whole manner whereof I have here
sent you as I had it from my Lord of Shrewsbury.

Enclosure: About nine o'clock in the morning Sir Charles
Cavendish, being at his new building, which is some quarter of a
mile from his little house where he and his Lady do lie, and
going from thence to a brick kiln, as far distant from that
building as that form his house, being attended by these three
persons only, Henry Ogle, Launcelot Ogle, his page, and one
horse-keeper, he discerned to the number of about 20 horse on
the side of a hill, which he thought to be Sir John Byron with
company hunting. But suddenly, they all galloping apace toward
him, he perceived he was betrayed, whereupon, being upon a
little nag, he put spurs to him, thinking to recover the new
building, but the tit [horse] fell with him, and before he could
draw his sword, two pistols were discharged upon him, and one
of them with a round bullet hit him in the inner side of the
thigh but missed the bone, and lies yet in the flesh near the
point of his buttock. He hath also diverse small shot in several
parts of his thigh and body thereabouts, which are thought came
out of the same pistol.

Notwithstanding, so strong was the hand of God with him as,
after this wound received, he and his two poor men and boy
unhorsed six of them and killed two in the place. A third fell
down in the forest and is thought dead also, and the fourth was
left behind in the same place so sore hurt as it not thought he
can recover, and lieth in the village ajoining. Upon this some of
the workmen came towards them, being without weapons. John
Stanhope, who was the hindmost during all the fight, was now
the foremost in running away, carrying all the rest of the
hirelings with him.

Sir Charles is hurt also in the head and in the hand, but these
two are but small hurts, and the surgeons do assuredly hope that
there is no great danger in the other wounds with the pistol,
though by incision they intend to take out the bullet, which is

within an inch and a half of the skin. Sir Charles and his three had rapiers and daggers only.

They left behind them six good geldings, whereof some are worth twenty pounds apiece, two or three cloaks, two rapiers, two pistols, one sword and dagger, and some of their hats, all of which are safely kept by Sir Charles. All this company did all the morning before lie in the forest, seeming as though they had been hunting. One of them that were killed was a keeper, whom Stanhope that morning took with him as he found him in his park, without boots or weapon but a pike-staff which he had, and, as the fellow confessed before he died, he know not whither he was carried, or what to do, until he came to the hillside where they stayed so long.

This is the truth of that accident.

John Chamberlain, *Letters,* 1597-1626

Famous People

JOHN COLET
Dean of St Paul's and founder of St Paul's School

In his excursions he would sometimes make me one of his company, and then no man could be more easy and pleasant. He always carried a book with him, and seasoned his conversation with religion. He had an aversion from all impure and improper discourse, and loved to be neat and clean in his apparel, furniture, equipment, books and whatever belonged to him; but he held all pageantry and magnificence in contempt. Though it was then the custom for the higher clergy to appear in purple, his habit was invariably black. His upper garment, of plain woollen cloth, was in cold weather lined with fur.
Desiderius Erasmus, quoted in Revd Francis Wrangham's
The British Plutarch

ARCHBISHOP MORTON
'I pray you, Sir' (quoth I), 'have you been in our country?' 'Yea forsooth' (quoth he), 'and there I tarried for the space of four or five months together, not long after the insurrection, that the western English men made against their king; which by their own miserable and pitiful slaughter was suppressed and ended. In the mean season I was much bound and beholden to the right reverend father John Morton, Archbishop, and Cardinal of Canterbury, and at that time also Lord Chancellor of England; a man, master Peter (for master More knoweth already that I will say), not more honourable for his authority than for his prudence and virtue. He was of a mean stature, and though stricken in age yet bare he his body upright. In his face did shine such an amiable reverence, as was pleasant to behold. Gentle in communication, yet earnest and sage. He had great delight many times with rough speech to his suitors to prove, but without harm, what prompt wit and what bold spirit were in every man. In the which, as in a virtue much agreeing with his

199

nature, so that therewith were not joined impudency, he took great delectation; and the same person, as apt and meet to have an administration in the weal public, he did lovingly embrace. In his speech he was fine, eloquent and pithy. In the law he had profound knowledge; in wit he was incomparable; and in memory wonderful excellent. These qualities, which in him were by nature singular, he by learning and use had made perfect.

The King put much trust in his counsel: the weal public also in a manner leaned unto him, when I was there. For even in the chief of his youth he was taken from school into the Court, and there passed all his time in much trouble and business, and was continually tumbled and tossed in the waves of divers misfortunes and adversities. And so by many and great dangers he learned the experience of the world, which so being learned can not easily be forgotten.

Sir Thomas More, Utopia, Book I

JOHN DONNE

He was of a stature moderately tall, of a straight and equally proportioned body, to which all his words and actions gave an unexpressible addition of comeliness. The melancholy and pleasant humour were in him so contempered that each gave advantage to the other, and made his company one of the delights of mankind . . .

His aspect was cheerful and, as such, gave a silent testimony of a clear, knowing soul, and of a conscience at peace with itself. His melting eye showed that he had a soft heart, full of noble compassion; of too brave a soul to offer injuries, and too much a Christian not to pardon them in others.

Izaak Walton, Life of Dr Donne, 1640

BEN JONSON

. . . punched full of eyelet-holes like the cover of a warming pan . . . the most ungodly face . . . it looks for all the world like a rotten russet-apple, when 'tis bruised. It's better than a spoonful of cinnamon-water next my heart, for me to hear him speak; he sounds it so i' the nose, and talks and rants . . . it's cake and pudding to me to see his face make faces when he reads his songs and sonnets.

Thomas Dekker, Satiro-mastix, 1602

75. William Tyndale. Artist unknown. He described himself as being 'evil favoured in this world and without grace in the sight of men'. His life has been called one of 'utter disappointment and struggle — persecuted in one city, fleeing to another. Yet he was a noble scholar, a man of invincible faith who died a martyr. When the Authorized Version of the Bible appeared, it was mainly the work of Tyndale.

WILLIAM TYNDALE
Translator of the Bible; died at the stake at Vilvorde.

I believe, right worshipful, that you are not ignorant of what has been determined concerning me; therefore I entreat your lordship, and that by the Lord Jesus, that if I am to remain here during the winter, you will request the Procureur to be kind enough to send me from my goods which were in his possession, a warmer cap, for I suffer extremely from cold in the head, being afflicted with a perpetual catarrh, which is considerably increased in this cell. A warmer coat also, for that which I have is very thin; also a piece of cloth to patch my leggings; my overcoat is worn out; my shirts are also worn out. He has a woollen shirt of mine, if he will be kind enough to send it. I have also with him leggings of thicker cloth for putting on above; he also has warmer caps for wearing at night. I wish also his permission to have a lamp in the evening, for it is wearisome to sit alone in the dark.

William Tyndale, from his prison at Vilvorde,
to the Governor of the Castle, 1536

76. Thomas Cranmer, archbishop of Canterbury, by Gerlach Flicke, *c.* 1547. In Mary's reign he was condemned for heresy and burned at the stake, holding his right hand, which had written his recantation, firmly in the fire. Pollard says, 'he alone interceded for Fisher and More; for Anne Boleyn and the Princess Mary, for Thomas Cromwell and Bishop Tunstall. He maintained almost unaided a stubborn fight against the Act of the Six Articles'. He deserves to be called the founder of the Anglican Protestant Church and was the principal author of the English liturgy.

THOMAS CRANMER

Now, as touching his qualities wherewithal he was specially
endued, like as some of them were very rare and notable, so
ought they not to be put in oblivion. Wherefore among other
things it is to be noted that he was a man of such temperature of
nature, or rather so mortified, that no manner of prosperity or
adversity could alter or change his accustomed conditions: for,
being the storms never so terrible or odious, nor the prosperous
estate of the time never so pleasant, joyous, or acceptable, to the
face of [the] world his countenance, diet, or sleep commonly
never altered or changed, so that they which were most nearest
and conservant about him never or seldom perceived by no sign
or token of countenance how th'affairs of the Prince or the
realm went. Notwithstanding privately with his secret and special
friends he would shed forth many bitter tears, lamenting the
miseries and calamities of the world.

Again, he so behaved himself to the whole world, that in no
manner of condition he would seem to have any enemy, although
in very deed he had both many great and secret enemies, whom
he always bore with such countenance and benevolence that they
could never take good opportunity to practise their malice
against him but to their great displeasure and hindrance in
th'end, And as concerning his own regard towards slanders and
reproach by any man to him imputed or impinged, such as
entirely knew him can testify that very little he esteemed or
regarded the brute thereof, by cause he altogether travailed
evermore from giving of just occasion of detraction. Whereupon
grew and proceeded that notable quality or virtue he had: to be
beneficial unto his enemies, so that in that respect he would not
acknown to have any enemy at all. For whosoever he had been
that had reported evil of him or otherways wrought or done to
him displeasure, were the reconciliation never so mean or simple
on the behalf of his adversary, if he had anything at all relented,
the matter was both pardoned and clearly forgotten, and so
voluntarily cast into the satchel of oblivion behind the back part,
that it was more clear now out of memory, than it was in mind
before it was either commenced or committed; insomuch that if
any such person should have had any suit unto him afterwards,
he might well reckon and be as sure to obtain (if by any means
he might lawfully do it) as any other of his special friends. So
that on a time I do remember that D. Hethe, late Archbishop of
York, partly misliking this his overmuch lenity by him used, said
unto him, 'My Lord, I now know how to win all things at your

hands well enough.' 'How so?' (quoth my Lord). 'Marry,' (said D. Hethe,) 'I perceive that I must first attempt to do unto you some notable displeasure, and then by a little relenting obtain of you what I can desire.' Whereat my Lord bit his lip, as his manner was when he was moved, and said: 'You say well; but yet you may be deceived. Howbeit, having some consideration so to do, I may not alter my mind and accustomed condition, as some would have me to do.'

Anecdotes and Character of Cranmer by Ralph Morice,
his secretary

SIR THOMAS MORE

To begin with that side of More of which you know nothing, in height and stature he is not tall, nor again noticeably short, but there is such symmetry in all his limbs as leaves nothing to be desired here. He has a fair skin, his complexion glowing rather than pale, though far from ruddy, but for a very faint rosiness shining through. His hair is of a darkish blond, or if you will, a lightish brown, his beard scanty, his eyes bluish grey, with flecks here and there. ... His expression corresponds to his character, always shewing a pleasant and friendly gaiety, and rather set in a smiling look; and, to speak honestly, better suited to merriment than to seriousness and solemnity, though far removed from silliness and buffoonery. His right shoulder seems a little higher than the left, particularly when he is walking: this is not natural to him but due to force of habit, like many of the little habits which we pick up. There is nothing to strike one in the rest of his body; only his hands are somewhat clumsy, but only when compared with the rest of his appearance. He has always from a boy been very careless of everything to do with personal adornment, to the point of not greatly caring for those things which according to Ovid's teaching should be the sole care of men. One can tell even now, from his appearance in maturity, how handsome he must have been as a young man; although when I first knew him he was not more than three and twenty years old, for he is now barely forty.

His health is not so much robust as satisfactory, but equal to all tasks becoming an honourable citizen, subject to no, or at least very few, diseases: there is every prospect of his living long, as he has a father of great age — but a wondrously fresh and green old age. ... His voice is neither strong nor at all weak, but easily audible, by no means soft or melodious, but the voice of a clear speaker: for he seems to have no natural gift for vocal

77. Sir Thomas More by Hans Holbein. He succeeded Wolsey as Lord Chancellor under Henry VIII, but fell into disgrace by refusing to take the oath of Supremacy and was ultimately executed. His *Utopia* is a literary masterpiece. More was also a saint, there was in him 'a hard core of granite, a fibre strong as steel, which made him a formidable opponent in controversy, a severe critic where he felt his principles to be outraged'.

music, although he delights in every kind of music. His speech is wonderfully clear and distinct, with no trace of haste or hesitation.

He likes to dress simply, and does not wear silk or purple or gold chains, excepting where it would not be decent not to wear them. . . .

In social intercourse he is of so rare a courtesy and charm of manners that there is no man so melancholy that he does not gladden, no subject so forbidding that he does not dispel the tedium of it. From his boyhood he has loved joking, so that he might seem born for this, but in his jokes he has never descended to buffoonery, and has never loved the biting jest. . . .

In human relations he looks for pleasure in everything he comes across, even in the gravest matters. If he has to do with intelligent and educated men, he takes pleasure in their brilliance; if with the ignorant and foolish, he enjoys their folly. He is not put out by perfect fools, and suits himself with marvellous dexterity to all men's feelings. For women generally, even for his wife, he has nothing but jests and merriment. . . .

He diligently cultivates true piety, while being remote from all superstitious observance. He has set hours in which he offers to God not the customary prayers but prayers from the heart. With his friends he talks of the life of the world to come so that one sees that he speaks sincerely and not without firm hope. Such is More even in the Court. And then there are those who think that Christians are to be found only in monasteries!

A letter from Erasmus to Ulrich von Hutten, 1519, from
Epistles of Erasmus

THOMAS CROMWELL

As you desire me to give you a detailed account of secretary Cromwell and his origin, I will tell you that he is the son of a poor blacksmith, who lived and is buried at a small village distant one league and a half from this city [London]. His uncle, the father of a cousin of his, whom he has since considerably enriched, was cook to the last Archbishop of Canterbury [Warham]. In his youth Cromwell was rather ill-conditioned and wild. After being some time in prison he went to Flanders, Rome, and other places in Italy where he made some stay. On his return to England he married the daughter of a fuller, and for a time kept servants in his house who worked for him at that handicraft. Later on he became a solicitor, and thereby became known to the late Cardinal of York [Wolsey] who took him into

78. Thomas Cromwell, after the school of Holbein. He was a protégé of Wolsey, rose to high office under Henry VIII, and began the suppression of the monasteries. He was executed after the failure of the Anne of Cleves marriage, which had been one part of his policy of alliance with the German Protestant princes.

his service. At his master's fall he behaved very well towards him; and on the Cardinal's death, Master Wallop, now ambassador at the Court of France, somehow threatened and insulted him; whereupon, to save himself, he [Cromwell] asked and obtained an audience from King Henry, whom he addressed in such flattering terms and eloquent language — promising to make him the richest King in the world — that the King at once took him into his service, and made him councillor, though his appointment was kept secret for more than four months. Since then he has been constantly rising in power, so much so that he has now more influence with his master than the Cardinal ever had; for in the latter's time there were Compton, the Duke of Suffolk, and others, to whose advice the King occasionally listened, whereas nowadays everything is done at his bidding. The Chancellor [Audley] is but a tool in his hands.

Cromwell is eloquent in his own language, and, besides, speaks Latin, French and Italian tolerably well. He lives splendidly; is very liberal both of money and fair words, and remarkably fond of pomp and ostentation in his household and in building.

Eustace Chapuys, the Imperial Ambassador,
to Nicholas de Granvelle. 1535

WILLIAM CECIL, LORD BURGHLEY

I come now to the next, which was Secretary William Cecil, for on the death of the old Marquis of Winchester, he came up in his room, a person of a most subtle, and active spirit.

He stood not by the way of constellation, but was wholly intentive to the service of his Mrs and his dexterity, experience and merit therein, challenged a room in the Queen's favour, which eclipsed the others' overseeming greatness, and made it appear that there were others steered, and stood at the helm besides himself, and more stars in the firmament of grace, than *Ursa Major*.

He was born as they say, in Lincolnshire, but as some aver, upon knowledge of a younger brother, of the Cecils of Hertfordshire, a family of my own knowledge, though now private, yet of no mean antiquity; who being exposed, and sent to the City, as poor gentlemen use to do their sons, became to be a rich man on London Bridge, and purchased in Lincolnshire, where this man was born.

He was sent to Cambridge, and then to the Inns of Court, and so came to serve the Duke of Somerset, in the time of his protectorship as Secretary, and having a pregnancy to high inclinations, he came by degrees to a higher conversation, with the chiefest affairs of State and Counsels, but on the fall of the Duke, he stood some years in umbrage, and without employment, till the State found they needed his abilities, and although we find not that he was taken into place, during Mary's reign, unless (as some say) towards the last, yet the Council several times made use of him, and in the Queen's entrance, he was admitted Secretary of State, afterwards he was made Mr of the Court of Wards, then Lord Treasurer, a person of most excellent abilities, and indeed the Queen began to need and seek out men of both Guards, and so I conclude to rank . . . this great instrument amongst the Togatie [the peace party] for he had not to do with the sword, more than as the great pay-master, and contriver of the war, which shortly followed, wherein he accomplished much, through his theoretical knowledge at home and his intelligence abroad, by unlocking the counsels of the Queen's enemies.

Naunton, *Fragmenta Regalia*, 1641

For if he might ride privately in his garden, upon his little mule, or lie a day or two at his little lodge at Theobald's, retired from great business or too much company, he thought it his greatest

79. William Cecil, Lord Burghley, Secretary of State. 'Perhaps the greatest of nis achievements was that he managed by great tact, great wisdom and great integrity of purpose, along with a nice sense of what was practicable and possible, to advance from strength to strength.' C. Read. He became beyond any doubt Queen Elizabeth's first minister.

greatness ... He hated idleness and loved no idle persons ... and it was notable to see his continual agitation both of body and mind, for he was ever more weary of a little idleness than of great labour. If he had nothing of necessity to do, he would yet busy himself, either in reading, writing or meditation, and was never less idle than when he had most leisure to be idle.

One of his household, the account written by
Francis Peck in *Desiderata Curiosa,* 1732-1735

CARDINAL WOLSEY

This Cardinal is the person who rules both the King and the entire kingdom. On the ambassador's first arrival in England he used to say to him, 'His Majesty will do so and so': subsequently, by degrees, he went forgetting himself, and commenced saying, 'We shall do so and so': at this present he has reached such a pitch that he says, 'I shall do so and so'.

He is about forty-six years old, very handsome, learned, extremely eloquent, of vast ability, and indefatigable. He, alone, transacts the same business as that which occupies all the magistracies, offices, and councils of Venice, both civil and criminal; and all state affairs, likewise are managed by him, let their nature be what it may.

He is pensive, and has the reputation of being extremely just: he favours the people exceedingly, and especially the poor; hearing their suits, and seeking to despatch them instantly: he also makes the lawyers plead *gratis* for all paupers.

He is in very great repute — seven times more so than if he were Pope. He has a very fine palace, where one traverses eight rooms before reaching his audience chamber, and they are all hung with tapestry, which is changed once a week. He always has a sideboard of plate worth 25,000 ducats, wherever he may be; and his silver is estimated at 150,000 ducats. In his own chamber there is always a cupboard with vessels to the amount of 30,000 ducats, this being customary with the English nobility.

He is supposed to be very rich indeed, in money, plate, and household stuff.

The archbishopric of York yields him about 14,000 ducats; the bishopric of Bath 8,000. One-third of the fees derived from the great seal are his; the other two are divided between the King and the Chancellor. The Cardinal's share amounts to about 5,000 ducats. By the new year's gifts, which he receives in like manner as the King, he makes some 15,000 ducats.

Giustiniari, *Despatches*

80. Thomas Wolsey, Cardinal, Archbishop of York, Lord Chancellor. For a number of years he was supreme, and by his diplomacy did much to strengthen the King's power. When he failed to obtain papal sanction for Henry's divorce of Catherine he fell into disfavour. He is remembered for his foundation of Cardinal College, today, Christ Church, Oxford, for his palace at Hampton Court, and for the fact that he was one of the strongest supporters of the 'new learning'.

SIR EDWARD COKE

For three things he would give God solemn thanks: that he never gave his body to physic, nor his heart to cruelty, nor his hand to corruption . . .

His parts were admirable: he had a deep judgment, faithful memory, active fancy: and the jewel of his mind was put into a fair case, a beautiful body, with a comely countenance; a case which he did wipe and keep clean, delighting in good clothes well worn, and being wont to say 'that the outward neatness of our bodies might be a monitor of purity to our souls.'

Thomas Fuller, *Worthies of England*, 1662

EDMUND SPENSER

This was written by Spenser in 1596. Before the close of the year he had published the Prothalamion, *a superb 'spousal verse'.*

Having in the greener times of my youth composed these former two hymns in the praise of love and beauty, and finding that the same too much pleased those of like age and disposition, which being too vehemently carried with that kind of affection do rather suck out poison to their strong passion than honey to their honest delight, I was moved by one of you two most excellent ladies [the ladies Margaret, Countess of Cumberland, Mary, Countess of Warwick] to call in the same; but unable so to do, by reason that many copies thereof were formerly scattered abroad, I resolved at least to amend and by way of retraction to reform them, making (instead of those two hymns of earthly or natural love and beauty) two others of heavenly and celestial.

HUGH LATIMER

After him [Ridley] came Master Latimer in a poor Bristow frieze frock, all worn, with his buttoned cap, and a kerchief on his head all ready to the fire, a new long shroud hanging over his hose down to the feet; which at the first sight stirred men's hearts . . . very quickly suffered his keeper to pull off his hose, and his other array, which to look unto was very simple; and being stripped unto his shroud, he seemed as comely a person to them that were present as one should lightly see; and whereas in his clothes he appeared a withered and crooked silly old man, he now stood bolt upright, as comely a father as one might lightly behold.

John Foxe, *Book of Martyrs*, 1563

81. Sir Philip Sidney, poet, statesman and soldier. He was one of Elizabeth's favourites, a man of ability and courage. He wrote *Arcadia, Apology for Poetry,* and *Defence of Poetry*. In 1586 he was given a command in the Netherlands, and died heroically at the siege of Zutphen. Over two hundred poetic elegies mourned his loss.

SIR FRANCIS WALSINGHAM

Sir Francis Walsingham ... was a gentleman at first, of a good house, and of a better education, and from the University travelled for the rest of his learning; doubtless he was the only linguist of his times, how to use his own tongue whereby he came to be employed in the chiefest affairs of State.

He was sent Ambassador to France, and stayed there legarlong [Ambassador for a long time] in the heat of the Civil-wars, and at the same time that Monsieur was here a suitor to the Queen, and if I be not mistaken he played the very same part there, as since Gundamore [Gondomar] did here: at his return he was taken principal Secretary, and for one of the great engines of State, and of the times, high in his Mrs the Queen's favour, and a watchful servant over the safety of his Mrs. . . .

I must again profess that I have read many of his letters, for they are commonly sent to my Lord of Leicester, and of Burleigh, out of France, containing many fine passages. and secrets yet if I might have been beholding to his cyphers, they would have told pretty tales of the times ... with one observation more, that he was one of the greatest always of the Austerian embracements, for both himself, and Stafford that preceded him, might well have been compared to him in the Gospel, that sowed his tares in the night; so did they their seeds in division, in the dark, and as it is a likely report, that they father on him at his return, the Queen speaking to him with some sensibility of the Spanish designs on France: 'Madam,' he answered, 'I beseech you be content, and fear not, the Spaniards have a great appetite and an excellent digestion, but I have fitted him with a bone for these 20 years, that your Majesty should have no cause to doubt him, provided that if the fire chance to slake, which I have kindled, you will be ruled by me, and cast in some of your fuel which will revive the flame.'

Naunton, *Fragmenta Regalia*, 1641

ROBERT DUDLEY, EARL OF LEICESTER

It will be out of doubt, that my Lord of Leicester was one of the first whom she made Master of the Horse, he was the youngest son then living of the Duke of Northumberland, beheaded *primo Mariae*, and his father was that Dudley which our histories couple with Empson ... [who] was executed the first year of Henry VIII. . . .

He was a very goodly person, tall, and singularly well featured, and all his youth well favoured, of a sweet aspect, but high

82. Robert Dudley, Earl of Leicester. He was a favourite of Queen Elizabeth; there is no doubt she was in love with him. He was devoted to her. As she was the Queen it went no further. Both in this relationship underwent great strain. He commanded the English troops in the Netherlands, 1585-1587, and in England before the Armada. In 1578 he married Lettice, the widowed Countess of Essex. Elizabeth referred to her as 'that she-wolf'.

foreheaded which (as I should take it) was of no discommendation, but towards his latter, and which with old men was but a middle age, he grew high coloured, so that the Queen had much of her father, for excepting some of her kindred and some few that had handsome wits in crooked bodies, she always took personages in the way of election for the people hath it to this day, 'King Henry loved a man.'

Being thus in her grace, she called to mind the sufferings of his ancestors, both in her father's and sister's reigns, and restored his, and his brother's blood, creating Ambrose the elder, Earl of Warwick, and himself Earl of Leicester, and as he was *ex primiciis* or of her first choice, so he rested not there, but long enjoyed her favour, and therewith what he listed, till time and emulation, the companions of greatness, resolved of his period, and to colour him at his sitting in a Cloud [at Conebury] not by so violent a death, or by the fatal sentence of Judicature, as that of his father and grandfather's was, but as it is supposed by that poison which he had prepared for others, wherein they report him a rare artist.

I am not bound to give credit to all vulgar relations, or to the libels of his time ... but which binds me to think him no good man amongst other things of known truth, is that of my Lord of Essex his death in Ireland, and the marriage of his Lady, which I forbear to press, in regard he is long since dead, and others living whom it may concern.

To take him in the observation of his letters and writings, which should best set him off, for such as have fallen into my hands, I never yet saw a style or phrase more seemingly religious, and fuller of the strains of devotion, and were they not sincere, I doubt much of his well-being, and I fear he was too well seen in the aphorisms, and principles of Nicolas the Florentine, and in the reaches of Caesar Borgia. . . .

He was sent Governor by the Queen to the revolted states of Holland, where we read not of his wonders, for they say, he had more of Mercury, than he had of Mars, and that his device might have been without prejudice to the great Caesar, *Veni, vidi, redivi.*

Naunton, *Fragmenta Regalia,* 1641

RICHARD MULCASTER, A TUDOR SCHOOLMASTER

Richard Mulcaster was born [1530?] of an ancient extract in the north; but whether in this county [Westmorland] or Cumberland, I find not decided. From Eton school he went to

Cambridge, where he was admitted into King's College, 1548; but, before he graduated, removed to Oxford. Here such was his proficiency in learning, that by general consent he was chosen the first master of Merchant Taylors' School in London, which prospered well under his care, as, by the flourishing of Saint John's in Oxford, doth plainly appear.

The Merchant Taylors, finding his scholars so to profit, intended to fix Mr Mulcaster at his desk to their school, till death should remove him. This he perceived, and therefore gave for his motto, *Fidelis servus, perpetuus asinus.* But after twenty-five years he procured his freedom, or rather exchanged his service, being made Master of St Paul's School.

His method of teaching was this. In a morning he would exactly and plainly construe and parse the lessons to his scholars; which done, he slept his hour (custom made him critical to proportion it) in his desk in the school; but woe be to the scholar that slept the while. Awaking, he heard them accurately; and Atropos might be persuaded to pity, as soon as he to pardon, where he found just fault. The prayers of cockering mothers prevailed with him as much as the requests of indulgent fathers, rather increasing than mitigating his severity on their offending child.

In a word he was *plagosus Orbilius;* though it may be truly said (and safely for one out of his school) that others have taught as much learning with fewer lashes. Yet his sharpness was the better endured, because unpartial; and many excellent scholars were bred under him, whereof Bishop Andrewes was most remarkable.

Then quitting that place, he was presented to the rich parsonage of Stanford Rivers in Essex. I have heard from those who have heard him preach, that his sermons were not excellent, which to me seems no wonder: partly because there is a different discipline in teaching children and men; partly because such who make divinity not the choice of their youth, but the refuge of their age, seldom attain to eminency therein.

Thomas Fuller, *The Worthies of England,* 1662.

SIR FRANCIS DRAKE

This General of the Englishmen is a nephew of John Hawkins and is the same who, about five years back, took the port of Nombre de Dios. He is called Francisco Drac, and is a man of about 35 years of age, low of stature, with a fair beard, and is

FRANCISCVS DRAECK NOBILISSIMVS EQVES ANGLIÆ AN ÆT SVÆ 43

Habes Lector candide fortiß ac inuictiß Ducis Draeck ad viuum Imaginem qui toto terrarum orbe, duorum annorum, et aestium decem spatio, Zephyris fauen tibus circumduct: Anglium sedes proprias. 4. Cal Octob: anno à partu Virginis 1580 reuisit cum antea portu soluisset Id: Decem: anni 1577.

83. Sir Francis Drake, Admiral. 'He was a genius with all the merits and all the faults which go with genius. His intellect was brilliant and bold, his courage invincible, his patriotism deep and fiery. He was an unrivalled sailor — only Nelson is comparable with him ... He was one of the greatest of all naval tacticians ... the first to recognize that the ship was the fighting unit and not the soldiers on board.' C. R. N. Routh.

one of the greatest mariners that sail the seas, both as a navigator and as a commander. His vessel is a galleon of nearly four hundred tons, and is a perfect sailer. She is manned with a hundred men, all of service, and of an age for warfare, and all are as practised therein as old soldiers from Italy could be. Each one takes particular pains to keep his arquebus clean. He treats them with affection, and they treat him with respect. He carries with him nine or ten cavaliers, cadets of English noblemen. These form a part of his council, which he calls together for even the most trivial matter, although he takes advice from no one. But he enjoys hearing what they say and afterwards issues his orders. He has no favourite.

The aforesaid gentleman sits at his table, as well as a Portuguese pilot, whom he brought from England, who spoke not a word during the whole time I was on board. He is served on silver dishes with gold borders and gilded garlands, in which are his arms. He carries all possible dainties and perfumed waters. He said that many of these had been given to him by the Queen.

None of these gentlemen took a seat or covered his head before him, until he repeatedly urged him to do so. This galleon of his carries about thirty heavy pieces of artillery and a great quantity of firearms with the requisite ammunition and lead. He dines and sups to the music of viols. He carries trained carpenters and artisans, so as to be able to careen the ship at any time. Besides being new, the ship has a double lining. I understood that all the men he carries with him receive wages, because, when our ship was sacked, no man dared take anything without his orders. He shows them great favour, but punishes the least fault. He also carries painters who paint for him pictures of the coast in its exact colours. . . .

I managed to ascertain whether the General was well liked. and all said that they adored him.

Letter of Don Francisco da Zarate to Don Martin Enriquez,
Viceroy of New Spain, in New Light on Drake

SIR WALTER RALEIGH

He had in the outward man a good presence, in a handsome and well compacted person, a strong natural wit, and a better judgement, with a bold and plausible tongue, whereby he could

84. Sir Walter Raleigh, poet, historian, courtier, explorer, adventurer, sailor, soldier. He found favour at Elizabeth's court; began colonisation of Virginia in 1584; introduced potatoes and tobacco to England; served in defence against Spain; found gold in Guiana. He had a fearlessly independent mind, was restlessly energetic. He was sent to the Tower in the reign of James I and there wrote his *History of the World*. After another voyage he was tried and executed to conciliate Spain.

set out his parts to the best advantage, and these he had by the
adjuncts of some general learning, which by diligence he
enforced to a great augmentation, and perfection, for he was an
indefatigable reader, where by sea or land, and one of the best
observers both of men and of the times. And I am somewhat
confident, that among the second causes of his growth, that
there was variance between him and my Lord General Gray, in
his second descent into Ireland, was principal for it, drew them
both over to the Council table there to plead their own causes,
where what advantage he had in the case, in controversy I know
not, but he had much the better in the manner of telling his tale,
insomuch as the Queen and the Lords took no slight mark of the
man, and his parts for from thence he came to be known, and to
have access to the Lords. And then we are not to doubt how such
a man would comply to progression, and whether or no my Lord
of Leicester had then cast a good word for him to the Queen,
which would have done him no harm, I do not determine, but
trust it is, he had gotten the Queen's ear in a trice, and she
began to be taken with his election, and loved to hear his reasons
to her demands. And the truth is she took him for a kind of
oracle, which nettled them all, yea those that he relied on,
began to take this his sudden favour for an alarm, and to be
sensible of their own supplantation, and to project him, which
made him shortly after sing, 'Fortune my foe, why dost thou
frown', so that finding his favour declining, and falling
into a recess, he undertook a new peregrination to leave that
terra infirma of the Court for that of the waves, and by declining
himself, and by absence to expel his and the passion of his
enemies, which in Court was a strange device of recovery, but
that he then knew there was some ill office done him, yet he
durst not attempt to remedy it, otherwise than by going aside
thereby to teach envy a new way of forgetfulness, and not so
much as to think of him. Howsoever he always had it in mind,
never to forget himself, and his device took so well and in his
return he came in as rams do, by going backward with the
greater strength, and so continued to the last, great in her
favour and Captain of her Guard, where I must leave him, but
with this observation, though he gained much at the Court he
took it not out of the Exchequer, or merely out of the Queen's
purse but by his wit and by the help of the prerogative. For the
Queen was never profuse in delivering out of her treasure, but
paid most and many of her servants part in money, and the rest
with grace, which as the case stood, was then taken for good

payment leaving the arrears of recompense due for their merit, to her great successor, which paid them all with advantage.

Naunton, Fragmenta Regalia, 1641

WILLIAM SHAKESPEARE

I remember, the Players have often mentioned it as an honour to Shakespeare, that in his writing, (whatsoever he penned) he never blotted out line. My answer hath been, would he had blotted a thousand. Which they thought a malevolent speech. I had not told posterity this, but for their ignorance, who choose that circumstance to commend their friend by, wherein he most faulted. And to justify mine own candour, (for I loved the man, and do honour his memory (on this side Idolatry) as much as any.) He was (indeed) honest, and of an open, and free nature: had an excellent fantasy, brave notions, and gentle expressions: wherein he flowed with that facility, that sometime it was necessary he should be stopped: *Sufflaminandus erat;* as Augustus said of Haterius. His wit was in his own power; would the rule of it had been so too. Many times he fell into those things, could not escape laughter: As when he said in the person of Caesar, one speaking to him; *Caesar thou dost me wrong.* He replied: *Caesar did never wrong, but with just cause:* and such like; which were ridiculous. But he redeemed his vices with his virtues. There was ever more in him to be praised, than to be pardoned.

Ben Jonson, Discoveries, 1640

PERKIN WARBECK

On the 19th inst., by Vadino Gambarana of Saona, I advised your Excellency of the coming of Perkin to this realm and what was the general opinion about it; and on the 25th by way of the Genoese at Bruges, I sent word that Perkin had fled. Now with the arrival of the Venetian packet I will send a detailed account of what has taken place according to the relation of Messer Fra Zoan Antonio de Carbonariis of Milan, who was actually present in the city of Exeter.

On the 6th of this month Perkin landed in Cornwall at a port called Mount St. Michael with three small ships and about three hundred persons of various nationalities, who had followed him for some time before. As he had so few with him, it is thought that the Cornishmen must have invited him. In fact eight thousand peasants were forthwith in arms with him, although ill disciplined and without any gentlemen, who form the governing class of England.

To the Reader.

This Figure, that thou here feeſt put,
  It was for gentle Shakeſpeare cut;
Wherein the Grauer had a ſtrife
  with Nature, to out-doo the life:
O, could he but haue drawne his wit
  As well in braſſe, as he hath hit
Hisface ; the Print would then ſurpaſſe
  All, that was euer writ in braſſe.
But, ſince he cannot, Reader, looke
  Not on his Picture, but his Booke.
                                B. I.

85. Two portraits of Shakespeare are accepted as authentic, the bust in Stratford Church, and the frontispiece to the folio of 1623, shown above, engraved by Martin Droeshout (who may not have known Shakespeare personally). Title page to the Shakespeare First Folio of 1623.

They proclaimed Perkin as King Richard, and they paid for the victuals with which the commune provided them, as they had done when the Cornishmen were routed at London. They marched towards his Majesty, who did not hear of this movement until the 10th. . . .

Without waiting the royal command, the Earl of Devon, a lord of the County, opposed these people with about 1,500 men, but owing to the multitude of the enemy he withdrew to the city of Exeter. Perkin arrived at that place at the 22nd hour of the 17th of the month, and being refused admission, he began the attack on two of the gates. He burned one, but the Earl drove him off with stones, so that at the second hour on the following day Perkin asked for a truce for six hours. This was granted on the understanding that no one of Exeter should be allowed to follow him. The moment the truce was made, Perkin departed and went to a village called Minet, ten miles from Exeter, where he passed the night. On the 19th he came to another good village called Taunton, twenty-four miles from Exeter, and stayed there until the 21st. Among other things he published certain apostolic bulls affirming that he was the son of King Edward and that he meant to coin money and give money to all.

In the meantime his Majesty had sent the Lord Chamberlain against him with a good number of men, and announced that he would pardon all who laid down their arms. Accordingly the numbers with Perkin constantly lessened. He began to declare that he had a close understanding with some lords of the realm. As the bridges on the straight road were cut, he proposed to turn somewhat to the right and take another way. Subsequently at the fourth hour of the night, he silently departed from the camp with some ten thousand persons and at dawn the next morning the unfortunate Cornishmen discovered their plight and took to flight, to such an extent that by the third hour of the day not one was left in Taunton. . . .

A letter from Raimondo de Soncino to the Duke of Milan,
30 September 1497

ROBERT DEVEREUX, EARL OF ESSEX

My Lord of Essex, even of those that truly loved and honoured him, was noted for too bold an engrosser, both of fame and favour, and of this . . . I shall present the truth of a passage yet in memory.

My Lord of Mountjoy, who was another child of her [the Queen's] favour, being newly come and then but Sir Charles

Blount . . . had the good fortune to run one day very well at the Tilt and the Queen was therewith so well pleased, that she sent him in token of her favour a Queen at Chess in gold, richly enamelled which his servants had the next day fastened unto his arm, with a crimson ribbon, which my Lord of Essex, as he passed through the Privy Chamber, espying with his cloak cast under his arm, the better to command it to the view, enquired what it was, and for what cause there fixed: Sir Fulke Greville told him it was the Queen's favour, which the day before, and next after the Tilting, she had sent him; whereat my Lord of Essex in a kind of emulation and as though he would have limited her favour said, 'Now I perceive every fool must have a favour'. This bitter and public affront came to Sir Charles Blount's ear, at which he sent him the challenge which was accepted by my Lord and they met near Marybone Park [Marylebone], where my Lord was hurt in the thigh, and disarmed; the Queen missing of the men was very curious to learn the truth but at last it was whispered out, she swore by God's death it was fit that some one or other should take him down and teach him better manners, otherwise there would be no rule with him . . .

Now . . . at last, and with much ado, he obtained his own ends [the command in Ireland], and therewith his fatal destruction, leaving the Queen and the Court, where he stood impregnable and firm in her grace, to men that had long fought, and waited their times to give him the trip, and could never find any opportunity but this of his absence, and of his own creation, and those are true observations of his appetite and inclinations, which were not of any true proportion, but hurried and transported with an over-desire and thirstiness for fame, and that deceitful fame of popularity. And to help on his catastrophe, I observed likewise two sorts of people that had a hand in his fall: first was the soldiery which all flock unto him, as it were foretelling a mortality, and are commonly of blunt and too rough counsels . . . the other sort were of his family, his servants and his own creatures such as were bound by safety and obligations of fidelity, to have looked better after the steering of that boat, wherein they themselves were carried and not to have suffered it to fleet and run on ground with those empty sails of tumor of popularity and applause. Methinks one honest man or other, which had but the brushing of his clothes, might have whispered in his ear, My lord look to it, this multitude that follows you, will either devour you or undo you, do not strive to

over-rule all, for it will cost hot water, and it will procure envy,
and if your genius must have it so, let the Court and the Queen's
presence be your station, for your absence must undo you, but
as I have said, they have sucked too much of their Lord's milk,
and instead of withdrawing, they drew the coals of his ambition
and infused into him too much of the spirit of glory . . . There
were some of insufferable natures about him, that towards his
last gave desperate advice such as his integrity abhorred and his
fidelity forbade.

                              Naunton, *Fragmenta Regalia*, 1641

Historic Events

THE DIVORCE PROCEEDINGS ANNOUNCED TO THE HOUSE OF COMMONS BY THE LORD CHANCELLOR, 30 MARCH, 1531

'You of this worshipful House,

'I am sure you be not so ignorant but you know well that the Kyng our Sovereign Lorde hath maried his Brother's Wyfe; for she was both wedded and bedded with his Brother Prince Arthur, and therefore you may surely say that he hath maried his Brother's Wyfe, if this Mariage be good as so many Clerkes do doubt; Wherefore the Kyng, like a virtuous Prince, willing to be satisfied in his Conscience, and also for the Suretie of his Realme, hath, with great Deliberation, consulted with great Clerkes, and hath sent my Lorde of London, here present, to the chiefe Universities of all Christendome, to know their Opinion and Judgment in that Behalf. And altho' the Universities of Cambryge and Oxforde had been sufficient to discusse the Cause, yet, because they be in this Realme, and to avoyde all Suspicion of Partiality, he hath sent into the Realme of France, Italy, the Pope's Dominions, and Venetians, to know their Judgment in that Behalf; which have concluded, written, and sealed their Determinations, accordyng as you shall heare red.' Then Sir Brian Tuke took out of a Box twelve Writings sealed, and read them before the House as they were translated into the English Tongue.

Next follows, in Hall, the Judgment of the Foreign Universities; which were those of Paris, Orleans, Anjou, Bruges, Bononia, and Padua, at Length. These being somewhat foreign to our Purpose, we shall therefore content ourselves with observing, That the Question put to these learned Societies was, Whether the Pope's Dispensation for a Brother's marrying a Brother's Wife, after Consummation with her former Husband, was valid or not? Which, as the Question was stated, they all gave in the Negative.

These Determinations being all read in the House, there were produced abouve an Hundred different Books, wrote by foreign Civilians and Divines, against the Lawfulness of the Marriage; which, says Hall, because the Day was far spent, were not read. Then the Chancellor again said, 'Now you of this Commen House may reporte in your Countries what you have seene and heard; and then all Men shall openly perceyve that the Kyng hath not attempted this Matter of Wyll or Pleasure, as some Straungers reporte, but only for the Discharge of his Conscience, and Suretie of the Succession of his Realme. This is the Cause of our Repayre hyther to you, and now we wyl departe.'

Parliamentary History

KETT'S REBELLION, 1549
Here are the demands of the Rebels.

We certify your grace that whereas the lords of the manors hath been charged with certe free rente, the same lords hath sought means to charge the freeholders to pay the same rent, contrary to right.

We pray your Grace that no lord of no manor shall common upon the commons. . . .

We pray that reed ground and meadow ground may be at such price as they were in the first year of King Henry VII.

We pray that all marshes that are holden of the King's Majesty by free rent or of any other, may be again at the price that they were in the first year of King Henry VII. . . .

We pray that all marshes that are holden of the King's Majesty by free rent or of any other, may be again at the price that they were in the first year of King Henry VII. . . .

We pray that all freeholders and copyholders may take the profits of all commons, and there to common, and the lords not to common nor take profits of the same. . . .

We pray that copyhold land that is unreasonable rented may go as it did in the first year of King Henry VII, and that at the death of a tenant or at a sale the same lands to be charged with an easy fine as a capon or a reasonable [sum] of money for a remembrance. . . .

We pray that all bond men may be made free, for God made all free with his precious blood-shedding. . . .

We pray that your Grace to give licence and authority by your gracious commission under your great seal to such commissioners as your poor commons hath chosen, or as many of them as your Majesty and your council shall 'appoint and think meet, for to redress and reform all such good laws, statutes, proclamations, and all other your proceedings, which hath been hidden by your justices of your peace, sheriffs, escheators, and other your officers from your poor commons, since the first year of the reign of your noble grandfather King Henry VII.

We pray that those your officers that had offended your Grace and your commons, and so proved by the complaint of your poor commons, do give unto these poor men so assembled iiijd. every day so long as they have remained there.

We pray that no lord, knight, esquire nor gentleman do graze nor feed any bullocks or sheep if he may spend forty pounds a year by his lands, but only for the provision of his house.

By me, Robt. Kett

  ,, ,, Thomas Aldryche   Thomas Cod

Harleian MSS. 304 f.75. Printed by Russell,
Ket's Rebellion in Norfolk

THE BURNING OF THOMAS CRANMER, 1555

Then rising he [Archbishop Cranmer] said, 'Every man desireth, good people, at the time of their deaths to give some good exhortation, that other may remember after their deaths and be the better thereby. So I beseech God grant me grace that I may speak something at this my departing, whereby God may be glorified and you edified. . . .

And now I come to the great thing that troubleth my conscience more than any other thing that ever I said or did in my life; and that is, the setting abroad of writings contrary to the truth. Which here now I renounce and refuse as things written with my hand, contrary to the truth which I have in my heart, and writ for fear of death and to save my life, if it might be: and that is all such bills which I have written or signed with mine own hand since my degradation, wherein I have written many things untrue. And forasmuch as my hand offended in writing contrary to my heart, therefore my hand shall first be punished. For if I may come to the fire, it shall be first burned. And as for the Pope, I refuse him as Christ's enemy and Antichrist, with all his false doctrine.'

And here being admonished of his recantation and dissembling, he said, 'Alas, my lord. I have been a man that all my life loved plainness and never dissembled till now against the truth, which I am most sorry for.' He added hereunto, that for the Sacrament, he believed as he had taught in his book against the Bishop of Winchester. And here he was suffered to speak no more.

Then he was carried away, and a great number that did run to see him go so wickedly to his death, ran after him, exhorting him, while time was, to remember himself. And one Friar John, a godly and well-learned man, all the way travelled with him to reduce him. But it would not be. What they said in particular I cannot tell, but the effect appeared in the end. For at the stake he professed that he died in all such opinions as he had taught, and oft repented him of his recantation.

Coming to the stake with a cheerful countenance and willing mind, he put off his garments with haste, and stood upright in his shirt. And a Bachelor of Divinity, named Elye, of Brasenose College, laboured to convert him to his former recantation, with the two Spanish friars. But when the friars saw his constancy, they said in Latin one to another. 'Let us go from him, we ought not to be nigh him, for the devil is with him.' But the Bachelor in Divinity was more earnest with him. Unto whom he answered, that as concerning his recantation he repented it right sore, because he knew it to be against the truth, with other words more. Whereupon the Lord Williams cried, 'Make short, make short.' Then the bishop took certain of his friends by the hand. But the bachelor of divinity refused to take him by the hand, and blamed all others that did so, and said he was sorry that ever he came in his company. And yet again he required him to agree to his former recantation. And the bishop answered (shewing his hand), 'This is the hand that wrote it, and therefore shall it suffer first punishment.'

Fire being now put to him, he stretched out his right hand and thrust it into the flame, and held it there a good space, before the fire came to any other part of his body, where his hand was seen of every man sensibly burning, crying with a loud voice, 'This hand hath offended.' As soon as the fire was got up, he was very soon dead, never stirring or crying all the while.

His patience in the torment, his courage in dying, if it had been taken either for the glory of God, the wealth of his country, or the testimony of truth, as it was for a pernicious error and subversion of true religion, I could worthily have commended the example and matched it with the fame of any father of ancient time: but seeing that not the death, but the cause and quarrel thereof, commendeth the sufferer, I cannot but much dispraise his obstinate stubbornness and sturdiness in dying, and specially in so evil a cause. Surely his death much grieved every man, but not after one sort. Some pitied to see his body so tormented with the fire raging upon the silly carcass, that counted not of the folly. Other that passed not much of the body, lamented to see him spill his soul wretchedly, without redemption, to be plagued for ever. His friends sorrowed for love, his enemies for pity, strangers for a common kind of humanity whereby we are bound one to another. Thus I have enforced myself, for your sake, to discourse this heavy narration, contrary to my mind: and being more than half weary, I make a short end, wishing you a quieter life, with less honour and easier death, with more praise. The 23rd of March.

Yours J.A.

A letter signed J.A. in the Harleian MS. 422,
printed in John Strype's *Memorials of Archbishop Cranmer*

THE MURDER OF RIZZIO, 1565

Upon Saturday the 9th of March, conform to the King's ordinance and device, the said Earl of Morton, Lord Ruthven, and Lord Lindsay, having their men and friends in a readiness, abiding the King's advertisement; the King having supped the sooner for the same purpose; and the Queen's Majesty in her cabinet, within her inner-chamber at supper, the King sent for the said Earl, Lords, and their accomplices, and desired them to make haste and come to the Palace, for he should have the door of the privy-chamber open, and should be talking with the Queen before their coming. The said Earl Morton, Lords Ruthven and Lindsay, with their accomplices, entering the Palace by the King's commandment, and the said Earl Morton to the King's outer-chamber, and certain with him; and the said Lord Ruthven the other way, through the King's chamber to the cabinet, up to the privy way to the Queen's chamber, as the King directed them, and through the chamber to the cabinet, where they found her Majesty at supper, at a little table, the Lady Argyll at the one end, and David at the other end, his cap on his head, the King speaking with her Majesty, with his hand about her waist.

The said Lord Ruthven at his entering in, said unto the Queen's Majesty, 'let it please your Majesty that yonder man David come forth of your privy chamber, where he hath been overlong'. The Queen answered, 'what offence hath he done?' Ruthven answered, that he made a greater and more heinous

offence to her Majesty's honour, the King her husband, the
Nobility and the Commonwealth. 'If it please your Majesty, he
hath offended your honour, which I dare not be so bold to
speak of. As to the King your husband's honour, he hath
hindered him of the Crown-Matrimonial, which your Grace
promised him, besides many other things which are not
necessary to be expressed; and hath caused your Majesty to
banish a great part of the Nobility, and to forfeit them, that he
might be made a Lord'. . . .

Then the said Lord Ruthven said to the King, 'Sir, take the
Queen your wife and sovereign to you', who stood all amazed
and wist not what to do. Then her Majesty rose upon her feet,
and stood before David, he holding her Majesty by the plates of
her gown, leaning back over the window, his dagger drawn in
his hand, and Arthur Erskine, and the Abbot of Holyroodhouse,
and the Lord Keith, master of the household, with the French
pothecary; and one of the chamber began to lay hands on the
Lord Ruthven, none of the King's party being there present.
Then the said Lord Ruthven pulled out his dagger, and
defended himself until more came in, and said to them, 'Lay no
hands on me, for I will not be handled.' At the coming in of
others into the cabinet, the said Lord Ruthven put up his
dagger; and with the rushing in of men, the board fell into the
wall, meat and candles being thereon, and the Lady of Argyll
took one of the candles in her hand. At the same instant the
Lord Ruthven took the Queen in his arms and put her into the
King's arms, beseeching her Majesty not to be afraid, for there
was no man there that would do her body any more harm than
they would do their own hearts; and assured her Majesty that all
that was done was the King's own deed. And the remnant of the
gentlemen being in the cabinet took David out of the window,
and after they had him out of the Queen's chamber, the said
Lord Ruthven followed, and bade take him away down to the
King's chamber the privy way; and the said Lord returned to the
cabinet, thinking that the said David had been taken down to the
King's chamber; the press of the people hurled him forth to the
outer-chamber, where there was a great number standing who
were vehemently moved against him, so that they could not
abide any longer, but slew him at the Queen's foredoor in the
other chamber. . . .

and David was thrown down the stairs from the Palace where
he was slain, and brought to the Porter's lodge, who taking off
his clothes said, 'this was his destiny; for upon this chest was his

first bed when he came to this place, and now he lieth a very
niggard and misknown knave'. The King's dagger was found
sticking in his side. The Queen enquired at the King where his
dagger was? who answered that he wist not well. 'Well,' said the
Queen, 'it will be known hereafter.'

The Narrative of Lord Ruthven

THE DEATH OF SIR PHILIP SIDNEY, 1586

Thus they go on, every man in the head of his own troop, and
the weather being misty, they fell unawares upon the enemy,
who had made a very strong stand to receive them, near to the
very walls of Zutphen; by reason of which accident their troops
fell not only unexpectedly to be engaged within the level of the
great shot that played from the ramparts, but more fatally within
shot of their muskets, which were laid in ambush within their
own trenches. . . . Howsoever by this stand, an unfortunate hand
out of those fore-spoken trenches brake the bone of Sir Philip's
thigh with a musket shot. The horse he rode upon was rather
furiously choleric, than bravely proud, and so forced him to
forsake the field, but not his back, as the noblest and fittest bier
to carry a martial commander to his grave. In this sad progress,
passing along by the rest of the army, where his uncle the
General was, and being thirsty with excess of bleeding he called
for drink, which was presently brought him; but as he was
putting the bottle to his mouth, he saw a poor soldier carried
along, who had eaten his last at the same feast, ghastly casting
up his eyes at the bottle; which Sir Philip perceiving, took it
from his head before he drank, and delivered it to the poor man
with these words: 'Thy necessity is yet greater than mine!' And
when he had pledged this poor soldier, he was presently carried
to Arnhem. . . .

The last scene of this tragedy, was the parting between the two
brothers; the weaker showing infinite strength in suppressing
sorrow and the stronger infinite weakness in expressing of it. So
far did invaluable worthiness in the dying brother enforce the
living to descend beneath his own worth, and by soundance of
childish tears, bewail the public, in his particular loss. . . . And to
stop his natural torrent of affection in both, [Sir Philip] took his
leave with these admonishing words: 'Love my memory; cherish
my friends; their faith to me may assure you they are honest.
But above all govern your will and affections by the will and
word of your Creator; in me beholding the end of this world,
with all her vanities.' And with this farewell desired the company

to lead him away. Here this noble gentleman ended the too short scene of his life; in which path whosoever is not confident that he walked the next way to eternal rest, will be found to judge uncharitably. . . . For my own part, I confess, in all I have here set down of his worth and goodness, I find myself still short of that honour he deserved, and I desired to do him.

Sir Fulke Greville, Life of Sir Philip Sidney

THE EXECUTION OF MARY, QUEEN OF SCOTS, 1587 (N.S.)

Her prayers being ended, the executioners, kneeling, desired her Grace to forgive them her death: who answered, 'I forgive you with all my heart, for now, I hope, you shall make an end of all my troubles'. Then they, with her two women, helping her up, began to disrobe her of her apparel: then she, laying her crucifix upon the stool, one of the executioners took from her neck the *Agnus Dei*, which she, laying hands off it, gave to one of her women, and told the executioner he should be answered money for it. Then she suffered them, with her two women, to disrobe her of her chain of pomander beads and all other her apparel most willingly, and with joy rather than sorrow, helped to make unready herself, putting on a pair of sleeves with her own hands which they had pulled off, and that with some haste, as if she had longed to be gone.

All this time they were pulling off her apparel, she never changed her countenance, but with smiling cheer she uttered these words. 'that she never had such grooms to make her unready, and that she never put off her clothes before such a company' . . .

This done, one of the women having a Corpus Christi cloth lapped up three-corner-ways, kissing it, put it it over the Q. of Sc. face, and pinned it fast to the caul [the back part of a woman's cap] of her head. Then the two women departed from her, and she kneeling down upon the cushion most resolutely, and without any token or fear of death, she spake aloud this Psalm in Latin, *In Te Domine confido, non confundar in eternam,* etc. Then, groping for the block, she laid down her head, putting her chin over the block with both hands, which, holding there still, had been cut off had they not been espied. Then lying upon the block most quietly, and stretching out her arms cried, *In manus tuas, Domine,* etc. three or four times. Then she, lying very still upon the block, one of the executioners holding her

86. In the sixteenth and seventeenth centuries 'beheading was a privilege'. This pen-and-ink sketch shows the arrangements for the execution of Mary, Queen of Scots at Fotheringhay Castle, 8 February 1587. First we see the Queen's entry, top left; then taking off her cloak and ruff, front of platform; and behind her, on the right, the executioner preparing for the deed.

Dressed in red satin she died with dignity and courage.

slightly with one of his hands, she endured two strokes of the other executioner with an axe, she making very small noise or none at all, and not stirring any part of her from the place where she lay: and so the executioner cut off her head, saving one little gristle, which being cut asunder, he lift up her head to the view of all the assembly and bade 'God save the Queen'. Then, her dress of lawn falling off from her head, it appeared as grey as one of threescore and ten years old, polled very short, her face in a moment being so much altered from the form she had when she was alive, as few could remember her by her dead face. Her lips stirred up and down a quarter of an hour after her head was cut off. . . .

Then one of the executioners, pulling off her garters, espied her little dog which was crept under her clothes, which could not be gotten forth but by force, yet afterward would not depart from the dead corpse, but came and lay between her head and her shoulders, which being imbrued with her blood was carried away and washed.

Report to Lord Burghley and endorsed in his hand
8th Feb. 1586 (O.S.), Printed in Ellis,
Original letters, Second Series

THE SPANISH ARMADA, 1588

Elizabeth's speech to her troops at Tilbury, one of the greatest in our history. This was on 18th of August when the English were not convinced that the Armada had been defeated.

My loving people, we have been persuaded by some that are careful of our safety, to take heed how we commit ourselves to armed multitudes, for feat of treachery. But I assure you, I do not desire to live to distrust my faithful and loving people. Let tyrants fear. I have always so behaved myself that, under God, I have placed my chiefest strength and safeguard in the loyal hearts and good will of my subjects; and therefore I am come amongst you, as you see, at this time, not for my recreation and disport, but being resolved, in the midst and heat of the battle, to live or die amongst you all, to lay down for my God, and for my kingdom, and for my people, my honour and my blood even in the dust. I know I have the body of a weak and feeble woman, but I have the heart and stomach of a King, and of a King of England too, and think foul scorn that Parma or Spain, or any prince of Europe should dare to invade the borders of my realm; to which, rather than any dishonour shall grow by me, I myself will take up arms. I myself will be your general, judge, and rewarder of every one of your virtues in the field. I know, already for your forwardness you have deserved rewards and crowns; and we do assure you, in the word of a prince, they shall be duly paid you.

Warfare and Insurrection

THE PILGRIMAGE OF GRACE, 1536

All these things [the insurrection in Lincolnshire] thus ended, the country appeased and all things in quiet, the King's Majesty returned and brake up his army.

But see! even within six days following was the King truly certified that there was a new insurrection made by the Northern men, which had assembled themselves into a huge and great army of warlike men, and well appointed both with captains, horse, harness and artillery to the number of 40,000 men, which had encamped themselves in Yorkshire. And these men had each of them to other bound themselves by their oath to be faithful and obedient to his captain; they also declared by their proclamations solemnly made that this their insurrection, should extend no farther but only to the maintenance and defence of the faith of Christ and deliverance of Holy Church, sore decayed and oppressed, and also for the furtherance as well of private as public matters in the realm, touching the wealth of all the King's poor subjects. They named this, their seditious and traitorous voyage, an holy and blessed pilgrimage. They also had certain banners in the field, whereupon was painted Christ hanging on the Cross on the one side and chalice with a painted cake on it on the other side, with divers other banners of like hypocrisy and feigned sanctity. The soldiers also had a certain cognisance or badge embroidered or set upon the sleeves of their coats, which was the similitude of the five wounds of Christ, and in the midst thereof was written the name of our Lord; and this, the rebellious garrison of Satan, with his false and counterfeited signs of holiness set forth and decked themselves, only to delude and deceive the simple and ignorant people.

Edward Hall, *Chronicle*, 1548

WYATT'S REBELLION, 1554

In the mean season, to wit the third day of February, about three of the clock in the afternoon, Sir Thomas Wyatt and the Kentishmen marched forward from Deptford towards London with five ensigns, being by estimation about two thousand; and so soon as their coming was perceived, there were shot off out of the White Tower, six or eight shots, but missed them — sometimes shooting over and sometimes short. After knowledge thereof was once had in London, forthwith the drawbridge was cut down, and the bridge gates shut. The mayor and sheriffs, harnessed, commanded each man to shut up their shops and windows and to be ready harnessed at their doors, what chance soever might happen. By this time was Wyatt entered into Kent Street and so by St George's Church into Southwark.

On Shrove Tuesday, the sixth of February, Sir Thomas Wyatt removed out of Southwark toward Kingston, where the bridge was broken and kept on the other side by two hundred men; wherefore Wyatt caused two pieces of ordnance to be laid on the end of the bridge, which so frightened them on the other side that they durst not abide; then caused he three or four of his soldiers to leap into the Thames and to swim to the other side; and they loosed the western barges which lay there tied, and so brought them over; and by that means he passed the water and came that night almost to Brainford, or ever they were described by the Queen's scouts.

Wyatt hearing the Earl of Pembroke was come into the fields, stayed at Knightsbridge until day, his men being very weary with marching that night and the day before, and also partly feebled and faint, having received small sustenance since their coming out of Southwark restless. There was no small ado in London, and likewise the Tower made great preparation of defence. By ten of the clock the Earl of Pembroke had set his troop of horsemen on the hill in the highway above the new bridge over against St James'; his footmen were set in two battles, somewhat lower and nearer Charing Cross, at the lane turning down by the brick wall from Islingtonward, where he had set also certain other horsemen and he had planted his ordnance upon the hillside. ... The Queen's whole battle of footmen standing still, Wyatt passed along by the wall toward Charing Cross, where the said horsemen that were there, set upon part of them, but were soon forced back. Wyatt with his men marched still forward all along to Temple Bar, and so through Fleet Street, till he came to the *Belle Sauvage*, an inn nigh unto Ludgate, without resistance,

his men going not in any good order or array, most with their
swords drawn. Some cried: 'Queen Mary hath granted our
request, and given us pardon!' Others said: 'The Queen hath
pardoned us!'

Thus some of Wyatt's men — some say it was Wyatt himself —
came even to Ludgate and knocked, calling to come in, saying,
there was Wyatt, whom the Queen had granted to have their
requests; but the Lord William Howard stood at the gate and
said: 'Avaunt, traitor! thou shalt not come in here.' Wyatt a while
stayed and rested him upon a stall over against the *Belle Sauvage*
gate, and at the last seeing he could not get into the city, and
being deceived by the aid he hoped for, returned back again, till
he came to Temple Bar, where a herald came and said to Master
Wyatt: 'Sir, you were best by my counsel to yield; you see this
day is gone against you.' Wyatt, herewith being somewhat
astonished, said: 'Well, if I shall needs yield, I will yield me to a
gentleman.' And to him Sir Maurice Berkeley came straight and
bade him leap up behind him; and another took Thomas
Cobham and William Kennet, and so carried them behind them
upon their horses to the Court.

John Stow, *Chronicles of England,* 1580

THE LOSS OF CALAIS, 1558

On Wednesday [5th January], the enemy continued their battery
on the town, without great hurt done, because they could not
beat the foot of the wall, for that the *contremure* was of a good
height, and we reinforced the breach, in the night, with timber,
wool, and other matter sufficiently; and we looked that the
enemy would have attempted the assault the same evening;
whereupon I caused two flankers to be made ready, and also
placed two bombards, by the help of the soldiers, appointing
weapons and fireworks to be in readiness at the said breach. At
which time, my Lord commanded the soldiers of the garrison to
keep their ordinary wards, and Master Grimston to the breach
with the residue of the best soldiers. And then my Lord
exhorted all men to fight, with other good words as in such cases
appertaineth. And my Lord told me, divers times, that 'although
there came no succour; yet he would never yield, nor stand to
answer the loss of such a town.'

On Thursday, began one other battery to the Castle; which
being a high and weak wall without ramparts, was made
saultable the same day. Whereupon, the Captain of the Castle
desired some more help to defend this breach, or else to know

what my Lord thought best in that behalf. Then, after long debating, my Lord determined to have the towers overthrown, which one Saulle took upon him to do; notwithstanding, I said openly that 'if the Castle were abandoned, it should be the loss of the Town.'

The same night, my Lord appointed me to be at the breach of the town with him: and, about eight of the clock, the enemy waded over the haven, at the low water, with certain harquebussiers, to view the breaches; and coming to the Castle, found no resistance, and so entered. Then the said Saulle failed to give fire unto the train of powder.

Then my Lord, understanding that the enemy were entered into the Castle, commanded me to give order for battering of the Castle: whereupon incontinent there were bent three cannons and one saker before the gate, to beat the bridge; which, being in the night, did not greatly annoy.

The same time, Master Marshall with divers soldiers, came towards the Castle, lest the enemy should enter the town also. And after we had skirmished upon the bridge, seeing no remedy to recover the Castle, we did burn and break the said bridge: and there was a trench immediately cast before the Castle, which was only help at that time.

Within one hour after, upon a necessity of things [my Lord] determined to send a trumpet with a herald, declaring that 'If the Frenchmen would send one gentleman, then he would send one other in gage'. Whereupon my Lord sent for me, and commanded that I should go forth of the town for the same purpose; wherein I desired his Lordship that he would send some other, and rather throw me over the walls. Then he spake likewise to one Windebanke, and to Massingberd, as I remember, which were both to go unto such service.

Then my Lord sent for me again, in Peyton's house; and being eftsoons commanded by the Council there, I went forth with a trumpet, and received in a French gentleman: who, as I heard, was brought to my Lord Deputy's house, and treated upon some articles; which were brought, within one hour, by one Hall, merchant of the staple.

Then Monsieur D'Andelot entered the town with certain French gentlemen; and the said Hall and I were brought to Monsieur De Guise, who lay in the sand hills by Rysbank, and there the said Hall delivered a bill: we were sent to Monsieur D'Estree's tent.

The Friday after [7th January], Monsieur D'Estrees told me

that Lord Deputy had agreed to render the town with loss of all the goods, and fifty prisoners to remain.

By John Highfield, Master of the Ordnance at Calais

THE REBELLION OF THE CATHOLIC NORTHERN EARLS, 1569
Letter written by Sir George Bowes to William Cecil, Lord Burghley, 14 December 1569

It may please your honourable mastership: yesternight I received a letter from the Queen's Majesty, of the 26th of Nov. last, with another letter from you of the same date ... being then commanded by her Grace's several commissions to me and others direct, to levy power, to be in readiness to attend upon the Lord Lieutenant, to suppress this rebellion, I had gathered together both horsemen and also footmen, and keeping them at Barnard Castle with me, to repair to the Lord Lieutenant upon his Lordship's call, as he had directed me. I was, in the meantime, besieged by the rebels, and continuing there in straight siege, with very hard diet and great want of bread, drink and water, which was our only drink, save I mixed it with some wine.

I found the people in the Castle in continual mutinies, seeking not only by great numbers to leap the walls and run to the rebels, but also by all means to betray the piece, and with open force to deliver it and all in it, to the rebels. So far, as in one day and night, two hundred and twenty-six men leaped over the walls and opened the gates and went to the enemy, of which number thirty-five broke their necks, legs or arms in the leaping. Upon which especial extremities, and that day our water that we had, by the intelligence of them that fled from us, being straight or taken away, and by other great occasions, I was forced, by composition offered, to leave the piece, taking with me all the men, armour, weapons and horses, leaving my household stuff, which I made no account of in this time of service, though the value were great, so as the enemies received only the bare piece and stuff aforesaid, which, by the causes aforesaid, I could hold no longer. And I am come with my whole number, which this day will be three hundred horse and one hundred footmen, to the Lo. Lieutenant to serve her Highness with all my force and ready heart, trusting it will please her Grace's goodness to accompt in good part these my doings, intended only to save her Grace's good subjects from the force of the rebels, and to bring them again in place of service rather than to preserve my life, the danger whereof shall never draw me any whit back from her Highness' service with my full duty. . . . At my coming abroad, my storers and keepers of my houses repaired to me with the same speech that Job's servants to him (save only my children): for I am utterly spoiled of all my goods, both within and without: my houses fully defaced by pulling away of the doors, windows, irons of the windows, ceiling, and all my brew vessels and other vessels and chimneys appertaining to my kitchen, so that now I possess nothing but my horse, armour and weapon brought out from Barnard Castle, which I more esteem than twenty times so much of other things, for that by it I am enabled to serve my good Queen, whom God preserve, and I weigh not all my losses. And thus I pray God preserve you.

From Sysaye the 14th of December, 1569.

Memorials of the Rebellion of 1569

ARMOUR AND AMMUNITION

In times past the chief force of England consisted in their long bows. But now we have in manner generally given over that kind

87. Tudor bow-men and a halberdier.

of artillery, and for long bows indeed do practice to short compass for our pastime: which kind of shooting can never yield any smart stroke, nor beat down our enemies, as our countrymen were wont to do at every time of need.

Certes, the Frenchmen deriding our new archery in respect of their corselets, will not let, in open skirmish, if any leisure serve to turn up their tails and cry 'Shoot English!' and all because our strong shooting is decayed and laid in bed. ... So our countrymen wax skilful in sundry other points, as in shooting in small pieces, the caliver, the handling of the pike, in the several uses whereof they are become very expert.

Our armour differeth not from that of other nations, and therefore consisteth of corselets, almaine rivets, shirts of mail, jacks quilted and covered over with leather, fustian, or canvas, over thick plates of iron that are sewed in the same, and of which there is no town or village that hath not her convenient furniture. The said armour and munition likewise is kept in one several place of every town, appointed by the consent of the whole parish, where it is always ready to be had and worn within an hour's warning ... Certes there is almost no village, so poor in England (be it never so small) that hath not sufficient furniture in a readiness to set forth three or four soldiers, as one archer, one gunner, one pike, and a billman at the least ... so that, it shall be impossible for the sudden enemy to find us unprovided ...

The names of our greatest ordinance are commonly these: *Robinet*, whose weight is two hundred pounds; and it hath one inch and a quarter within the mouth; *Falcon*, hath eight hundred pounds, and two inches and a half within the mouth; *Cannon*, seven thousand pounds, and seven inches within the mouth; *Basilisk*, nine thousand pounds, eight inches and three quarters within the mouth ...

Seldom shall you see any of my countrymen above eighteen or twenty years old to go without a dagger at the least at his back or by his side, although they be aged burgesses or magistrates of any city who in appearance are most exempt from brabling and contention. Our nobility wear commonly swords or rapiers with their daggers, as doth every common serving man also that followeth his lord and master.

Finally no man travelleth by the way without his sword or some such weapon.

William Harrison, *Description of England*, 1587

SOLDIERS' PAY, 1598

The establishment was signed by the Queen the four and twenty of March, being the last day (after the English account) of the year 1598.

It contained: first the pay of the chief officers in the Army: the Lord Lieutenant General ten pound a day; the Lieutenant of the Army three pound a day; the General of the Horse forty shillings a day; the Marshal of the Camp thirty shillings a day; the Sergeant Major twenty shillings a day; the Lieutenant of the Horse twenty shillings a day; the Quartermaster twenty shillings a day; the Judge Marshal twenty shillings a day; the Auditor General thirteen shillings four pence a day; the Controller General of the victuals ten shillings a day; the Lieutenant of the Ordnance ten shillings a day; the Surveyor six shillings eight pence; two clerks of Munitions each five shillings a day; four Corporals of the field six shillings eight pence a day a piece; one Commissary of victuals eight shillings, and three other, each six shillings a day; the Carriage Master six shillings eight pence a day; and twenty Colonels, each ten shillings a day . . .

It contained further the pay of thirteen hundred horse, divided into six and twenty bands each band having a Captain at four shillings a day, a Lieutenant at two shillings six pence a day, a Cornet at two shillings a day, and fifty horsemen each at fifteen pence a day . . .

It contained further the pay of sixteen thousand footmen, distributed into one hundred and sixty bands, each band having a Captain at four shillings a day, a Lieutenant at two shillings a day, an Ensign eighteen pence a day, two Sergeants, a Drum, and a Surgeon, each at twelve pence a day, and ninety-four soldiers . . . at eight pence each by the day . . .

Lastly it contained an extraordinary supply of six thousand pounds to be allowed . . . for spies, guides, messengers, boat-hiring, keeping of prisoners, buildings, reparations, rewards, and like charges.

Fynes Moryson, Itinerary

England and the Sea

DRAKE'S GOLDEN TOOTHPICK, 1573

Our Captain, Francis Drake, had prepared to take his journey for Panama by land; he gave Ellis Hixom charge of his own ship and company, and especially of those Spaniards whom he had put into the great prize, which was hauled ashore to the island, which we termed Slaughter Island (because so many of our men died there), and used as a storehouse for ourselves, and a prison for our enemies.

All things thus ordered, our Captain, conferring with his company, and the chiefest of the Cimaroons*, what provisions were to be prepared for this great and long journey, what kind of weapons, what store of victuals, and what manner of apparel: was especially advised, to carry as great store of shoes as possible he might, by reason of so many rivers with stone and gravel as they were to pass. Which, accordingly providing, prepared his company for that journey, entering it upon Shrove-Tuesday (3rd February, 1573). At what time, there had died twenty-eight of our men, and a few whole men were left aboard with Ellis Hixom to keep the ship, and attend the sick, and guard the prisoners.

At his departure our Captain gave this Master Ellis Hixom, straight charge, in any case not to trust any messenger, that should come in his name with any token, *unless he brought his handwriting*: which he knew could not be counterfeited by the Cimaroons or Spaniards.

After some three weeks' absence, the little band of Englishmen, sick, weary and hungry struggled back to the coast, where their ship was hidden.

From this place within three leagues off the secret port where our ship lay, at our first entrance in the evening, on Saturday (22nd February, 1573), our Captain despatched a Cimaroon with a token and certain order to the Master: who had, these three

*Natives, who helped Drake against the Spaniards.

246

weeks, kept good watch against the enemy, and shifted in the woods for fresh victual, for the relief and recovery of our men left aboard.

As soon as this messenger was come to the shore, calling to our ship, as bringing some news, he was quickly fetched aboard by those which longed to hear of our Captain's speeding; but when he showed the toothpike of gold, which he said our Captain had sent for a token to Ellis Hixom, with charge to meet him at such a river: though the Master knew well the Captain's toothpike; yet by reason of his admonition and caveat (*warning*) given him at parting, he (though he bewrayed no sign of distrusting the Cimaroon) yet stood as amazed, least something had befallen our Captain, otherwise than well. The Cimaroon, perceiving this, told him, that it was night when he was sent away, so that our Captain could not send any letter, but yet with the point of his knife, he wrote something upon the toothpick, 'which,' he said, 'should be sufficient to gain credit to the messenger.'

Thereupon, the Master looked at it, and saw written. *By me, Francis Drake*: wherefore he believed, and according to the message, prepared what provision he could, and repaired to the mouth of the river of Tortugos, as the Cimaroons that went with him then named it.

That afternoon towards three a clock, we were come down to that river, not past half-an-hour before we saw our pinnace ready come to receive us: which was unto us all a double rejoicing: first that we saw them, and next, so soon. Our Captain with all our company praised GOD most heartily, for that we saw our pinnace and fellows again.

Richard Hakluyt, *Sir Francis Drake Revived*, 1589

FROBISHER AMONG THE ICE, 1576

This extract from Hakluyt's Principall Navigations *is Martin Frobisher's search for the North West Passage in America.*

This was a more fearful spectacle for the fleet to behold, for that the outrageous storm which presently followed threatened them the like fortune and danger, For the fleet being thus compassed, as aforesaid, on every side with ice, having left much behind them, through which they passed, and finding more before them, through which it was not possible to pass, there arose a sudden terrible tempest at the south-east, which blowing from the main sea directly upon the place of the Straits, brought together all the ice a-seaboard of us upon our backs, and thereby debarred us of turning back to recover sea-room again; so that being thus compassed with danger on every side, sundry men with sundry devices sought the best way to save themselves. Some of the ships, where they could find a place more clear of ice, and get a little berth of sea-room, did take in their sails, and they lay adrift. Other some fastened and moored anchor upon a great island of ice, and rode under the lee thereof, supposing to be better guarded thereby from the outrageous winds, and the danger of the lesser fleeting ice. And again some were so fast shut up, and compassed in amongst an infinite number of great countries and islands of ice, that they were fain to submit themselves and their ships to the mercy of the unmerciful ice, and strengthened the sides of their ships with junks of cables, beds, masts, planks, and such like, which being hanged overboard on the sides of their ships, might the better defend them from the outrageous sway and strokes of the said ice. But as in greatest distress men of best valour are best to be discerned, so it is greatly worthy commendation and noting with what invincible mind every captain encouraged his company, and with what incredible labour the painful mariners and poor miners, unacquainted with such extremities, to the everlasting renown of our nation, did overcome the brunt of these so great and extreme dangers. For some, even without board upon the ice, and some within board upon the sides of their ships, having poles, pikes, pieces of timber, and oars in their hands, stood almost day and night without any rest, bearing off the force, and breaking the sway of the ice with such incredible pain and peril, that it was wonderful to behold; which otherwise no doubt had stricken quite through and through the sides of their ships, notwithstanding our former provision; for planks of timber of more than three inches thick, and other things of greater force and bigness, by the surging of the sea and billow with the ice, were shivered and cut in sunder, at the sides of our ships, so that it will seem more than credible to be reported of. And yet (that which is more) it is faithfully and plainly to be proved, and that by many substantial witnesses, that our ships, even those of greatest burdens, with the meeting of contrary waves of the sea, were heaved up between islands of ice, a foot well-near out of the sea, above their watermark, having their knees and timbers within board both bowed and broken therewith.

And amidst these extremes, whilst some laboured for defence of the ships, and sought to save their bodies, other some, of more milder spirit, sought to save the soul by devout prayer and meditation to the Almighty; thinking indeed by no other means possible than by a divine miracle to have their deliverance. So that there was none that were either idle, or not well occupied; and he that held himself in best security had, God knoweth, but only bare hope remaining for his best safety. Thus all the gallant fleet and miserable men, without hope of ever getting forth again, distressed with these extremities, remained here all the whole night and part of the next day, excepting four ships, that is, the *Anne Francis*, the *Moon*, the *Francis of Foy*, and the *Gabriel*; which being somewhat a-seaboard of the fleet, and being fast ships by a wind, having a more scope of clear, tried it out, all the time of the storm, under sail, being hardly able to bear a-coast of each other.

And albeit, by reason of the fleeting ice, which was dispersed here almost the whole sea over, they were brought many times to the extremest point of peril, mountains of ice ten thousand times scaping them scarce one inch, which to have stricken had been their present destruction, considering the swift course and way of the ships, and the unwieldiness of them to stay and turn as a man would wish; yet they esteemed it their better safety, with such peril, to seek sea-room, than, without hope of ever getting liberty, to lie striving against the stream, and beating amongst the icy mountains; whose hugeness and monstrous greatness was such that no man could credit but such as, to their pains, saw and felt it. And these four ships by the next day at noon got out to sea, and were first clear of the ice. Who now enjoying their own liberty, began anew to sorrow and fear for their fellows' safeties; and, devoutly kneeling about their mainmast, they gave unto God humble thanks, not only for themselves, but besought Him likewise highly for their friends' deliverance.

Richard Hakluyt, *Principall Navigations,*
Voiages and Discoveries of the English Nation, 1589

A MEETING WITH SIR FRANCIS DRAKE AT SEA

Realejo, Nicaragua, 16th of April, 1579.

I sailed out of the port of Acapulco on the 23rd of March and navigated until Saturday, the fourth of April, on which date, half an hour before dawn, we saw, by moonlight, a ship very close to ours. Our steersman shouted that she was to get out of the way and not come alongside of us. To this they made no answer, pretending to be asleep. The steersman then shouted louder, asking them where their ship hailed from. They answered 'from

Peru', and that she was 'of *Miguel Angel*', which is the name of a well-known captain of that route. . . .

The ship of the adversary carried her bark at her prow as though she were being towed. Suddenly, in a moment, she crossed our poop, ordering us 'to strike sail' and shooting seven or eight arquebuse shots at us.

We thought this as much of a joke as it afterwards turned out to be serious.

On our part there was no resistance, nor had we more than six of our men awake on the whole boat, so they entered our ship with as little risk to themselves as though they were our friends. They did no personal harm to any one, beyond seizing the swords and keys of the passengers. Having informed themselves as to who were on board ship, they ordered me to go in their boat to where their general was — a fact I was glad of, as it appeared to me that it gave me more time in which to recommend myself to God. But in a very short time we arrived where he was, on a very good galleon, as well mounted with artillery as any I have seen in my life.

I found him promenading on deck and, on approaching him, I kissed his hands. He received me with a show of kindness, and took me to his cabin, where he bade me be seated and said: 'I am a friend of those who tell me the truth, but with those who do not I get out of humour. Therefore you must tell me (for this is the best road to my favour) how much silver and gold does your ship carry?' I said to him, 'None'. He repeated his question. I answered, 'None, only some small plates that I use and some cups — that is all that is in her.' He kept silent for a while, then renewing the conversation asked me if I knew Your Excellency, I said, 'Yes'. . . .

This corsair, like a pioneer, arrived two months before he intended to pass through and during that time for many days there were great storms. So it was that one of the gentlemen, whom he had with him, said to him: 'We have been a long while in this strait and you have placed all of us, who follow or serve you, in danger of death. It would therefore be prudent for you to give order that we return to the North Sea, where we have the certainty of capturing prizes, and that we give up seeking to make new discoveries. You see how fraught with difficulties these are.'

This gentleman must have sustained this opinion with more vigour than appeared proper to the General. His answer was that he had the gentleman carried below deck and put in irons.

On another day, at the same hour, he ordered him to be taken out, and to be beheaded in presence of all. [In July 1578 in Port St. Julian, Drake with his own hand executed the man, Thomas Doughty, for stirring up mutiny and treachery.]

The term of his imprisonment was no more than was necessary to substantiate the lawsuit that was conducted against him. All this he told me, speaking much good about the dead man, but adding that he had not been able to act otherwise, because this was what the Queen's service demanded. He showed me the commissions that he had received from her and carried. I tried to ascertain whether any relatives of the dead man had remained on board. They told me that there was only one, who was one of those who ate at his table. During all this time that I was on board, which was fifty-five hours, this youth never left the ship, although all the others did so, in turn. It was not that he was left to guard me. I think that they guarded him.

I managed to ascertain whether the General was well liked, and all said that they adored him.

This is what I was able to find out during the time I spent with him. . . .

A letter from Don Francisco da Zarate to Don Martin Enriquez, Viceroy of New Spain. This extract is taken from an English translation published in *New Light on Drake*

HOW THE ENGLISH EXTENDED TRADE BY SEA AND RIVER

The English also settled through the Muscovite with the Tartars on the banks of the Volga to allow the free passage of their merchandise down the river to the Caspian Sea; whilst the Persian . . . should give them leave to trade and distribute their merchandise, through Media and Persia, in exchange for goods which reach the Persians by the rivers that run from the East Indies to the Caspian Sea. This privilege was granted. . . .

Two years ago they opened up the trade, which they still continue, to the Levant, which is extremely profitable to them, as they take great quantities of tin and lead thither. . . . In order to carry on the trade with more safety and speed . . . [they] requested permission of the Turk to go from Azov by the Don and Port Euxine and sell their goods from Media and Persia by the Caspian Sea and the river Volga to the river Don, the distance between the two rivers at one point not being more than a German league. . . . A depot was thus to be formed to concentrate the trade of the two rivers . . . and to serve as a

point of distribution for goods brought from England, for ...
the whole of the Levant, without their having to pass, as at
present, by Italy.

The Spanish Ambassador, Mendoza, to Philip II, 15 May 1582

THE NAVY

If you regard the form and the assurance from peril, of the sea
and therewithal the strength and nimbleness of such [vessels] as
are made in our time, you shall easily find that ours are of more
value than theirs. For as the greatest vessel is not always the
safest, so that of most huge capacity is not always the aptest to
shift, and brook the seas: as might be seen by the *Great Henry*,
the hugest vessel that ever England framed in our times. Neither
were the ships of old like unto ours in mould and manner of
building above the water (for of low galleys in our seas we make
small account) nor so full of ease within, since time hath
engendered more skill in the wrights, and brought all things to
more perfection than they had in the beginning. ...

The navy of England may be divided into three sorts, of which
the one serveth for the wars, the other for burden, and the third
for fishermen which get their living by fishing on the sea. How
many of the first order are maintained within the realm it
passeth my cunning to express. ... Certes there is no prince in
Europe that hath a more beautiful or gallant sort of ships than
the queen's majesty of England at this present, and those
generally are of such exceeding force that two of them, being
well appointed and furnished as they ought, will not let to
encounter with three or four of those of other countries, and
either bowge them to put them to flight, if they may not bring
them home. ...

The common report that strangers make of our ships amongst
themselves is daily confirmed to be true, which is, that for
strength, assurance, nimbleness, and swiftness of sailing, there
are no vessels in the world to be compared with ours. ...

The queen's highness hath at this present which is the
four-and-twentieth year of her reign, already made and
furnished to the number of four-and-twenty great ships, which
lie for the most part in Gillingham Road, besides three galleys,
of whose particular names and furniture (so far forth as I can
come by them) it shall not be amiss to make report at this time.

*The names of so many ships belonging to her majesty as I could come
by at this present:*

    The Bonadventure.   *Foresight.*

Elizabeth Jonas.	*Swift Suit.*
White Bear.	*Aid.*
Philip and Mary.	*Handmaid.*
Triumph.	*Dreadnought.*
Bull.	*Swallow.*
Tiger.	*Genet.*
Antelope.	*Bark of Bullen.*
Hope.	*Achates.*
Lion.	*Falcon.*
Victory.	*George.*
Mary Rose.	*Revenge.*

Besides these, her grace hath other in hand also. . . . She hath likewise three notable galleys: the *Speedwell* the *Try Right,* and the *Black Galley,* with the sight whereof and the rest of the navy royal, it is incredible to say how greatly her grace is delighted: and not without great cause (I say) since by their means her coasts are kept in quiet and sundry foreign enemies put back, which otherwise would invade us. . . .

If the report of one record be anything at all to be credited, there are 135 ships that exceed 500 ton; topmen under 100 and above forty, 656; hoys, 100; but of hulks, catches, fisherboats and crayres, it lieth not in me to deliver the just account, since they are hardly to come by. . . .

I might take occasion to tell of the notable and difficult voyages made into strange countries by Englishmen, and of their daily success there; but as these things are nothing incident to my purpose, so I surcease to speak of them. . . .

For the journeys also of our ships, you shall understand that a well-builded vessel will run or sail commonly three hundred leagues or nine hundred miles in a week, or peradventure some will go 2,200 leagues in six weeks and a half. . . . There be of them that will be here, at the West Indies, and home again in twelve or thirteen weeks from Colchester, although the said Indies be eight hundred leagues from the cape or point of Cornwall, as I have been informed.

William Harrison, *Description of England,* 1587

SKILFUL TACTICS AGAINST THE ARMADA, 1588

Certainly, he that will happily perform a fight at sea, must be skilful in making choice of vessels to fight in; he must believe that there is more belonging to a good man-of-war upon the waters than great daring; and must know that there is a great deal of difference between fighting loose or at large, and grappling. The guns of a slow ship pierce as well, and make as great holes, as those in a swift. To clap ships together without consideration belongs rather to a madman than to a man of war; for by such an ignorant bravery was Peter Strossie lost at the Azores, when he fought against the Marquis of Santa Cruz. In like sort had the Lord Charles Howard, Admiral of England, been lost in the year 1588, if he had not been better advised than a great many malignant fools were, that found fault with his demeanour. The Spaniards had an army aboard them, and he had none; they had more ships than he had, and of higher building and charging; so that, had he entangled himself with those great and powerful vessels, he had greatly endangered this kingdom of England. For twenty men upon the defences are equal to an hundred that board and enter; whereas then, contrariwise, the Spaniards had an hundred for twenty of ours, to defend themselves withal.

But our admiral knew his advantage, and held it; which had he not done, he had not been worthy to have held his head.

88. The 'Ark Royal', Lord Howard of Effingham's flagship against the Armada. Woodcut, c. 1588. This ship was built by Sir Walter Raleigh for his own use, and sold to the Queen as her flagship against Spain. Wynter, the Vice Admiral, writes from the Downs, 'I pray you tell her Majesty from me that her money was well given for the 'Ark Raleigh' — for I think her the odd ship in all the world for all conditions . . .'

Here to speak in general of sea-fight (for particulars are fitter for private hands than for the press) I say, that a fleet of twenty ships, all good sailers and good ships, have the advantage, on the open sea, of an hundred as good ships and of slower sailing.

Sir Walter Raleigh, *History of the World*

THE LAST OF THE *REVENGE*, 1591

This ship fought fifteen Spanish ships for fifteen hours off Flores.

All the powder of the *Revenge* to the last barrel was now spent, all her pikes broken, forty of her best men slain, and the most part of the rest hurt. In the beginning of the fight she had but one hundred free from sickness, and fourscore and ten sick, laid in hold upon the ballast. A small troop to man such a ship, and a weak garrison to resist so mighty an army. By those hundred all was sustained, the volleys, boardings, and enterings of fifteen ships of war, besides those which beat her at large. On the contrary, the Spanish were always supplied with soldiers brought from every squadron: all manner of arms and powder at will. Unto ours there remained no comfort at all, no hope, no supply of either ships, men, or weapons; the masts all beaten overboard, all her tackle cut asunder, her upper work altogether rased, and in effect evened she was with the water, but the very foundation or bottom of a ship, nothing being left overhead either for fight or defence. Sir Richard [Grenville] finding himself in this distress, and unable any longer to make resistance, commanded the Master-gunner, whom he knew to be a most resolute man, to split and sink the ship; that thereby nothing might remain of glory or victory to the Spaniards, seeing in so many hours' fight, and with so great a navy they were not able to take her, and persuaded the company, or as many as he could induce, to yield themselves unto God, and to the mercy of none else; but as they had like valiant resolute men repulsed so many enemies, they should not now shorten the honour of their nation, by prolonging their own lives for a few hours, or a few days. The Master-gunner readily condescended, and divers others; but the Captain and the Master were of another opinion, and besought Sir Richard to have care of them.

And as the matter was thus in dispute, and Sir Richard refusing to hearken to any of those reasons, the Master of the *Revenge* (while the Captain was unto him the greater party) was convoyed aboard the *General* Don Alonso Bassan. Who finding none over hasty to enter the *Revenge* again, doubting lest Sir Richard would have blown them up and himself, and perceiving by the report of the Master of the *Revenge* his dangerous disposition: yielded that all their lives should be saved, the company sent for England, and the better sort to pay such reasonable ransom as their estate would bear, and in the mean season to be free from galley or imprisonment. To this he so much the rather condescended as well, as I have said, for fear of further loss and mischief to themselves, as also for the desire he had to recover Sir Richard Grenville; whom for his notable valour he seemed greatly to honour and admire.

When this answer was returned, and that safety of life was promised, the common sort being now at the end of their peril, the most drew back from Sir Richard and the Master-gunner, being no hard matter to dissuade men from death to life. The Master-gunner finding himself and Sir Richard thus prevented and mastered by the greater number, would have slain himself with the sword, had he not been by force withheld and locked into his cabin. Then the General sent many boats aboard the *Revenge,* and divers of our men fearing Sir Richard's disposition, stole away aboard the *General* and other ships. Sir Richard, thus overmatched, was sent unto by Alonso Bassan to remove out of the *Revenge,* the ship being marvellous unsavoury, filled with blood and bodies of dead and wounded men like a slaughter house. Sir Richard answered that he might do with his body what he list, for he esteemed it not, and as he was carried out of the ship he swooned, and reviving again desired the company to pray for him. The General used Sir Richard with all humanity, and left nothing unattempted that tended to his recovery, highly commending his valour and worthiness, and greatly bewailed the danger wherein he was, being unto them a rare spectacle, and a resolution seldom approved, to see one ship turn towards so many enemies, to endure the charge and boarding of so many huge Armadoes, and to resist and repel the assaults and entries of so many soldiers. . . .

Sir Richard died, as it is said, the second or third day aboard the *General,* and was by them greatly bewailed. What became of his body, whether it were buried in the sea or on the land we know not: the comfort that remaineth to his friends is, that he hath ended his life honourably in respect of the reputation won to his nation and country, and of the same to his posterity, and that being dead, he hath not outlived his own honour.

Sir Walter Raleigh, *A Report of the Fight about the Isles of Azores, 1591, betwixt the 'Revenge' and an Armada of the King of Spain*

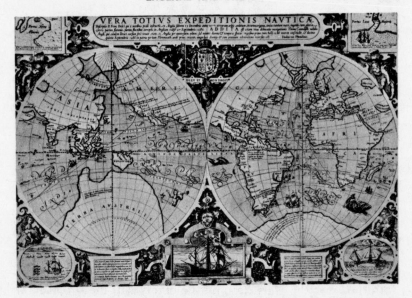

89. World map depicting the circumnavigations of Drake (1577-80) and
Cavendish (1586-8); engraved *c.* 1590 by Jocodus Hondius, probably in London.

THE ATTACK ON CADIZ, 1596
A letter written by Sir Walter Raleigh.
This being agreed on, and both the Generals persuaded to lead
the body of the fleet, the charge for the performance thereof
[was] (upon my humble suit) granted and assigned unto me.

The Lord Thomas Howard — because the *Meere-Honour,*
which he commanded, was one of the greatest ships — was also
left behind with the Generals; but being impatient thereof,
pressed the Generals to have the service committed unto him,
and left the *Meere-Honour* to Mr Dudley, putting himself into the
Nonpareill, For mine own part, as I was willing to give honour to
my Lord Thomas, having both precedency in the army, and being
a nobleman whom I much honoured, so yet I was resolved to
give and not take example for his service, holding mine own
reputation dearest, and remembering my great duty to her
Majesty. With the first peep of day, therefore, I weighed anchor,
and ᵇbare with the Spanish fleet, taking the start of all ours a
good distance. . . .

Having, as aforesaid, taken the leading, I was first saluted by
the fort called *Philip,* afterwards by the ordnance on the curtain,

and lastly by all the galleys, in good order. To show scorn to all
which, I only answered first the fort, and afterwards the galleys,
to each piece a blurr with a trumpet: disdaining to shoot one
piece at any one or all of those esteemed dreadful monsters. The
ships that followed beat upon the galleys so thick that they soon
betook them to their oars, and got up to join with the
galleons in the strait, as aforesaid; and then, as they were driven
to come near me, and enforced to range their sides towards me,
I bestowed a benediction amongst them.

But the *St Philip,* the great and famous Admiral of Spain, was
the mark I shot at; esteeming those galleys but as wasps in
respect of the powerfulness of the other; and being resolved to
be revenged for the *Revenge,* or to second her with mine own
life, I came to anchor by the galleons; of which the *Philip* and
Andrew were two that boarded the *Revenge.* I was formerly
commanded not to board, but was promised fly-boats, in which,
after I had battered a while, I resolved to join unto them.

My Lord Thomas came to anchor by me, on the one hand,
with the *Lyon;* the *Mary Rose,* on the other, with the *Dreadnaught;*
the Marshal [Sir Francis Vere] towards the side of Puntall; and
towards ten of the clock, my Lord General Essex, being
impatient to abide far off, hearing so great thunder of ordnance,
thrust up through the fleet, and headed all those on the left
hand, coming to anchor next unto me on that side; and
afterward came in the *Swiftsure,* as near as she could. Always I
must, without glory, say for myself, that I held single in the head
of all.

Now, after we had beat, as two butts, one upon another almost
three hours (assuring your Honour that the volleys of cannon
and culverin came as thick as if it had been a skirmish of
musketeers), and finding myself in danger to be sunk in the
place, I went to my Lord General in my skiff, to desire him that
he would enforce the promised fly-boats to come up, that I
might board; for as I rid, I could not endure so great battery
any long time. My Lord General was then coming up himself; to
whom I declared that if the fly-boats came not, I would board
with the Queen's ship, for it was the same loss to burn, or sink,
for I must endure the one. The Earl finding that it was not in
his power to command fear, told me that, whatsoever I did, he
would second me in person, upon his honour. My Lord Admiral,
having also a disposition to come up at first, but the river was so
choked as he could not pass with the *Ark,* came up in person into
the *Nonpareill,* with my Lord Thomas.

While I was thus speaking with the Earl, the Marshal who thought it some touch to his great esteemed valour to ride behind me so many hours, got up ahead my ship; which my Lord Thomas perceiving headed him again; — myself being but a quarter of an hour absent. At my return, finding myself from being the first to be but the third, I presently let slip anchor, and thrust in between my Lord Thomas and the Marshal, and went up further ahead than all them before, and thrust my self athwart the channel; so as I was sure none should outstart me again, for that day. My Lord General Essex, thinking his ship's side stronger than the rest thrust the *Dreadnaught* aside, and came next the *Warspight* on the left hand; ahead all that rank, but my Lord Thomas. The Marshal, while we had no leisure to look behind us, secretly fastened a rope on my ship's side towards him, to draw himself up equally with me; but some of my company advertising me thereof, I caused it to be cut off, and so he fell back into his place, whom I guarded, all but his very prow, from the sight of the enemy.

Now if it please you to remember, that having no hope of my fly-boats to board, and that the Earl and my Lord Thomas both promised to second me, I laid out a warp by the side of the *Philip* to shake hands with her (for with the wind we could not get aboard): which when she and the rest perceived, finding also that the *Repulse* (seeing mine) began to do the like, and the Rear-Admiral my Lord Thomas, they all let slip, and ran aground, tumbling into the sea heaps of soldiers, so thick as if coals had been poured out of a sack in many ports at once; some drowned and some sticking in the mud. The *Philip* and the *St Thomas* burnt themselves: the *St Matthew* and the *St Andrew* were recovered with our boats ere they could get out to fire them. The spectacle was very lamentable on their side; for many drowned themselves; many, half burnt, leapt into the water; very many hanging by the ropes' ends by the ships' side, under the water even to the lips; many swimming with grievous wounds, strucken under water, and put out of their pain: and withal so huge a fire, and such tearing of the ordnance in the great *Philip*, and the rest, when the fire came to them, as, if any man had a desire to see Hell itself, it was there most lively figured. Ourselves spared the lives of all, after the victory; but the Flemings, who did little or nothing in the fight, used merciless slaughter, till they were by myself, and afterwards by my Lord Admiral, beaten off. . . .

This being happily finished, we prepared to land the army,

and to attempt the town; in which there were, of all sorts, some five thousand foot burghers, one hundred and fifty soldiers in pay, and some eight hundred horse of the gentry and cavalleros of Xerez, gathered together upon the discovery of our fleet two days before, while we were becalmed off Cape St Mary. The horsemen sallied out to resist the landing; but were so well withstood that they most took their way toward the bridge which leadeth into the Main, called Puento Souse; the rest retired to the town, and so hardly followed, as they were driven to leave their horses at the port (which the inhabitants durst not open, to let them in), and so they leapt down an old wall into the suburbs; and being so closely followed by the vanguard of our footmen, as, when the General perceived an entrance there, he thought it was possible for ours to do the like; upon which occasion the town was carried with a sudden fury, and with little loss. . . .

The town of Cales was very rich in merchandize, in plate, and money; many rich prisoners given to the land commanders; so as that sort are very rich. Some had prisoners for sixteen thousand ducats; some for twenty thousand; some for ten thousand; and, besides, great houses of merchandize. What the Generals have gotten, I know least; they protest it is little. For my own part, I have gotten a lame leg, and a deformed.

E. Edwards, *The Life of Sir Walter Raleigh*

Colonies

JOHN CABOT
A letter from Lorenzo Pasqualigo to his brothers at Venice, 23 August 1497.

London, 23rd August, 1497
Our Venetian, who went with a small ship from Bristol to find new islands, has come back and says he has discovered, seven hundred leagues off, the mainland of the country of the Great Khan and that he coasted along it for 300 leagues, and landed, but did not see any person. But he has brought here to the King certain snares' spread to take game, and a needle for making nets; and he found some notched trees, from which he judged that there were inhabitants. Being in doubt, he came back to the ship. He has been away three months on the voyage, which is certain, and in returning he saw two islands to the right, but he did not wish to land, lest he should lose time, for he was in want of provisions. This King has been much pleased. He says that the tides are slack, and do not make currents as they do here. The King has promised for another time, ten armed ships as he desires, and has given him all the prisoners, except such as are confined for high treason, to go with him, as he has requested; and has granted him money to amuse himself till then. Meanwhile he is with his Venetian wife and his sons at Bristol. His name is Zuam Cabot and he is called the Great Admiral, great honour being paid to him, and he goes dressed in silk. The English are ready to go with him, and so are many of our rascals. The discoverer of these things has planted a large cross in the ground with a banner of England, and one of St Mark, as he is a Venetian; so that our flag has been hoisted very far away.

COLONIES ENLARGE NAVIGATION AND BRING TRADE
Here Hakluyt gives us a REPORT OF THE LATE DISCOVERIES OF SIR HUMPHREY GILBERT: By this western voyage our navy and

navigation shall be enlarged. Besides this, it will prove a general benefit unto our country, not only a great number of men which do now live idly at home shall thereby be set at work, but also children of twelve or fourteen years of age, or under, may be kept from idleness, in making of a thousand kinds of trifling things which will be good merchandise for that country. And moreover, our idle women (which the realm may well spare) shall also be employed in plucking, drying and sorting of feathers, in pulling, beating and working of hemp, and in gathering of cotton, and divers things right necessary for dyeing. And the men may employ themselves in dragging for pearl, working for mines and in matters of husbandry and likewise in hunting the whale; besides in fishing for cod, salmon and herring, drying, salting and barrelling the same, and felling of trees, hewing and sawing of them, and suchlike work meet for those persons that are no men of Art or Science.

Sir George Reckshaw, *A True Report of the late Discoveries of Sir Humphrey Gilbert,* 1583, Hakluyt's *Voyages*

THE COLONISATION OF NEWFOUNDLAND, 1583
Written by Mr Edward Haie, gentleman and principall actour in the same voyage, who alone continued unto the end, and by God's speciall assistance returned home with his retinue safe and entire.

We began our voyage upon Tuesday the eleventh day of June in the year of our Lord 1583, having in our fleet (at our departure from Causet Bay [near Plymouth] these ships as followeth: (The *Delight*; the Barke *Raleigh,* 'set forth by Mr Walter Raleigh'; the *Golden Hinde*; the *Swallow*; and the *Squirrel*.)

We were in number in all about 260 men: among whom we had of every faculty good choice, as ship-wrights, masons, carpenters, smiths, and such like requisite to such an action: also mineral men and refiners. Besides, for solace of our people, and allurement of the savages, we were provided of music in good variety: not omitting the least toys, as Morris dancers, hobby horses, and May-like conceits to delight the savage people, whom we intended to win by all fair means possible. And to that end we were indifferently furnished of all petty haberdashery wares to barter with those simple people. . . .

Saturday the 27 of July, we might descry not far from us, as it were mountains of ice driven upon the sea, being then in 50 degrees, which were carried southward to the weather of us.

Before we come to Newfoundland, about 50 leagues on this side, we pass the bank, which are high grounds rising within the

sea and under water, yet deep enough and without danger. . . .
The breadth of this bank is somewhere more, and somewhere
less. The Portugals and French chiefly have a notable trade of
fishing upon the bank, where are sometimes 100 or more sails of
ships, who commonly begin the fishing in April, and have ended
by July. . . .

(Aug. 3 — Saturday.) Trending this coast we came to the
island called Baccalaos, being not past two leagues from the
main. . . .

Monday following [August 5], the general [Sir Humphrey
Gilbert] had his tent set up, who being accompanied with his
own followers, summoned the merchants and masters, both
English and strangers, to be present at his taking possession of
these countries. Before whom openly was read and interpreted
unto the strangers his commision: by virtue whereof he took
possession in the same harbour of St John, and 200 leagues
every way; invested the queen's majesty with the title and dignity
thereof; had delivered unto him (after the custom of England) a
rod and a turf of the same soil, entering possession also for him
and his heirs and assigns for ever: And signified unto all men
that from that time forward, they should take the same land as
territory appertaining to the Queen of England. . . . At the same
time, for a beginning, he proposed and delivered three laws to
be in force immediately. . . .

The first, for religion, which in public exercise should be
according to the Church of England. The second, for
maintenance of her majesty's right and possession of those
territories, against which if anything were attempted prejudicial,
the party or parties offending should be adjudged and executed
as in case of high treason, according to the laws of England. The
third, if any person should utter words sounding to the
dishonour of her majesty, he should lose his ears, and have his
ship and goods confiscate. . . . After this the assembly was
dismissed. And afterward were erected not far from that place
the arms of England engraven in lead, and infixed upon a pillar
of wood. Yet further and actually to establish this possession
taken in right of her majesty, and to the behoof of Sir
Humphrey Gilbert, Knight, his heirs, and assigns for ever, the
general granted in fee farm divers parcels of land lying by the
water side, both in this harbour of St John, and elsewhere.

[*The expedition having met with storm and discomfort in their further
sailings and investigation, and their supply of food growing scanty,*]

Upon Saturday in the afternoon the 31st of August we

changed our course, and returned back for England.

Richard Hakluyt, *Principall Navigations, Voiages,*
and Discoveries of the English Nation, 1589

THE FIRST LANDING IN VIRGINIA, 1585

This Island had many goodly woods, and full of deer, coneys, hares and fowl, even in the midst of Summer, in incredible abundance. The woods are not such as you find in Bohemia, Moscovia, or Hyrcania, barren and fruitless, but the highest and reddest cedars of the world, far bettering the cedars of the Azores, of the Indies, or of Libanus; pines, cypress, sassafras, the lentisk, or the tree that beareth the mastic; the tree that beareth the rind of black cinnamon, of which Master Winter brought from the Straits of Magellan; and many other of excellent smell and quality. We remained by the side of this Island two whole days before we saw any people of the country. The third day we espied one small boat rowing towards us, having in it three persons. This boat came to the land's side, four arquebus-shot from our ships; and there two of the people remaining, the third came along the shore side towards us, and we being then all within board, he walked up and down upon the point of the land next unto us. Then the Master and the Pilot of the Admiral, Simon Ferdinando, and the Captain, Philip Amadas, myself, and others, rowed to the land; whose coming this fellow attended, never making any show of fear or doubt. And after he had spoken of many things not understood by us, we brought him, with his own good liking, aboard the ships, and gave him a shirt, a hat, and some other things, and made him taste of our wine and our meat, which he liked very well; and, after having viewed both barks, he departed, and went to his own boat again, which he had left in a little cove or creek adjoining. As soon as he was two bow-shot into the water he fell to fishing, and in less than half an hour he had laden his boat as deep as it could swim, with which he came again to the point of the land, and there he divided his fish into two parts, pointing one part to the ship and the other to the pinnace. Which, after he had as much as he might requited the former benefits received, departed out of our sight.

The next day there came unto us divers boats, and in one of them the King's brother, accompanied with forty or fifty men, very handsome and goodly people, and in their behaviour as mannerly and civil as any of Europe. His name was *Granganameo,* and the king is called *Wingina;* the country, *Wingandacoa,* (and now by her Majesty *Virginia*). The manner of his coming was in this sort: he left his boats altogether as the first man did, a little from the ships by the shore, and came along to the place over against the ships, followed with forty men. When he came to the place, his servants spread a long mat upon the ground, on which he sat down, and at the other end of the mat four others of his company did the like; the rest of his men stood round about him somewhat afar off. When we came to the shore to him, with our weapons, he never moved from his place, nor any of the other four, nor never mistrusted any harm to be offered from us; but, sitting still, he beckoned us to come and sit by him, which we performed; and being set, he makes all signs of joy and welcome, striking on his head and his breast and afterwards on ours, to show we were all one, smiling and making show the best he could of all love and familiarity. After he had made a long speech unto us we presented him with divers things, which he received very joyfully and thankfully. None of the company durst to speak one word all the time; only the four which were at the other end spake one to the other's ear very softly.

Richard Hakluyt, *Principall Navigations, Voiages and Discoveries of the English Nation,* 1589

VIRGINIA

A letter from Ralph Lane, Governor of Virginia 1585-1587.

In the meanwhile you shall understand, that since Sir Richard Grenville's departure from us, as also before, we have discovered the main to be the goodliest soil under the cope of heaven, so abounding with sweet trees, that bring such sundry rich and pleasant gums, grapes of such greatness, yet wild, as France, Spain nor Italy have no greater, so many sorts of apothecary drugs, such several kinds of flax, and one kind like silk, the same gathered of a grass, as common there, as grass is here. And now within these few days we have found here maize or Guinea wheat, whose ear yieldeth corn for bread 400, upon one ear, and the cane maketh very good and perfect sugar, also *Terra Samia,* otherwise *Terra sigillata.* Besides that, it is the goodliest and most pleasing territory of the world: for the continent is of an huge unknown greatness, and very well peopled and towned, though savagely, and the climate so wholesome, that we had not one sick since we touched the land here. To conclude, if Virginia had but horses and kine in some reasonable proportion, I dare assure myself being inhabited with English, no realm in Christendom were comparable to it. For this already we find, that what commodities soever Spain, France, Italy or the East parts so yield unto us, in wines of all sorts, in oils, in flax, in resins, pitch, frankincense, currants, sugars, and such like, these parts do abound with the growth of them all, but being savages that possess the land, they know no use of the same. And sundry other rich commodities, that no parts of the world, be they West or East Indies, have, here we find great abundance of. The people naturally are most courteous, and very desirous to have clothes, but especially of coarse cloth rather than silk, coarse canvas they also like well of, but copper carrieth the price of all, so it be made red. Thus good M. Hakluyt and M. H., I have joined you both in one letter of remembrance, as two that I love dearly well, and commending me most heartily to you both, I commit you to the tuition of the Almighty. From the new fort in Virginia, this third of September, 1585.

Your most assured friend Ralph Lane.

Hakluyt, *Principal Navigations*

SEA VOYAGES BRING NEW INDUSTRIES

The first making of Venice glasses in England began at the Crotched Friars in London about the beginning of the reign of Queen Elizabeth, by one Jacob Venaline, an Italian.

The cutting of iron bars in a mill for the ready use of smiths, to make long rods and all sorts of nails, was brought first into England in the year 1590, by Godfrey Box of the Province of Liege. He likewise set up the first mill for the making of copper plate. And upon the same river, called Dartford River, not long before, was set up a mill to make white paper, by Master John Spilman (a German); this was the first mill in England, wherein fine paper was made. In the reign of King James coarse paper (commonly called brown paper) was first made in divers places, serving for grocers and such like.

John Stow, *Annales*, 1592

MERCHANT ADVENTURERS

Increasing trade in the sixteenth century brought more exploration.
Adventurers invested many pounds. This led to the granting of charters.
This kingdom hath continued the making of great store of excellent cloth, which all nations hitherto have always desired for their general use. For transport thereof, certain merchants obtained a strong Company for themselves, calling themselves the Merchant Adventurers. At first their usual voyages were but Calais, and after that to Antwerp, their skill in navigation was

then but small in comparison of this time; and it is recorded in the Guild Hall in London for a most memorable matter that in those days there was one citizen who adventured fifty pounds. At this day there are a great number of merchants that adventure five thousand pounds and some twenty thousand pounds; not only such that are of the Merchant Adventurers, but also Merchants of other companies, as the Muscovy, Turkey, Spain, Barbary and now lastly the East Indian Company, which company Queen Elizabeth, upon good consideration, granted a charter.

John Stow, *Annales,* 1592

THE DISCOVERY OF GUIANA, 1596

And so the fifteenth day at sea we discovered afar off the mountains of Guiana to our great joy, and towards the evening had a slight breeze of a northerly wind that blew very strong, which brought us in sight of the great river of Orenoque, out of which this river descended wherein we were. We descried afar off three other canoes as far as we could discern them, after whom we hastened with our barge and wherries, but two of them passed out of sight. And the third entered up the great river on the right hand to the westward, and there stayed out of sight, thinking that we meant to take the way eastward towards the province of Carapana, for that way the Spaniards keep, not daring to go upwards to Guiana, the people in those parts being all their enemies. And those in the canoes thought us to have been those Spaniards that were fled from Trinidado, and had escaped killing. And when we came so far down as the opening of that branch into which they slipped, being near them with our barge and wherries, we made after them, and ere they could land, came within call, and by our interpreter told them what we were, wherewith they came back willingly aboard us. And of such fish and Tortugas eggs as they had gathered, they gave us, and promised in the morning to bring the lord of that part with them, and to do us all other services they could.

When we ran to the tops of the first hills of the plains adjoining to the river, we beheld that wonderful breach of waters, which ran down Caroli. We might from that mountain see the river how it ran in three parts, above twenty miles off, and there appeared some ten or twelve overfalls in sight, every one as high over the other as a church-tower, which fell with that fury that the rebound of waters made it seem as if it had been all covered over with a great shower of rain. And in some places we took it at the first for a smoke that had risen over some great town. For mine own part, I was well persuaded from thence to have returned, being a very ill footman, but the rest were all so desirous to go near the said strange thunder of waters, as they drew me on by little and little, till we came into the next valley, where we might better discern the same. I never saw a more beautiful country, nor more lively prospects, hills so raised here and there over the valleys, the river winding into divers branches, the plains adjoining without bush or stubble, all fair green grass, the ground of hard sand easy to march on, either for horse or foot, the deer crossing in every path, the birds towards the evening singing on every tree with a thousand several tunes, cranes and herons of white, crimson, and carnation perching on the river's side, the air fresh with a gentle easterly wind, and every stone that we stooped to take up, promised either gold or silver by his complexion.

Sir Walter Raleigh, *Discovery of the Empire of Guiana*, 1596

GUIANANS

Those Guianans ... are marvellous great drunkards, in which vice I think no nation can compare with them and at the times of their solemn feasts when the emperor carouseth with his captains, tributaries, and governors, the manner is thus. All those that pledge him are first stripped naked, and their bodies anointed all over with a kind of white balm (by them called Curcas) of which there is great plenty and yet very dear amongst them, and it is of all other the most precious, whereof we have had good experience: when they are anointed all over, certain servants of the emperor having prepared gold made into a fine powder blow it through hollow canes unto their naked bodies, until they be all shining from the foot to the head, and in this sort they sit drinking by twenties and hundreds and continue in drunkenness sometimes six or seven days together.

Sir Walter Raleigh, *The Discovery of Guiana*, 1596

IN PRAISE OF SEAFARING MEN IN HOPES OF GOOD FORTUNE

Who seeks the way to win renown,
Or flies with wings of high desire;
Who seeks to wear the laurel crown,
Or hath the mind that would aspire:
Tell him his native soil eschew,
Tell him go range and seek anew.

To pass the seas some think a toil,
Some think it strange abroad to roam,
Some think it grief to leave their soil,
Their parents, kinsfolk and their home;
Think so who list, I like it not,
I must abroad to try my lot.

Sir Richard Grenville

SELECT BIBLIOGRAPHY

AUERBACH, ERNA, *Tudor Artists*

BERESFORD, M., *The Lost Villages of England*

BINDOFF, S. T., *Tudor England*

BLACK, J. B., *The Reign of Elizabeth* (Oxford)

BOAS, F. S., *An Introduction to Tudor Drama* (Oxford)

CAMPBELL, M., *The English Yeoman under Elizabeth and the Early Stuarts* (Yale)

CASPARI, F., *Humanism and the Social Order in Tudor England* (Chicago)

CLAPHAM, J. H., *Concise Economic History of Britain* (Cambridge)

CRUICKSHANK, C. G., *Elizabeth's Army* (Oxford)

DODD, A. H., *Life in Elizabethan England* (Batsford)

ELTON, G. R., *England under the Tudors* (Methuen)

GARNER, T. and STRATTON, A., *The Domestic Architecture of England during the Tudor Period*

HARRISON, G. B., *An Elizabethan Journal*

JUDGE, A. V., *Elizabethan Underworld*

KNAPPEN, M. M., *Tudor Puritanism* (Chicago)

LEE, SIR SIDNEY and ONIONS, C. T., *Shakespeare's England*

LEWIS, C. S., *English Literature in the Sixteenth Century excluding Drama* (Oxford)

MACKIE, J. D., *The Earlier Tudors* (Oxford)

MORRIS, CHRISTOPHER, *The Tudors* (Batsford)

NEALE, J. E., *Queen Elizabeth I*

NORRIS, H., *Costume and Fashion: The Tudor Period*

PARKER, T. M., *The English Reformation to 1558*

PICKTHORN, K., *Early Tudor Government: Henry VII* (Cambridge)

QUINN, D. B., *Raleigh and the British Empire*

REESE, M. M., *Shakespeare his world and his work*

ROWSE, A. L., *The England of Elizabeth*

SALZMAN, F. L., *Building in England down to 1540* (Oxford)

TAWNEY, R. H., *The Agrarian Problem in the Sixteenth Century*

TAWNEY, R. H., *Religion and the Rise of Capitalism*

THIRSK, JOAN, *Tudor Enclosures* (Historical Association Pamphlet, 1959)
TILLYARD, E. M. W., *The Elizabethan World Picture* (Chatto)
TREVELYAN, G. M., *English Social History* (Longmans)
TREVOR-ROPER, H. R., *The Century 1540-1640* (Cambridge)
WALKER, E., *A History of Music in England* (Oxford)
WILLAN, T. S., *Studies in Elizabethan Foreign Trade* (Manchester)
WILLIAMS, PENRY, *Life in Early Tudor England* (Batsford)
WILLIAMSON, J. A., *The Age of Drake*
WILSON, F. P., *Elizabethan and Jacobean*

Biographies

ROGER ASCHAM (1515-1568), classical author, pioneer of the English language. Greek lecturer on Socratic dialogues at Cambridge. Tutor to Princess Elizabeth. Latin secretary to Queen Mary. Private tutor to Queen Elizabeth. His works include *Toxophilus, the Schoole of Shootinge*, 1545, and *The Scholemaster Or plaine and perfite way of teachying children to understand, write and speake, in Latin tong*, 1570.

JOHN AWDELEY (*fl*. 1559-1577), *Fraternitye of Vacabondes*, 1561.

JOHN BLAKMAN, (or Blacman) was a priest who knew Henry VI. It has been said that his *On the Virtues and Miracles of Henry VI* was written as he knew of the efforts Henry VII made to get Henry VI canonized.

ANDREW BOORDE (*c*. 1490-1549), traveller, physician, suffragan bishop of Chichester, 1521. *A Compendyous Regyment or a Dietary of Helth*, 1542; *Breviary of Helth*, 1547.

SIR GEORGE BOWES (1527-1580), military commander at Scottish war, 1549. Marshal of Berwick, 1558. Handled the rebellion of the northern earls which threatened the throne of Queen Elizabeth. A comment on his character was made in a letter to Burghley, 'He was the surest pyllore the queen's majesty had in these parts.'

WILLIAM BULLEIN (*d*. 1576), *Government of Health*, 1558; *Bulwark against all Sickness*, 1562; *Dialogue against Fever Pestilence*, 1564.

WILLIAM BYRD (1538?-1623), one of the great masters of music, especially of the madrigal, in this period. In 1575 letters patent were granted to Tallis and Byrd to print music 'for any and so many as they will of set song or songs in part.' *Psalms, Sonets, and songs of sadnes and pietie,* 1588; *Songs of sundrie natures,* 1589.

WILLIAM CAMDEN (1551-1623), antiquary and historian. Educated at St Paul's School and Christ Church, Oxford. Appointed headmaster of Westminster School in 1593. He published his *Britannia* in 1586, and his *Annales Rerum Anglicarum et Hibernicarum Regnante Elizabetha* in 1615. He founded a chair of history in Oxford University. He wrote chiefly in Latin. His *Britannia* was translated into English by Philemon Holland in 1610.

JEROME CARDAN (GIROLAMO CARDANO) (1501-1576), a distinguished Italian mathematician, and writer on medicine and occult studies.

RICHARD CAREW (1555-1620), *Godfrey of Bulloigne,* 1594 (translation of Tasso's *Jerusalem Delivered,* Cantos I-V); *Survey of Cornwall,* 1602; *Excellency of the English Tongue,* 1605.

GEORGE CAVENDISH (1500-1561?), lived in the home of Thomas Wolsey, and wrote a remarkable life of the Cardinal, *The Negotiations of Thomas Woolsey.* This was passed round in manuscript, and first printed in 1641.

WILLIAM CLOWES (1540-1604), was surgeon to St Bartholomew's Hospital from 1575 to 1585, served in the army, and was at the battle of Zutphen. He later joined the navy and was in the fleet against the Armada. An accurate observer, he wrote copiously. His best works are *A Prooved Practise for all young Chirurgians concerning Burning with Gunpowder,* 1591; and *A right frutefull and approved Treatise for the Artificiall Cure of the Struma or Evill,* 1602. He became surgeon to Queen Elizabeth.

THOMAS CROMWELL, EARL OF ESSEX (1485?-1540), secretary to Cardinal Wolsey and later to Henry VIII. He was adviser in ecclesiastical matters and began the dissolution of the monasteries. He was executed after the failure of the Anne of Cleves marriage, part of his policy of alliance with the Protestant princes of Germany.

SAMUEL DANIEL (1562-1619), poet, historian, writer of epistles and masques. He published *Delia,* a collection of sonnets, in 1592; *Complaynt of Rosamond* also in 1592; and *Cleopatra,* a Senecan tragedy, in 1594. Spenser refers to him as the 'new shepherd late up sprong', and William Browne praised him as 'well-languaged Daniel'.

THOMAS DAWSON (*fl.* 1580), *The Good Huswifes Jewell; Rare Devises for Conseites in Cookerie,* 1587.

THOMAS DEKKER (1570?-1632), dramatist, pamphleteer and satirist. Wrote plays in collaboration with Drayton, Ben Jonson, Middleton, Massinger and others. His comedies, *The Shoemaker's Holiday* and *Old Fortunatus,* appeared in 1600. Other plays were *Satiromastix,* 1602; *The Honest Whore,* 1604; his pamphlets include *The Wonderful Yeare 1603, The Seven deadly Sinnes of London* and *The Belman of London.* He also wrote *The Guls Hornebooke,* 1609.

THOMAS DELONEY (1543?-1600?), pamphleteer and ballad-writer, by trade a silk-weaver. His chief works were written between 1596 and 1600, and are prose narratives: *Thomas of Reading* (on the clothier's craft), *Jack of Newbury* (on the weaver's craft), and *The Gentle Craft* (on shoemaker's work). From the last Dekker wrote *The Shoemaker's Holiday.*

DESIDERIUS ERASMUS (1466-1536), the great Dutch humanist and philosopher. He came to England several times and was welcomed by the great scholars, More, Colet, and Grocyn. He was appointed Lady Margaret Reader at Cambridge, lecturing on Greek from 1511 to 1514. His principal works were the *Novum Instrumentum,* Latin version of the New Testament, 1516; *Encomium Moriae,* 1509; *Enchiridion Militis Christiani,* 1503. His *Colloquia,* 1529, reveals much of contemporary life.

PETER ERONDELL (*fl.* 1600), *The French Garden,* a conversation manual, published in 1605.

SIMON FISH (*d.* 1531), a gentleman of Gray's Inn who had to leave London about 1525 for acting in a play which touched upon Cardinal Wolsey. He, like Tyndale, fled abroad, and there wrote *The Supplication for the Beggars,* 1529. Another work is *The Sum of Scripture.*

ST. JOHN FISHER (1459-1535), master of Michaelhouse, 1497, later part of Trinity College, Cambridge. Became bishop of Rochester 1504. He persuaded Erasmus to lecture on Greek at Cambridge. He opposed the Reformation and was imprisoned in the Tower. He was beheaded in 1535 as he refused to acknowledge the King as supreme head of the Church.

JOHN FITZHERBERT (*fl.* 1520), *The Booke of Husbandrie*, 1523; *Book of Surveying*, 1523; *A Pleasaunt Instruction of the Parfit ordering of Bees*, 1568.

JOHN FOXE (1516-1587), pamphleteer, prebendary of Salisbury in 1563. He preached at Paul's Cross a famous sermon 'On Christ Crucified' in 1570. His *Actes and Monuments* (commonly called 'Book of Martyrs') appeared in 1563 and was so popular that it was placed in all churches by appointment. However, it was sometimes derided as 'Foxe's Golden Legend'.

THOMAS FULLER (1608-1661), became a prebendary of Salisbury in 1631, and rector of Broadwindsor, Dorset, in 1634. His *History of the Holy Warre* was published in 1639, and *The Holy State and the Profane State* in 1642. His finest work, *The Worthies of England*, appeared after his death, in 1662.

JOHN GERARD (1545-1612), herbalist, who looked after Lord Burghley's gardens in the Strand. He went botanizing in 'the fields of Holborn near unto Gray's Inn'. His renowned *Herball or generall Historie of Plantes* appeared in 1597.

JOHN GERARD (1564-1637), Jesuit priest, educated at Oxford, at Donia, and Rheims. For Jesuit colleges he worked vigorously in the Low Countries; was Confessor to an English college at Rome. His *Autobiography* shows him to be courageous, energetic, and of unquestioning faith.

GEORGE GIFFORD (*d.* 1620), *Discourse of Subtill Practices of Devils*, 1587; *Dialogue concerning Witches and Witchcraft*, 1593.

STEPHEN GOSSON (1554-1624), satirist, critic, playwright, poet, Rector of Great Wigborough, 1591; and of St. Botolph's, Bishopsgate, 1600. He attacked players and poets in his *Schoole of Abuse* in 1579, and in the same year wrote *Apologie for Schoole of Abuse*. His plays are not now extant; his other work includes *The Ephemerides of Plato*, 1579; and *Plays confuted in Five Actions*, 1582.

ROBERT GREENE (1560-1592), educated at Cambridge and Oxford. Dramatist, lyric poet, satirist, 'conny-catching' pamphleteer, University Wit. His work includes *The Honorable Historie of Friar Bacon and Friar Bungay*, acted in 1594; *Menaphon*, 1589; among his pamphlets appear *Green's Mourning Garment*, 1590; *Greene's Never Too Late*, 1590, and *Groatsworth of Wit*, 1592.

SIR RICHARD GRENVILLE (1541-1591), the naval commander of the *Revenge*, who fought fifteen Spanish ships for fifteen hours off Flores till fatally wounded.

SIR FULKE GREVILLE, FIRST BARON BROOKE (1554-1628), came to court with his friend Sir Philip Sidney, became favourite of Queen Elizabeth. He wrote *Tragedy of Mustapha*, 1609; *Certain Learned and Elegant Works* and *The Life of the renowned Sir Philip Sidney*. These were both published after his tragic death, murdered by his servant Haywood, who thought he was not in his master's will.

JOHN HACKET (1592-1670), wrote *Life of Archbishop Williams*, and a Latin comedy *Loiola*, about 'an unscrupulous Jesuit'.

RICHARD HAKLUYT (1553-1616), educated at Westminster School and Christ Church, Oxford. Chaplain to Sir Edward Stafford, ambassador at Paris, 1583-1588. Devoted himself to the study of English explorations. He wrote *Diverse Voyages touching Discovery of America*, 1582; *Voyages made into Florida*, 1587; *Principall Navigations, Voyages and Discoveries*, 1589.

EDWARD HALL (d. 1547), wrote *The Union of the Noble and Illustre Families of Lancastre and York*, which was prohibited by Queen Mary. It has splendid descriptions of the days of Henry VIII.

JOSEPH HALL (1574-1656), educated at Emmanuel College, Cambridge, and was bishop of Exeter 1627-1641, and Norwich 1641-1647. He was impeached in 1642, and expelled from his palace in 1647. He published his *Virgidemiarum Sex Libri* in 1597, and his *Characters in Virtues and Vices* in 1608. His controversial works show him to be one of the early English satirists.

THOMAS HARMAN (fl. 1560), *Caveat or Warening for Commen Cursetors Vulgarely called Vagabones*, 1567.

SIR JOHN HARINGTON (1561-1612), godson of Queen Elizabeth, was educated at Eton and Christ's College, Cambridge. He translated Ariosto's *Orlando Furioso* by the Queen's direction. His *Metamorphosis of Ajax*, 1596, and other satires led to his banishment from court. He joined Essex on his way to Ireland. His *Nugae Antiquae* appeared 1769-1775.

WILLIAM HARRISON (1534-1593), was educated at Cambridge and Oxford, became rector of Radwinter and canon of Windsor. He wrote the valuable *Description of England*, 1587, which is included in the *Chronicles* of Holinshed.

SAMUEL HARSNETT (1561-1631), was at King's College, Cambridge; became archbishop of York. He was in high favour at court. Fuller commends his 'great learning, strong parts, and stout spirit', and also calls him a 'zealous asserter of ceremonies'.

SIR JOHN HAYWARD (1564-1627), author of historical works. His *First Part of the Life and Raigne of Henrie the IIII*, 1599, displeased Elizabeth and led to his imprisonment. His other chief works were *Lives of the III Normans, Kings of England*, 1613; *Raigne of King Edward the Sixt*, 1630; and *The Beginning of the Reign of Elizabeth*, 1636.

PAUL HENTZNER, a German from Brandenburg, who visited England in 1598, praised the handsomeness and cleanliness of Cheapside. He described college life both at Oxford and Cambridge as 'almost monastic'. His *Travels in England* appeared in 1598.

JOHN HEYWOOD (1497-1580), pageant-writer, poet, translator, dramatist. Master of the choir school at Court. His works include *The Four P.P.*, 1545; *Proverbs*, 1546; *Two Hundred Epigrams*, 1555; *Spider and the Fly*, 1556; *Fourth Hundred of Epigrams*, 1560.

THOMAS HEYWOOD (1574-1641), a member of the lord admiral's company in 1598, and later one of the queen's players. His chief plays are *Edward the Fourth*, 1599; *A Woman Kilde with Kindnesse*, 1607; *The Fair Maid of the West*, 1631; and *The English Traveller* (printed in 1633).

278

LADY MARGARET HOBY, married three times: first to Walter Devereux, younger brother of the Earl of Essex; then to Thomas Sidney, Sir Philip's younger brother; lastly to Sir Thomas Posthumous Hoby. Her valuable diary of the day covers the years 1599 to 1605.

RAPHAEL HOLINSHED (*d.* 1580?), said by Anthony à Wood to have been a 'minister of God's word'. Several writers contributed to his *Chronicles,* 1577. He himself wrote the *Historie of England.* His work was a source-book for Elizabethan dramatists.

CLAUDIUS HOLLYBAND (*fl.* 1575), a Huguenot refugee who, in Elizabeth's reign, established a school first in Lewisham and then in Paul's Churchyard. His works, often in dialogue form, include *French Littleton,* 1576; *French Schoolemaester,* and *Campo di Fior.*

JAMES VI OF SCOTLAND, King of England 1603-1625. *Prentice in Art of Poesie,* 1584; *Demonologie,* 1597; *Basilikon Doron,* 1599; *True Law of Free Monarchies,* 1603; *Counterblast to Tobacco,* 1604.

BENJAMIN JONSON (1572-1637) ('Ben Jonson'), educated at Westminster School under William Camden, later worked with his stepfather, a bricklayer. In 1597 joined Henslowe's company as player and playwright. A friend of Shakespeare and one of the great poets and dramatists of his age. Virtually poet laureate in 1616. Among his best works are: *Every Man out of his Humour,* 1600; *Sejanus,* 1605; *Volpone,* 1607; *The Alchemist,* 1612; *Bartholomew Fayre,* 1614; *The Staple of News,* 1625; *Timber: or discoveries,* 1640.

THOMAS KYD (1558?-1594?), dramatist, poet, translator; last of the University Wits. His plays showed sound construction of plot and effective stage situations. *The Spanish Tragedie,* 1594; *Pompey the Great,* 1595; *Cornelia,* 1594; *Soliman and Perseda,* ?1599.

ROBERT LANEHAM (*fl.* 1575), *A letter; wherein the Entertainment at Killingworth Castle is signified,* 1575.

THOMAS LODGE (1558?-1625), educated at Merchant Taylors' School, London, and Trinity College, Oxford. He was at Lincoln's Inn, then turned from law to literature, excelling as a lyric poet. He is remembered for *Honest Excuses: a defence of poetry, music and stage plays*, 1579; *Rosalynde: Euphues golden legacie*, 1590; *Phillis: pastorall sonnets*, 1593; *A Fig for Momus: satyres, eclogues, and epistles*, 1598.

WALTER MAP, *(fl.* 1200), a Welshman, who was archdeacon of Oxford under Henry II. He wrote *De nugis curialium*, which included *Dissuasio Valerii ad Rufinum de non ducenda uxore.*

THOMAS MIDDLETON (1570?-1627), wrote satirical and romantic comedies, often in collaboration with Dekker, Munday, Rowley. He also wrote a number of masques. His plays were popular and include *Micron-cynicon: sixe snarling satyres*, 1599; *The Roaring Girle*, 1611; *The Changeling*, 1623; *Women beware Women*, 1657; his pageants and masques include *The Triumphs of Truth*, 1613; *The World Tost at Tennis*, 1620.

SIR THOMAS MORE (ST) (1478-1535), author, scholar, judge, politician, ambassador, statesman. At Canterbury Hall, Oxford, was a pupil of Grocyn and Linacre. Brought up in the household of Cardinal Morton. He was strikingly successful when called to the bar. More was a close friend of Colet and Erasmus. He entered parliament in 1504, was an envoy to Flanders, privy councillor in 1518, and succeeded Wolsey as Lord Chancellor in 1529. He refused to take an oath weakening the pope's authority, disapproved of Henry's divorce from Queen Catherine, 1534, and was imprisoned in the Tower. He was tried for high treason, found guilty, and beheaded. His chief works are *Utopia*, 1516; *Dialogue*, 1528; *Apologye*, 1533; *History of Richard the Thirde*, 1544.

THOMAS MORLEY (1557-1603), a pupil of Byrd, wrote the most famous English musical textbook of the day, *A plain and easy introduction to practical music*. Chiefly known for his madrigals and ballets. Contributor to *The Triumphs of Oriana.*

RICHARD MULCASTER (1530?-1611), educated at Eton and Christ Church, Oxford, was headmaster of Merchant Taylors' School and high-master of St Paul's School. He wrote *De Laudibus Legum Angliae*, 1567; *Positions wherein those Circumstances be examined Necessarie for the Training up of Children*, 1581; *Elementarie*, 1582.

THOMAS NASHE (1567-1601), was a sizar of St John's College, Cambridge. Settled in London after touring France and Italy. He took part under the name of 'Pasquil' in the Martin Marprelate controversy, and wrote *A Countercuffe given to Martin Junior,* 1589. The conflict continued with *Pierce Pennilesse his Supplication to the Divell,* 1592. Some repentance is shown in *Christes Teares over Jerusalem,* 1593. Nashe pointed the way to the novel of adventure with *The Unfortunate Traveller, or the Life of Jacke Wilton,* 1594. *Nashes Lenten Stuffe,* 1599, has some of the vigour of Rabelais.

SIR ROBERT NAUNTON (*fl.* 1640), *Fragmenta Regalia, or Observations on Queen Elizabeth her Times and Favorites,* 1641.

JOHN NORTHBROOKE (*fl.* 1570), preacher and writer against plays. In 1568 he was 'Minister and Preacher of the Worde of God' at St Mary de Redcliffe, Bristol. In his tract *Address to the Reader,* 1577, is the first mention by name in print of the playhouses — the Theatre and Curtain.

FRANCIS PECK (1692-1743), antiquary. Curate of Kingscliff in Northamptonshire. He wrote about antiques in *Desiderata Curiosa. Divers Curious Historical Pieces* contains a long account of Queen Elizabeth's entertainment at Oxford in 1592.

GEORGE PETTIE (1548-1589), *Petite Pallace of Pettie his Pleasure,* 1576; translation of *Civile Conversations of Stefano Guazzo,* 1581.

SIR HUGH PLATT (1552-1608), writer on agriculture, gardening, domestic economy; also known for his mechanical inventions. He also wrote on distilling, cookery, housewifery, and cosmetics. *The Jewell House of Art and Nature,* 1594; *Delightes for Ladies, to adorne their Persons, Tables, Closets and Distillatories,* 1602.

THOMAS PLATTER (*fl.* 1590), *Thomas Platters des Jüngeren Englandfahrt im Jahre 1599.*

ELLIS PRICE (1505?-1599), Welsh administrator, received the rectory of Llandrillo yn Rhos and Llanuwchllyn 1538, was also a tenant of the Earl of Leicester, Lord of Denbigh.

SIR WALTER RALEIGH (1522-1618), educated at Oriel College, Oxford. He entered Elizabeth's court where he found favour, helped in the plantation of Munster, began colonisation of Virginia in 1584, served in defence against Spain; was committed to the Tower in 1592 on account of his relations with Elizabeth Throgmorton. They subsequently married. Raleigh was reprieved. In 1616 went to the Orinoco in search of gold. The expedition failed; at the demand of the Spanish ambassador he was arrested and executed in 1618. In prose he published *The Report of the Fight about the Azores*, 1591; *The Discoverie of Guiana*, 1596; *A Historie of the World*, 1614. He had 'one of the most enterprising and original minds of the age'.

HUGH RHODES (*fl.* 1550), born and bred in Devonshire. He was gentleman of the King's Chapel. For the benefit of the children of the chapel he prepared his *Boke of Nurture, or Schoole of good Maners*, 1550; also *Boke of Nurture for Men, Servants and Children*, 1545. He wrote the 'Song of the Chyld byshop', which was sung before the Queen in 1555.

PATRICK RUTHVEN, THIRD LORD RUTHVEN (1520?-1566), Privy Councillor of Mary Queen of Scots. Sheriff-clerk of Perthshire. Mary's Italian secretary, Rizzio, was dragged from the queen's presence, and brutally murdered at the Palace of Holyroodhouse in March 1566. Ruthven was present and described the murder in *The Narrative*.

REGINALD SCOT (1538?-1599), educated at Hart Hall, Oxford. M.P. for New Romney, 1588-9. He wrote *A Perfite Platforme of a Hoppe Garden* in 1574, the first book to deal with the Kentish industry of hop growing. In 1584 *The Discoverie of Witchcraft* was published, and here he set out to prove that the belief in witchcraft was heretical and not based upon fact.

EDMUND SPENSER (1552?-1599), was educated at Merchant Taylors' School and Pembroke Hall, Cambridge. In 1578 he obtained a place in Leicester's household, and with Sir Philip Sidney, Dyer and others, formed the literary club 'Areopagus'. In 1579 he began *The Faerie Queene*, and published *The Shepheards Calendar*. In 1580 he was appointed secretary to the Lord Deputy of Ireland and received Kilcolman Castle in County Cork. Here he wrote his elegy *Astrophel* on Sir Philip Sidney. *Amoretti* and his splendid *Epithalamion* appeared in 1595. Different books of *The Faerie Queene* were published, and *Prothalamion* was printed in 1596. In an insurrection in 1598 his castle was burnt, and Spenser with his wife and four children escaped to Cork and then to London.

JOHN STOW (1525?-1605), antiquary and chronicler. He began by transcribing manuscripts, and then became 'the most accurate and businesslike of the historians of his century'. His chief works are: *Summarie of Englyshe Chronicles*, 1565; Matthew of Westminster's *Flores Historiarum*, 1567; *The Chronicles of England*, 1580, in following editions called *The Annales of England; A Survey of London*, 1598.

JOHN STRYPE (1643-1737), ecclesiastical historian, educated at St Paul's School, Jesus College and St Catharine's Hall, Cambridge. He formed a superb collection of original documents, mostly of the Tudor age, now in the Harleian and Lansdowne MSS. He enlarged Stow's *Survey of London* in 1720.

PHILIP STUBBES (*fl.* 1583-1591), a Puritan pamphleteer who detested stupidity and cruelty. He denounces the evil customs of the time in *The Anatomie of Abuses*, 1583. Thomas Nashe answers him in his *Anatomie of Absurditie*, 1589.

GEORGE TURBERVILLE (1540?-1610?), scholar of Winchester and fellow of New College, Oxford. He published *Epitaphs, Epigrams, Songs and Sonets*, 1567; *The Booke of Faulconrie or Hauking*, 1575; *The Noble Art of Venerie or Hunting*, 1575.

THOMAS TUSSER (1524?-1580), was educated at Eton and Trinity Hall, Cambridge. He farmed at Cattiwade, Suffolk, and became an agricultural writer and poet. He published his *Hundreth Good Points of Husbandrie* in 1557, in sharp effective verse. He continued his advice on conduct and good farming in *Five Hundreth Pointes of Good Husbandrie*, 1573.

WILLIAM TYNDALE (*d.* 1536), the translator of the Bible, studied at Oxford and Cambridge. He visited Luther at Wittenberg, and began printing his translation of the New Testament at Cologne in 1525, finishing it at Worms. Copies were destroyed in England at St Paul's Cross. He became a Zwinglian, an active pamphleteer and wrote *An answere unto Sir Thomas Mores dialoge* in 1531. He was betrayed and arrested for heresy and imprisoned at Vilvorde in 1535. He was burnt there at the stake. Tyndale was a great leader of the Reformation.

EMANUEL VAN METEREN (*fl.* 1570), *Nederlandtsche Historie,* 1575.

WILLIAM VAUGHAN (1577-1641), *Golden Grove,* 1600; *Fifteen Directions to Preserve Health,* 1600; *Golden Fleece,* 1626.

GILBERT WALKER (*fl.* 1530), *A Manifestation of Dice-play,* 1532.

IZAAK WALTON (1593-1683), was apprenticed to an ironmonger in London. He was the friend of Donne, Drayton, Wotton, Ben Jonson and of Bishop Morley. He published his biographies of John Donne in 1640, of Sir Henry Wotton in 1651, of Richard Hooker in 1665, of George Herbert in 1670, and of Bishop Sanderson in 1678. *The Compleat Angler* first appeared in 1653, was largely rewritten in the second edition. As Saintsbury commenced, he has a 'singular and golden simplicity'.

WILLIAM WEST (1568-1594), student of the Inner Temple, author of *Symbolaeographia,* 1590, *the Art, Description, or Image of Instruments, Covenants, Contracts,* etc., held in great esteem at the time. The new edition was dedicated to Edward Coke.

WILLIAM WESTON (1550?-1615), Jesuit, also known as Edmonds and Hunt. Educated at Oxford, and friend of Edmund Campion, Was a priest at San Lucar, Cadiz and Seville. In London he gained fame by his reported exorcisms of devils. He wrote *Book of Miracles,* only known from extracts printed in *A Declaration of Egregious Popish Impostures . . . practised by Edmonds alias Weston a Jesuit,* published by Samuel Harsnett in 1603.

THOMAS WHYTHORNE (1528-1596), educated at Magdalen College School and Magdalen College, Oxford. He lived in the household of John Heywood, and became a music teacher and composer of madrigals. His autobiography, *A Book of Songs and Sonetts*, was discovered in manuscript in 1955 and published in 1961.

FREDERICK, DUKE OF WÜRTEMBERG. This noble sightseer visited England in 1592, commented on the 'masterly paintings at Hampton Court' and on Burghley's hall at Theobalds. He is forthright in many of his descriptions — of English roads, towns, customs. He counted on the poles of London Bridge thirty-four heads of those executed as traitors. He is in Rye's book, *England as Seen by Foreigners*.

INDEX

Figures in **bold** refer to illustrations.

285